Rome
day BY day®
4th Edition

by Sylvie Hogg Murphy

FrommerMedia LLC

Contents

15 Favorite Moments   1
15 Favorite Moments   2

1 The Best Full-Day Tours   7
The Best in One Day   8
The Best in Two Days   14
The Best in Three Days   18

2 The Best Special-Interest Tours   21
Ancient Rome   22
The Best Museums   28
Baroque Rome   32
Rome's Best Piazzas   36
Rome's Best Churches   40
Romantic Rome   44
Underground Rome   46
Vatican City   48

3 The Best Neighborhood Walks   51
Piazza Navona & the Pantheon   52
Campo de' Fiori   56
Trastevere   58
Tridente   60
Monti   64
Jewish Ghetto & Tiber Island   66
Pigneto   70
Testaccio   72

4 The Best Shopping   75
Shopping Best Bets   76
Rome Shopping A to Z   81

5 The Great Outdoors   89
Villa Borghese   90
Appia Antica (Appian Way)   94
Other Rome Parks to Explore   98

6 The Best Dining 101
Dining Best Bets 102
Rome Restaurants A to Z 107

7 The Best Nightlife 117
Nightlife Best Bets 118
Rome Nightlife A to Z 123

8 The Best Arts & Entertainment 129
Arts & Entertainment Best Bets 130
Rome A&E A to Z 133

9 The Best Lodging 137
Lodging Best Bets 138
Rome Hotels A to Z 144

10 The Best Day Trips & Excursions 151
Tivoli: Hadrian's Villa 152
Ostia Antica 154
Pompeii & Naples 156
Castelli Romani 158
Beaches & Etruscan Sites
   Near Rome 160

The Savvy Traveler 163
Before You Go 164
Getting There 166
Getting Around 167
Fast Facts 168
A Brief History 172
Roman Architecture 174
Useful Phrases 175
Useful Websites 177

Published by:

FrommerMedia LLC

ISBN: 978-1-628-87023-7 (paper); 978-1-628-87053-4 (ebk)

Editorial Director: Pauline Frommer
Editor: Anuja Madar
Production Editor: Jana M. Stefanciosa
Photo Editor: Meghan Lamb
Cartographer: Liz Puhl
Page Compositor: Jennifer Goldsmith
Indexer: Kelly Henthorne

For information on our other products and services, please go to Frommers.com/contactus.

Frommer's also publishes its books in a variety of electronic formats. Some content that appears in print may not be available in electronic formats.

Manufactured in China

5 4 3 2 1

A Note from the Editorial Director

Organizing your time. That's what this guide is all about.

Other guides give you long lists of things to see and do and then expect you to fit the pieces together. The Day by Day guides are different. These guides tell you the best of everything, and then they show you how to see it *in the smartest, most time-efficient way.* Our authors have designed detailed itineraries organized by time, neighborhood, or special interest. And each tour comes with a bulleted map that takes you from stop to stop.

Hoping to relive the glory days of ancient Rome or to tour the highlights of Vatican City? Planning a walk through Piazza Navona or a whirlwind tour of the very best that Rome has to offer? Whatever your interest or schedule, the Day by Days give you the smartest routes to follow. Not only do we take you to the top attractions, hotels, and restaurants, but we also help you access those special moments that locals get to experience—those "finds" that turn tourists into travelers.

The Day by Days are also your top choice if you're looking for one complete guide for all your travel needs. The best hotels and restaurants for every budget, the greatest shopping values, the wildest nightlife—it's all here.

Why should you trust our judgment? Because our authors personally visit each place they write about. They're an independent lot who say what they think and would never include places they wouldn't recommend to their best friends. They're also open to suggestions from readers. If you'd like to contact them, please send your comments our way at support@frommermedia.com, and we'll pass them on.

Enjoy your Day by Day guide—the most helpful travel companion you can buy. And have the trip of a lifetime.

About the Author

Sylvie Hogg Murphy has been writing guidebooks and travel articles about Italy and her favorite city in the world, Rome, for more than a decade. Her insider and intimate knowledge of the Eternal City both past and present come from her degree in Classical Archaeology and from her experience as an expatriate in Rome, where she pounded the cobblestones as a tour guide for 5 years. A native Californian, Sylvie lives in Overland Park, Kansas, with her husband and three boys, and teaches Italian in the Kansas City area.

An Additional Note

Please be advised that travel information is subject to change at any time—and this is especially true of prices. We therefore suggest that you write or call ahead for confirmation when making your travel plans. The authors, editors, and publisher cannot be held responsible for the experiences of readers while traveling. Your safety is important to us, however, so we encourage you to stay alert and be aware of your surroundings.

Star Ratings, Icons & Abbreviations

Every hotel, restaurant, and attraction listing in this guide has been ranked for quality, value, service, amenities, and special features using a **star-rating system.** Hotels, restaurants, attractions, shopping, and nightlife are rated on a scale of zero stars (recommended) to three stars (exceptional). In addition to the star-rating system, we also use a **kids icon** to point out the best bets for families. Within each tour, we recommend cafes, bars, or restaurants where you can take a break. Each of these stops appears in a shaded box marked with a coffee-cup-shaped bullet 🍵.

The following **abbreviations** are used for credit cards:

AE	American Express	DISC	Discover	V	Visa
DC	Diners Club	MC	MasterCard		

Frommers.com

Frommer's travel resources don't end with this guide. Frommer's website, **www.frommers.com,** has travel information on more than 4,000 destinations. We update features regularly, giving you access to the most current trip-planning information and the best airfare, lodging, and car-rental bargains. You can also listen to podcasts, connect with other Frommers.com members through our active-reader forums, share your travel photos, read blogs from guidebook editors and fellow travelers, and much more.

A Note on Prices

In the "Take a Break" and "Best Bets" sections of this book, we have used a system of dollar signs to show a range of costs for 1 night in a hotel (the price of a double-occupancy room) or the cost of an entree at a restaurant. Use the following table to decipher the dollar signs:

Cost	Hotels	Restaurants
$	under $130	under $15
$$	$130–$200	$15–$30
$$$	$200–$300	$30–$40
$$$$	$300–$395	$40–$50
$$$$$	over $395	over $50

How to Contact Us

In researching this book, we discovered many wonderful places—hotels, restaurants, shops, and more. We're sure you'll find others. Please tell us about them, so we can share the information with your fellow travelers in upcoming editions. If you were disappointed with a recommendation, we'd love to know that, too. Please write to: Support@FrommerMedia.com

15 Favorite
Moments

15 Favorite Moments

VATICAN CITY

Vatican Museums

Sistine Chapel

St. Peter's Basilica

PRATI

Piazzale d. Eroi

Piazzale S.M. d.'Grazie

Largo Trionfale

V. Trionfale

V. Campanella

Viale delle Milizie

Viale Giulio Cesare

Lepanto

V. Andrea Doria

V. Barletta

V. Vespasiano

V. Leone IV

Ottaviano

Via Germanico

Via de Gracchi

Via Cola di Rienzo

Via Crescenzio

Piazza d. Quiriti

Piazza Cola di Rienzo

Piazza d. Risorgimento

V. Orazio

V. Virgilio

V. di Pta. Angelica

Borgo Angelico

Borgo Vittorio

Borgo Pio

V. Corridori

Piazza S. Pietro

Via della Conciliazione

Borgo Santo Spirito

Piazza S. Uffizio

Castel Sant' Angelo

Pza Pia

Lung. Vaticano

Lung. Castello

Piazza Adriana

Palazzo di Giustizia

Piazza Cavour

Piazza d. Liberta

Piazza Cinque Giornate

Ponte G. Matteotti

Lung. Armando da Brescia

Lung. Michelangelo

Ponte Reg. Margherita

Ponte Cavour

V. Visconti

V. G. Belli

V. Luci Caro

Lung. Prati

Lung. Mellini

Lung. Marzio

Pza. S. Salvatore

L. di Tor di Nono

Umberto I

Pte. S.

Lung. G. Zanardelli

Cor. dei Rinascimento

PIAZZA NAVONA

Piazza P. Paoli

Piazza d'Oro

Piazza d. Rovere

Lung. Gianicolense G.

Cor. Vitt. Emanuele II

Piazza di Chiesa Nuova

V. dei Vecchio

PIAZZA CAMPO D. FIORI

Via Monserrato

Via Giulia

Lung. dei Tebaldi

Lung. d. Farnesina Pte. Sisto

V. Pettinari

V. di Vallati

L. R. Sanzio

Ponte Garibaldi

JANICULUM HILL

VILLA ABAMELEK

Piazzale G. Garibaldi

PARCO GIANICOLENSE

Via Garibaldi

Piazza Trilussa

Piazza da Renzi

Piazza S. Egidio

Piazza di S. Cosimato

Piazza Mastai

V. Pta Cavalleggeri

Piazza Gregorio VII

Piazza S. Maria a Fornaci

V. Innocenzo III

Via delle Fornaci

Viale delle Mura Aurelie

V. Nuova delle Fornaci

Via A. Ceriani

Via Aurelia

VILLA DORIA PAMPHILI

Via di S. Pancrazio

V. d. Vascello

V.dei Quattro Venti

Via Garibaldi

TRASTEVERE

Piazza di S. Cosimato

VILLA SCIARRA

Viale Trastevere

Via Trastevere

Piazza di Pta. Portese

0   1/4 mi
0   0.25 km

1 Roman Forum
2 Pincio terraces
3 Campo de' Fiori
4 Via Appia Antica
5 Riding a scooter
6 Trastevere
7 Circus Maximus
8 Bar Sant'Eustachio

Previous page: Overlooking the city from the perenially romantic Pincio terraces.

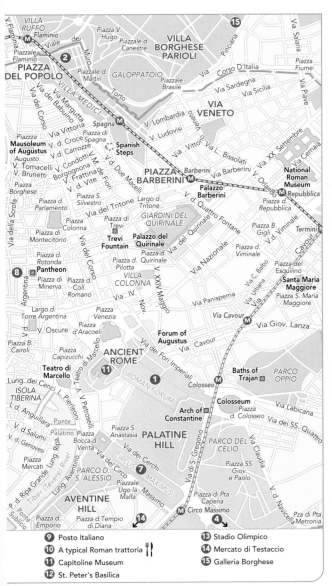

9 Posto Italiano
10 A typical Roman trattoria 🍴
11 Capitoline Museum
12 St. Peter's Basilica

13 Stadio Olimpico
14 Mercato di Testaccio
15 Galleria Borghese

When it comes to experiencing the best of Rome, sun-drenched days at the Colosseum are only the beginning—the Eternal City virtually bombards you with ways to enjoy yourself, from the visual to the gastronomical. With its unrivalled concentration of art and history, romantic scenery, and vibrant people, Rome embraces all with a monumental, irresistible charm. Here are the most sublime moments in our ongoing love affair.

1 **Gazing over the ruins of the Roman Forum and Palatine from the Capitoline Hill terraces in the evening** and, from there, strolling down Via dei Fori Imperiali, where strategically placed floodlights cast dramatic glows over solitary columns and the arches of the Colosseum. The ruins of Rome at night are truly, disarmingly spectacular. *See p 24.*

2 **Taking your lover to the Pincio terraces,** whose theatrical ivy-covered stone balustrades and view are virtually unchanged since the Renaissance, when maidens, courtiers, and the occasional knave no doubt met here for trysts and double-crossings. *See p 45.*

3 **After a long day of sightseeing, joining the rest of Rome for an aperitivo** at one of the outdoor bars on Campo de' Fiori. Take a seat, praise Bacchus for having created inexpensive, drinkable wine, and watch the world go by. *See p 56.*

4 **Treading the ancient paving stones along the leafy Via Appia Antica,** and leaving the hustle and bustle of the *centro* far behind. From the Catacombs to the ruined villas of Roman patricians, there's a quiet but heavy sense of history here. Umbrella pines and farmland perfume the air, transporting you back to the time when this was Rome's *Regina Viarum* (Queen of Roads). *See p 97.*

5 **Riding a scooter,** half-fearing for your life, over the broad cobblestone avenues of Rome's archaeological areas, past umbrella pines and 2,000-year-old ruins. Whether driven yourself, or as a passenger

The famous Roman sporting arena, Circus Maximus.

The traditional Roman dish, rigatoni alla carbonara.

on a chauffeured bike, it's a thrill ride and history lesson all in one.

⑥ **Wandering the untouristed, narrow back streets of Trastevere** and discovering shops, eateries, and slices of local life not listed in any guidebook. Separated from the rest of the old city by the river, this picturesque neighborhood has been able to maintain its own identity since ancient times, when it was simply called Trans Tiberim ("across the Tiber"). *See p 58.*

⑦ **Standing along the high western rim of the Circus Maximus** and absorbing the view from among the umbrella pines across to the ruins of Palatine Hill. As you do, imagine being one of the 300,000 fans cheering on the raucous, ancient Roman chariot races. *See p 27.*

⑧ **Mastering the art of taking a caffè at a real Roman bar.** Walk into the bar, greeting all with a smile and *"Buon giorno."* Pay for your drink at the *cassa,* and take your receipt to the bar counter. Slip a 10- or 20-cent tip on top of the receipt, and place your order with the *barista.* Drink your coffee as the Romans do—standing up at the bar.

⑨ **Buying Italian leather shoes** that look and feel as good as big-name designer—for a fraction of the price. Italy's sophisticated, lesser-known labels are a much more authentic souvenir than Gucci or Prada, and they'll still make your friends back home green with envy. Posto Italiano is a good place to start. *See p 87.*

⑩ **Spending hours over lunch or dinner** at a typical Roman trattoria or pizzeria, with a steady, wonderfully affordable flow of wine, water, and delicious food. Look for such Roman classics as *spaghetti alla carbonara* (pasta with bacon, black pepper, and eggs) or *saltimbocca alla romana* (thin slices of veal with cheese, ham, and sage). *See p 101.*

⑪ **Going to the Capitoline Museum's Palazzo Nuovo** in late afternoon on a crisp winter day, when no one else is there. Your only companions are half-drunk, smirking fauns and busts of Hadrian and Homer. *See p 31.*

⑫ **Taking your first step over the threshold of St. Peter's Basilica.** When the ethereal light of the low afternoon sun is broken into

Taking in a football game.

celestial beams by the basilica's well-placed windows, Bernini's stained-glass dove of the Holy Spirit against the church's terminal apse flickers with searing tones of amber. *See p 48.*

⓭ **Going to a Roma or Lazio football *(calcio)* game** on a sunny Sunday afternoon and joining in the infectious, unbridled exhilaration that floods the stadium when the home team scores. You're likely to be hugged and spun around by complete strangers. *See p 136.*

⓮ **Mixing with locals at the lively Mercato di Testaccio.** No other market in the city has such a strong sense of community: Yuppies and jovial retirees shuffle from stall to stall, passionately debating the latest political scandal—or *calcio* (football) league standings—while they expertly pick out the freshest culinary delights. Perhaps more so than any other Roman neighborhood, Testaccio has a salt-of-the-earth flavor drawn from its working-class slaughterhouse past. *See p 74.*

⓯ **Encountering Bernini's sculptures at Galleria Borghese.** Grimace in determination as *David* does against daunting adversary Goliath, or gape at the amazing detail of *Apollo and Daphne*. The paintings and ceiling frescoes throughout the gallery make for colorful counterpoints. *See p 30.* ●

Scenic Villa Borghese park.

1

The Best
Full-Day Tours

The Best **in One Day**

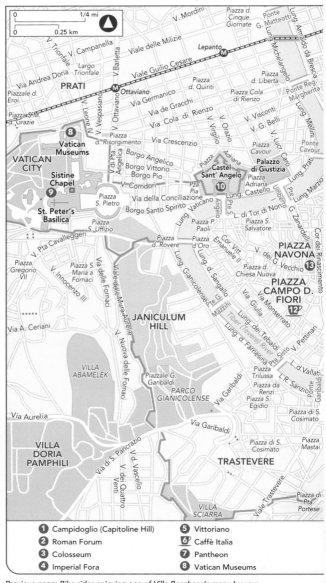

0   1/4 mi
0   0.25 km

❶ Campidoglio (Capitoline Hill)   ❺ Vittoriano

❷ Roman Forum   ❻ Caffè Italia

❸ Colosseum   ❼ Pantheon

❹ Imperial Fora   ❽ Vatican Museums

Previous page: Bike rider enjoying one of Villa Borghese's many byways.

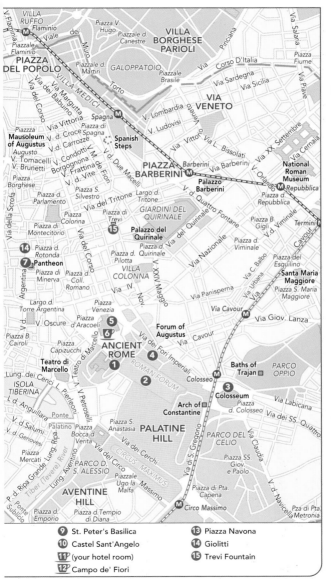

9 St. Peter's Basilica

10 Castel Sant'Angelo

11ª (your hotel room)

12ª Campo de' Fiori

13 Piazza Navona

14 Giolitti

15 Trevi Fountain

Seeing the top sights of Rome in 1 day requires an early start, discipline, and a bit of stamina, but it's actually quite doable. This "greatest hits" itinerary begins with an overview of the highlights of ancient Rome; after lunch, cross town and spend a few hours at the Vatican. Conclude your day with a leisurely evening walking tour of the gorgeously floodlit fountains and piazzas of the centro storico.
START: Take bus 30, 40, 62, 64, 70, 87, 95, 170, 492, or 628 to Piazza dell'Ara Coeli and climb the stairs to Piazza del Campidoglio.

Travel Tip

On this 1-day odyssey through the greatest hits of monumental Rome, be extra-vigilant for pickpockets, who are particularly predatory among the milling crowds at the Trevi Fountain and in the line for the Vatican Museums.

❶ ★★★ Campidoglio (Capitoline Hill). The most sacred of Rome's hills was given its present look in the 1500s, when Michelangelo designed the star-patterned square and surrounding buildings of the Capitoline Museums (see p 31, ❻). The bronze statue of

Ruins of the Roman Forum.

Marcus Aurelius in the center of the piazza is a copy; the 2nd-century-A.D. original is inside the museum. The western slopes of the hill, with their steep red tufa walls and tangled vegetation, still look much the same as they would have in the primordial days before the rise of Rome. Don't miss the majestic view of the Roman Forum from the south-facing terraces on either side of the bell-towered Palazzo Senatorio (city hall). ⏱ 15–30 min. Also gorgeous—and deserted—at night. Bus: 34, 40, 62, 64, 70, 87, 170, 492, or 571.

❷ ★★★ Roman Forum. While the Forum is not one of the better-preserved archaeological sites of ancient Rome, it is the most historically significant. The Forum was the nerve center of the most powerful Western civilization in history for the better part of a thousand years, where political decisions were made, public speeches were heard, and market activities took place. The remains here—of 2,000-year-old temples, law courts, and victory monuments—are impressive but skeletal, and can be difficult to decipher. Be sure to follow the detailed Roman Forum tour or consider hiring a guide. ⏱ 30–45 min. See p 24, ❼ for full details.

❸ ★★★ Colosseum. The Flavian amphitheater (A.D. 72–80) never fails to impress—for its elegant, enduring bulk and its disturbing former function as a theater of slaughter. At the height of the Roman Empire, games were held

Bloody battles were staged in the Colosseum.

almost every other day; in times of special celebration, games could last for weeks or months on end. Free *tesserae* (tickets) were distributed to about 65,000 Romans, who could be seated in the arena in a matter of minutes, thanks to an efficient system of 80 numbered *vomitoria* (entrance/exit passageways). Against slashing swords and gnashing lions' teeth, gladiators and *bestiarii* (animal fighters) fought to the death, hoping to someday win their freedom. (In the Colosseum's 400-year history, fewer than 100 men ever did.) A visit inside the massive structure is certainly rewarding, but if you're pressed for time or cash, a walk around the exterior is fine. If there's a long queue, buy your tickets at the Palatine (p 26, **8**) and go straight to the turnstiles.
🕐 *30–45 min. See p 26,* **10** *for full details.*

4 ★★ **Imperial Fora.** Mussolini blazed the broad thoroughfare of Via dell'Impero—now Via dei Fori Imperiali—to trumpet the glories of his ancient forebears and propagate his own ambitions of empire. Along the east side of the boulevard, the ruins of the forums built by emperors Nerva, Augustus, and Trajan can be seen protruding from the ancient street level, 7.6m (25 ft.) below. On the west side, near the Colosseum, don't miss the

fascinating marble maps (also from the Fascist period) charting the spread of the Roman Empire, which reached as far east as Iran (Parthia).
🕐 *30 min. Via dei Fori Imperiali.*

5 ★ **Vittoriano.** Locals revile the 100-year-old monument to Victor Emanuel II, the first king of united Italy, as a tasteless and over-the-top neoclassical "typewriter," but tourists can't seem to take their eyes off the plus-size marble confection on the south side of Piazza Venezia. Take the elevators (*ascensori panoramici*) to the uppermost level, the Terrazza delle Quadrighe, for the most thrilling view in Rome.
🕐 *30–45 min. Piazza Venezia.*
☎ *06-6780664. Elevators to upper terrace 7€. Mon–Thurs 9:30am–6:30pm, Fri–Sun 9:30am–7:30pm. Bus: 30, 40, 60, 62, 64, 70, 85, 87, or 492.*

Take a breather at **6** ★ **Caffè Italia**; this alfresco cafe is halfway up the summit of the Vittoriano, to the left of the gigantic bronze statue of the king on horseback. *Il Vittoriano.* ☎ *06-6780905. $–$$.*

7 ★★★ **Pantheon.** As the best-preserved and most elegant ancient building in the city—and perhaps the whole world—the Pantheon ("temple to all gods") merits multiple visits. It was designed and built under Hadrian from A.D. 118 to 125, in a form governed by circles and squares—shapes which, as Vitruvius wrote (and Leonardo later immortalized in his drawing *Vitruvian Man*), the human body most naturally occupies. The Pantheon's perfectly hemispherical, poured-concrete dome is 43m (141 ft.) tall and wide—1m (3 ft.) wider than the dome of St. Peter's. ⏲ *15–30 min. See p 54,* ⓫. *Take a taxi from the Pantheon to the Vatican Museums.*

⑧ ★★★ **Vatican Museums.** After lunch, the crowds have left the Vatican, making it much more pleasant to explore. Stay focused, however, and make sure you see the stirring ancient sculptures—the gut-wrenching emotion and dynamism of *Laocoon,* the transcendent composure of *Apollo Belvedere*—in the Pio-Clementine section of the museums, and then hightail it for the Vatican's biggest guns, Raphael's *stanze*

and Michelangelo's frescoes in the Sistine Chapel. The art here, by two of the greatest painters in history, is a triumph of Renaissance achievement, bold in color, lofty in concept, and monumental in scale. ⏲ *at least 1½ hr. See p 49,* ⑥ *for a more comprehensive review.*

⑨ ★★★ **St. Peter's Basilica.** The incomprehensibly voluminous Vatican basilica is packed with incalculable riches, from the marble and gold that cover its every surface to masterpieces like Michelangelo's *Pietà* and Bernini's *Baldacchino.* ⏲ *at least 30 min. Ascent to dome not absolutely necessary if pressed for time. See p 48,* ❷.

⑩ ★★ **Castel Sant'Angelo.** You probably won't have the time or energy to go inside, but the view of this mausoleum-turned-fortress, from ★★ **Ponte Sant'Angelo**—where angels by Bernini wince and

Michelangelo's masterful Pietá.

The spectacular nave of St. Peter's Basilica.

moan—is one of the most iconic images in Rome and not to be missed. ⏱ *15 min. See p 53,* **1** *for full details.*

By now it's 4 or 5pm—a good time to return to **11** your hotel room, rest your feet, and freshen up before heading back out for dinner and your evening walking tour. Just don't crash completely. If it's after 5pm and you're feeling energetic, skip the hotel and proceed directly to **12**, below.

By early evening (6–6:30pm), **13** ★★★ **Campo de' Fiori** in the very heart of the centro storico is abuzz with all kinds of people taking an aperitivo at the many outdoor bars. (I recommend Vineria Reggio.) Later in the evening, it's a younger scene. Campo de' Fiori and nearby Piazza Navona, the starting points of your evening tour, are also prime zones for dinner. ⏱ *1 hr. Bus: 30, 40, 62, 64, 70, 87, 116, or 492. $–$$.*

14 ★★★ **Piazza Navona.** The most famous baroque square in Rome, built on the site of the ancient athletic stadium of Domitian, boasts Bernini's fantastic

Fountain of the Four Rivers and Borromini's church of Sant'Agnese in Agone, as well as the smaller Fontana del Moro and Fontana di Nettuno. There are also a number of cafes to tempt you with after-dinner treats—it's unabashedly touristy, but the setting sure is pretty. ⏱ *20–30 min. See p 38,* **1**, *and p 54,* **6**. *Bus: 30, 40, 62, 64, 70, 87, 116, or 492.*

At **15** ★★ **Giolitti,** the centro storico's best-loved gelato shop, the setting is elegant and the ritual is fun. Pay the cashier up front, then negotiate your way through the crowds in back, where gracious servers scoop up enormous helpings of almost 100 flavors. *Via Uffici del Vicario 40.* ☎ *06-6991243. www. giolitti.it. $.*

16 ★★★ **Trevi Fountain.** Rome's most celebrated fountain, designed by Nicola Salvi and built from 1732–62, is delightful enough during the day, but at night, the floodlights make it look cleaner and doubly spectacular—so gorgeous that you won't even mind the crowds. ⏱ *20 min. Piazza di Trevi. Bus: 62, 85, 95, 175, or 492.*

Crowds wane at Trevi by night.

The Best in Two Days

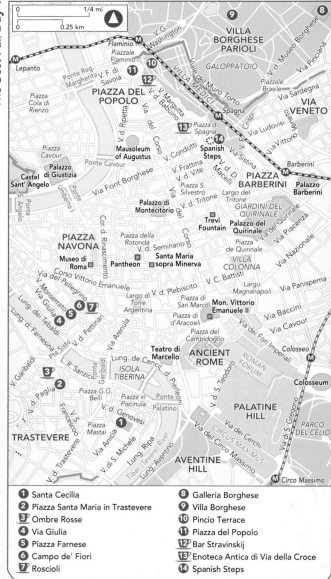

1 Santa Cecilia
2 Piazza Santa Maria in Trastevere
3 Ombre Rosse
4 Via Giulia
5 Piazza Farnese
6 Campo de' Fiori
7 Roscioli

8 Galleria Borghese
9 Villa Borghese
10 Pincio Terrace
11 Piazza del Popolo
12 Bar Stravinskij
13 Enoteca Antica di Via della Croce
14 Spanish Steps

On your second day, spend the morning wandering the picturesque squares and alleys of Trastevere and Campo de' Fiori, Rome's oldest and most authentic quarters. Have lunch, and then cross town to feast your eyes on the crown jewels of baroque art in the Galleria Borghese. Go for a stroll through the Villa Borghese, making your way to the Pincio terraces and their enchanting view over the city and the Vatican. Finish the day by visiting the elegant Tridente district below, where such *dolce vita* activities as shopping, drinking, and eating abound. Allow 2½ hours for the morning tour of Trastevere and Campo de' Fiori. START: **Take bus 23, 271, or 280 to Lungotevere degli Anguillara, and then walk to Piazza di Santa Cecilia; or take bus H, 780, or tram 8 to Piazza G. G. Belli, and walk.**

① ★ **Santa Cecilia.** This incredibly peaceful basilica—an 18th-century reworking of a medieval church—is dedicated to the patron saint of music, who was martyred here in the 3rd century A.D. Inside, altar mosaics dazzle, and fragments of Pietro Cavallini's wonderful 13th-century fresco of the *Last Judgment* can be seen at limited times. Cecilia was exhumed from her tomb in the crypt here in 1599, long enough for Stefano Maderno to sculpt the lovely (but disturbing—her throat is slashed) statue of the saint's still-uncorrupted body below the altar. The church is one of the most popular in Rome for weddings, evidenced by omnipresent grains of rice on the ground near the front door. ○ *20 min. Piazza di Santa Cecilia.* ☎ *06-5899289. Admission (for crypt and Cavallini frescoes): 2.50€. Daily 9:30am–1pm and 4–6:30pm. Cavallini frescoes: Mon–Sat 10:15am–12:15pm; Sun*

Abundant fresh produce in Campo de' Fiori.

11:30am–12:30pm. Bus: 23, 271, 280, or H. Tram: 3 or 8.

2 ★★ **Piazza and Basilica di Santa Maria in Trastevere.** The first church in Rome dedicated to the Virgin Mary is spectacular inside and out, with a landmark Roman-esque brick bell tower, colorful fres-coes, mosaics, and loads of recycled ancient marbles. The eponymous square in front of the church acts as a kind of common living room for the neighborhood—it seems that every resident of Trastevere crosses the wide expanse of cobblestones here at some point during the day. See also p 39, **8**, and p 43, **8**. ⏲ 20 min. Piazza Santa Maria in Trastevere. ☎ 06-5819443. Daily 7:30am–9pm. Bus: 23, 271, 280, or H. Tram: 8.

3 ★ **Ombre Rosse** cafe, with a porchlike view over a charming piazza, is more stylish than the average neighborhood bar. It's still frequented by born-and-bred, local trasteverini, and perfect for cappuccino-sipping and people-watching. Piazza Sant' Egidio 12. ☎ 06-5884155. www.ombrerosse-caffe.it. $–$$.

4 ★★ **Via Giulia.** Bearing straight from the Vatican from Ponte Sisto, this former pilgrim route is home to many art galleries and high-end, original boutiques. Via Giulia's most fetching feature is an arch—with overgrown ivy draped luxuriously toward the pitch-black cobblestones—that spans the road behind Palazzo Farnese. ⏲ 15 min. Bus: 23, 271, or 280.

5 ★★ **Piazza Farnese.** Sophis-ticated and regal Piazza Farnese is where locals come to read the newspaper or to push a stroller in

peace, against the stately, yellow-brick backdrop of 16th-century Palazzo Farnese. The sleepy square seems a world away—in reality, it's only a block—from the hubbub of Campo de' Fiori. See also p 39, **10**, and p 56, **3**. ⏲ 15 min. Bus: 23, 30, 40, 62, 64, 70, 87, 116, 271, 492, or 571. Tram: 8.

6 ★★★ **Campo de' Fiori.** Rome's market square par excel-lence, the Campo is the perfect embodiment of the myth of Italy. Every morning from Monday to Sat-urday, the square hosts a lively fruit, vegetable, and trinket bazaar. By early evening, where grocery shop-pers eyed pachino tomatoes a few hours before, Rome's bright young things are scoping each other out over sparkling wine and efferves-cent conversation, indulging in the carefree atmosphere of this always busy outdoor salon. See also p 39, **11**, and p 56, **1**. ⏲ 20–30 min. Bus: 23, 30, 40, 62, 64, 70, 87, 116, or 492. Tram: 8.

Break for lunch at **7** **Roscioli,** around Campo de' Fiori, before beginning the second part of the day's tour. For savory pizza-bread sandwiches stuffed with charcuterie goodness, Antico Forno Roscioli can't be beat (p 57, **7**). $.

8 ★★★ **Galleria Borghese.** Reel in amazement at sculptures by Bernini (and other masterpieces) at one of the world's most outstand-ing small museums. Visits must be booked at least 1 day in advance: Go for the 1 or 3pm time slot. See also p 30, **3**. ⏲ 1 hr. Piazzale Museo Borghese. ☎ 06-32810. www.galleriaborghese.it. Admission 11€ plus 2€ booking fee. Tues–Sun 9am–7pm (last visit 5pm). Bus: 116 or 910.

The iconic Spanish Steps.

introduction to the "good life" in the Tridente district, which spreads out pronglike to the south. See also p 38, ④, and p 61, ❶. ⏱ *15 min. Metro: Flaminio.*

Forget the cheesy sidewalk cafes of Via Veneto—these days, celebs hounded by the paparazzi duck into the (pricey) **⓬** ★★ **Bar Stravinskij** inside the glamorous Hotel de Russie. In warm weather, sit outside in the gorgeous interior garden, sloping up toward the Pincio; in winter, get cozy at the piano bar's indoor tables. *Via del Babuino 9.* ☎ *06-32888874. $$$–$$$$.*

⓭ ★★ **Enoteca Antica di Via della Croce.** For a more budget-friendly snack, grab a barstool or sidewalk seat and enjoy some wine and tantalizing plates of meats, cheeses, and olives at this friendly spot. A favorite of expats living in Rome. *Via della Croce 76B.* ☎ *06-6790896. www.anticaenoteca. com. $$.*

❾ ★★ **Villa Borghese.** Go for a relaxing stroll among the refreshing greenery of Rome's most central public park. Boats can be rented at the picturesque *laghetto.* See also p 92. ⏱ *at least 30 min. Daily 6am–sunset. Metro: Spagna. Bus: 52, 53, 63, 116, or 910. Tram: 3 or 19.*

❿ ★★★ **Pincio Terrace.** Hearts flutter at the impressive perspective on the Vatican from this panoramic spot above Piazza del Popolo. It's gloriously sun-filled by day, ultraromantic by night. See also p 45, ❸. ⏱ *15 min. Metro: Flaminio.*

⓫ ★★ **Piazza del Popolo.** Romans and tourists alike bask in the late-afternoon sun that floods this vast, traffic-free oval space just below the Pincio. Graced in the center by a massive, hieroglyphed pink-granite obelisk, the "Square of the People" is wonderfully elegant and uncluttered—perfect for idling and gelato-licking, and a fitting

⓮ ★★★ **Spanish Steps.** Fortunately, the sweeping beauty of the Scalinata di Piazza di Spagna transcends the sometimes-ugly crowds of tourists that populate the square day and night. The climb to the high terrace covers 12 curving flights of steps of varying width—you'll trip if you don't watch where your feet are—but the view from the top is exhilarating. Come between 2 and 6am, and you'll enjoy that rarest of Roman treats—having the fabulous stage of the Spanish Steps to yourself. See also p 63, ⓫. ⏱ *30 min. Metro: Spagna.*

The Best in Three Days

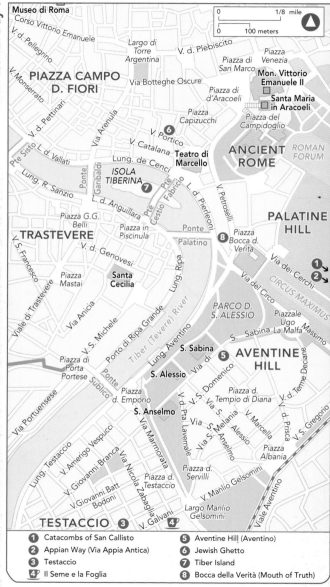

Museo di Roma
Corso Vittorio Emanuele
V. d. Pellegrino

0   1/8 mile
0   100 meters

Largo di Torre Argentina
V. d. Plebiscito
Piazza di San Marco
Piazza Venezia

PIAZZA CAMPO D. FIORI

Via Botteghe Oscure

Mon. Vittorio Emanuele II
Santa Maria in Aracoeli
Piazza del Campidoglio

V. Monserrato
V. d. Pettinari
Via Arenula
Pte Sisto L. d. Vallati
Lung. R. Sanzio
Ponte Garibaldi
Lung. de Cenci
L. d. Anguillara

6 V. Portico
V. Catalana
Piazza di d'Aracoeli
Piazza Capizucchi
Teatro di Marcello

ANCIENT ROME
ROMAN FORUM

ISOLA TIBERINA **7**
Pte Cestio Fabricio
L. d. Pierleoni
V. Petroselli

Piazza G.G. Belli
TRASTEVERE
V. d. Genovesi
Piazza in Piscinula
Ponte Palatino
8 Piazza Bocca d. Verita

PALATINE HILL

1 **2**
Via dei Cerchi
CIRCUS MAXIMUS

S. Francesco
Viale di Trastevere
Piazza Mastai
Santa Cecilia
Via Anicia
V. S. Michele
Porto di Ripa Grande
Lung. Ripa
Tiber (Tevere) River
Lung. Aventino

Via del Circo
PARCO D. S. ALESSIO
Piazzale Ugo La Malfa
S. Sabina Massimo

S. Sabina **5**
AVENTINE HILL

Via di

Piazza di Porta Portese
Via Portuensese
Ponte Sublicio
Piazza d. Emporio
S. Alessio
S. Anselmo
V. d. Pta. Lavernale
Via S. Domenico
Piazza d. Tempio di Diana
V. S. Melania
V. S. Alessio
Via S. Anselmo
Via S. Marcella
V. d. Prisca
Piazza Albania
V. d. Temte Deciane
V. S. Gregorio

Lung. Testaccio
V. Amerigo Vespucci
V. Giovanni Branca
V. Giovanni Batt Bodoni
Via Nicola Zabaglia
Piazza d. Testaccio
Piazza d. Servilli
V. Manlio Gelsomini
Viale Aventino

TESTACCIO **3**
V. Galvani
4 **2**
Largo Manlio Gelsomini

---

1 Catacombs of San Callisto

2 Appian Way (Via Appia Antica)

3 Testaccio

4 Il Seme e la Foglia

5 Aventine Hill (Aventino)

6 Jewish Ghetto

7 Tiber Island

8 Bocca della Verità (Mouth of Truth)

One of the best and most surprising things about Rome is how quickly you can escape the urban chaos and enjoy the rustic tranquility of the city's greener areas, just a few miles away from the tourist hordes. On your third day, visit the catacombs and breathe the spicy, rural air along the history-saturated Appian Way. Then, go for a stroll in the contrasting, adjacent neighborhoods of Testaccio and the Aventine. Finish the day back in the *centro storico* with a walk through the Jewish Ghetto and Tiber Island. (Alternatively, get out of town entirely, and go for a day trip to Ostia Antica or Tivoli. See p 155 and 152.) START: **Take bus 118 or a taxi to the Catacombe di San Callisto on the Appian Way (the entrance is 3.2km/2 miles south of Porta San Sebastiano gate).**

❶ ★★★ Catacombs of San Callisto. Nineteen kilometers (12 miles) and four levels of hand-dug tunnels make up the underground network of Rome's largest catacombs, home to the tombs of half a million Christians, buried here from the 1st to the 4th centuries A.D. Deep within the complex, a labyrinth of 9m-high (30-ft.) tunnels, whose walls are perforated up to the ceiling with *loculi* (tomb niches), is especially impressive (and uncannily reminiscent of college library stacks). See also p 46, ❶. ⏱ *45 min. Via Appia Antica 110.* ☎ *06-5130151. www.catacombe.roma.it. Admission 8€. Open Thurs–Tues 9am–noon, 2–5pm. Bus: 118.*

❷ ★★★ Appian Way. Few places in Rome transport you to ancient times as well as the Via

Fountain at Santa Sabina church, on peaceful Aventine Hill.

Appia Antica, whose black basalt cobblestones, still bearing the wheel ruts of ancient cart traffic, stretch south of the city from Porta San Sebastiano. A few miles from the city walls, a rustic, agrarian landscape opens up on either side of the 4th-century-B.C. highway; the scenery is scattered with imposing or modest remains of ancient tombs and villas, and shepherds drive flocks of sheep from pasture to pasture, right across the "Queen of Roads." Even the scent of the Appian Way is ripe with antiquity: Once you smell it, the combination of bright notes of umbrella pine needles, musty sunbaked brick and marble, and the acrid pungency of leaves burning in farmyards becomes indelible in your memory. See also p 94. ⏱ *1 hr. Bus: 118.*

❸ ★★ Testaccio. Anchored by an artificial hill made of ancient pottery cast-offs and populated by salt-of-the-earth *romani de' Roma* (and the odd sheep or goat), the authentic neighborhood of Testaccio oozes character. See also p 72. ⏱ *1 hr. Metro: Piramide. Bus: 30, 60, 75, 95, 118, or 170. Tram: 3.*

With views of the old slaughterhouse and the potsherds of Monte Testaccio, hip corner joint ❹ ★ Il **Seme e la Foglia** is a great place

Nuns walking along Via Panisperna in the Monti neighborhood.

for a casual, quick lunch of enormous and tasty salads and sandwiches. *Via Galvani 18.*
☎ *06-5743008. $–$$.*

⑤ ★★★ Aventine. Oblivious to the noise of the *centro* below, Aventine Hill is an elegant and mostly residential enclave, and home to several churches, whose dignified and simple redbrick exteriors and grassy grounds are a welcome contrast from the fussy facades and cramped quarters of many Roman churches. The 5th-century-A.D. church of Santa Sabina is cavernous and calming—a sublime example of the basilican form. ⓧ *1 hr. Metro: Circo Massimo. Bus: 30, 60, 75, 81, 95, 118, 175, or 628. Tram: 3.*

⑥ ★★ Jewish Ghetto. As the area where Roman Jews were confined from the 16th to the 19th centuries, the medieval quarter between the Capitoline and the Tiber has seen its share of dark days. Today, however, the Ghetto is an upbeat, characteristic part of the *centro storico* that many tourists miss. From towering ancient ruins like the Theater of Marcellus, to sculptural gems like the Fountain of the Tortoises in Piazza Mattei, to the triumphant synagogue, this small area has a lot to see. See also p 66. ⓧ *45 min. Bus: 30, 40, 62, 64, 70, 81, 87, 170, 271, 492, or 628. Tram: 8.*

⑦ ★★ Tiber Island. This boat-shaped protuberance in the middle

of the river, between the Ghetto and Trastevere, is an oasis of calm; ever since the Greek god of medicine, Aesculapius, washed up here disguised as a snake, the island has been the city's sanctuary of medicine. Check out the lower promenade (water level permitting), with its great views of the ancient bridges nearby. See also p 66. ⓧ *30 min. Bus: 23, 30, 40, 62, 64, 70, 81, 87, 170, 271, 280, 492, or 628. Tram: 8.*

⑧ ★Bocca della Verità. Wrap up day 3 with a visit to Rome's time-honored, silly touristic rite, the Mouth of Truth. Set inside the porch of Santa Maria in Cosmedin is an ancient sewer-cover with a face carved into it. According to legend, truthful tourists may stick their hands in its mouth worry-free, while liars will have their hands snapped off. Either way, just do it—you might even get a little nervous as your fingers slide into that stoic maw. See p 69 ⑭ for full details. ●

Tiber Island, looking upstream from Ponte Palatino.

Ancient Rome

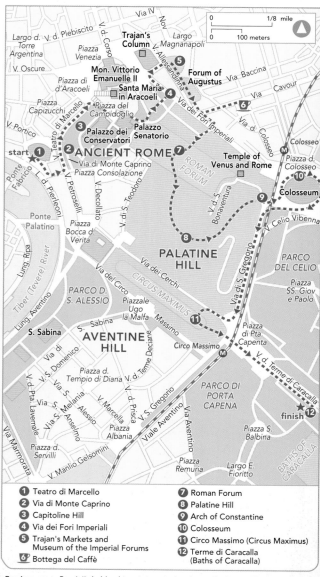

0   1/8 mile
0   100 meters

Via IV Nov

Largo d. V. d. Plebiscito

Largo Magnanapoli

Trajan's Column

Largo d.
Torre
Argentina

Piazza
Venezia

V. Oscure

V. d. Corso

Piazza di
d'Aracoeli

Mon. Vittorio Emanuelle II

V. Alessandrina

⑤

Forum of Augustus

Via d. Baccina

Via Cavour

Santa Maria in Aracoeli

④

Piazza
Capizucchi

Piazza del
Campidoglio

Via dei Fori Imperiali

⑥

Via d. Colosseo

V. Portico

③ Palazzo dei Conservatori

Palazzo Senatore

Colosseo

Piazza d.
Colosseo

V. Capizucchi

start **①**

② ANCIENT ROME

⑦

Temple of Venus and Rome

⑩

Ponte
Fabricio

L. d. Pierleoni

Via di Monte Caprino
Piazza Consolazione

V. di Teatro di Marcello

V. Petroselli

V. Decollato

ROMAN
FORUM

Colosseum

Piazza d.
Colosseo

Ponte
Palatino

Lung. Ripa

Tiber (Tevere) River

Piazza
Bocca d.
Verita

V. di S. Teodoro

V. di S. Bonaventura

⑧

PALATINE HILL

⑨

V. Celio Vibenna

PARCO DEL CELIO

Piazza
SS. Giov
e Paolo

Lung. Aventino

PARCO D.
S. ALESSIO

Via del Circo

Via dei Cerchi

CIRCUS MAXIMUS

Via di S. Gregorio

S. Sabina

AVENTINE HILL

Via di
S. Domenico

Via di S. Sabina

S. Sabina

Piazzale
Ugo
la Malfa

Massimo

⑪

Piazza
di Pta.
Capenta

V. d. Terme di Caracalla

Via Marmorata

V. d. Pta. Lavernale

Via S. Melania

V. S. Anselmo

V. S. Alessio

Piazza d.
Tempio di Diana

V. d. Terme Deciane

V. S. Prisca

V. Marcella

V. S. Gregorio

Viale Aventino

Circo Massimo

M

PARCO DI PORTA CAPENA

Piazza S.
Balbina

Piazza
Albania

Via Aventino

Piazza d.
Servilli

V. Manlio Gelsomini

Piazza
Remuria

Largo E.
Fioritto

finish ⑫

Piazza d.
Servilli

BATHS OF
CARACALLA

---

① Teatro di Marcello
② Via di Monte Caprino
③ Capitoline Hill
④ Via dei Fori Imperiali
⑤ Trajan's Markets and Museum of the Imperial Forums
⑥ Bottega del Caffè

⑦ Roman Forum
⑧ Palatine Hill
⑨ Arch of Constantine
⑩ Colosseum
⑪ Circo Massimo (Circus Maximus)
⑫ Terme di Caracalla (Baths of Caracalla)

Previous page: Bernini's baldacchino rises over the altar at St. Peter's Basilica.

In towering brick or crumbling marble, the awe-inspiring ruins of ancient Rome are concentrated in the archaeological park south of the *centro storico*. Here, in an undulating topography drenched in history and dotted with umbrella pines, lie such famed sights as the Forum and the Colosseum, as well as the most sacred hills of Rome, the Capitoline and the Palatine. Bring a bottle of water and a picnic, and wear comfortable shoes for this half- or full-day tour. In summer, avoid these sites during the intense heat of midday. START: **Take bus 30, 95, 170, or 628 to Via del Teatro di Marcello, or take bus 40, 62, 64, 70, 87, or 492 to Via d'Aracoeli or Piazza Venezia, and walk.**

❶ ★ Teatro di Marcello. The familiar arches of this 1st-century-B.C. theater, used for plays and concerts, inspired the design of the Colosseum, built 100 years later. *Via del Teatro di Marcello.*

❷ ★ Via di Monte Caprino. Past shade trees and weathered fountains, this charming path winds its way up the Capitoline Hill's western slope. In 390 B.C., the Gauls attempted to storm the Capitol under cover of darkness and the dense vegetation here, but the sacred geese of Rome, kept in a pen nearby, detected their movement and sounded the alarm, thwarting the raiders. (The Capitoline guard dogs, who slept through it, were later crucified.)

❸ ★★ Capitoline Hill. Analogous to the Acropolis in Athens, this was the citadel and religious nerve center of ancient Rome. Atop this spur of red tufa, augurs monitored the flight of birds for omens, and traitors were hurled from the infamous Tarpeian Rock. The temple of Jupiter here, now lost, dominated the Roman skyline for centuries. Though it was redubbed Campidoglio in the Middle Ages and architecturally restyled during the Renaissance, the Capitoline's air of antiquity remains palpable. Be sure to visit the hill's southern terraces for staggeringly gorgeous views over the Roman Forum. *See p 45, ❽ for Piazza del Campidoglio, and p 31, ❻ for the Capitoline Museums.*

❹ ★★ Via dei Fori Imperiali. Mussolini created this tree-lined boulevard, running dead-straight from his balcony at Palazzo Venezia

The arched walls of the Teatro di Marcello.

to the Colosseum, to showcase the reminders of Rome's glory days and military might. On the east side of the street, from north to south, are the forums of Trajan, Augustus, and Nerva; on the west side are the Forum of Julius Caesar and the original Roman Forum.

⑤ ★★ Trajan's Markets & Museum of the Imperial Forums.

Majestic and overtly phallic, the 40m-high (130-ft.) marble Column of Trajan was dedicated in A.D. 113 to commemorate the Romans' victory over Dacia (modern Romania). The ascending spiral band of sculptured reliefs depicts all stages of the military campaign, down to the finest detail. The most dominant feature in Trajan's Forum is the massive, concave-fronted brick structure known as Trajan's Markets. Built on three levels, the markets were the world's first mall, housing 150 shops and commercial offices. Recent restorations converted part of Trajan's Markets into exhibition space for the Museum of the Imperial Forums, which has excellent visual displays that help you imagine what these grand public squares and temples used to look like. ⏱ 45 min. Via IV Novembre 94. ☎ 06-69923521. 11€. Tues–Sun 9am–7pm. Bus: 30, 40, 60, 62, 64, 70, 85, 87, 95, 170, 175, or 492.

Grab a bite and people-watch at busy alfresco ⑥ **Bottega del Caffè**, just up the hill from the Forum (and a world away from the predatory tourist snack carts down there). Pastries, salads, and panini are available, as are wine, beer, coffee, and soft drinks. *Piazza Madonna dei Monti 5 (at Via dei Serpenti).* ☎ *06-4741578. $–$$.*

⑦ ★★★ Roman Forum.

The Forum was the beating heart of republican and imperial Rome and the most important civic space in all of Western civilization for much of antiquity. It was here, in temples, basilicas, and markets—that range in date from the 6th century B.C. to the 5th century A.D.—that the Roman people carried out their daily religious, political, and commercial activities. Today, the Forum is a picturesque and evocative ruin that bears the deep scars of Roman "recycling"; when power over Rome passed from the emperors to the popes, church fathers dismantled the pagan buildings for their precious marble and bronze. From the late Middle Ages, dirt, debris, and cow manure accumulated in the Forum, reaching a height of 9m (30 ft.) by the 1890s, when excavations began.

The Roman Forum seen from Piazza del Campidoglio.

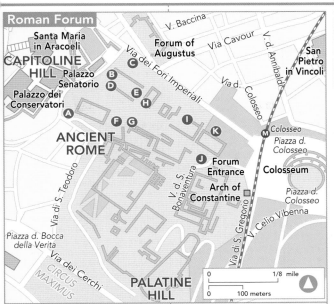

The eight columns of the **7A** ★ **Temple of Saturn** indicate the former height of all the structures here. Nearby, the **7B** ★★ **Arch of Septimius Severus** was erected in the 3rd century A.D. to celebrate that emperor's triumph in Parthia (modern Iran). The tall brick **7C** ★★ **Curia Julia** (29 B.C.) is where the Roman senate met. The low, brown **7D** ★ **Rostra,** or orator's stage, is where Mark Antony addressed friends, Romans, and countrymen. All that's left of the one-time hexastyle (six-columned front) **7E** ★ **Temple of Julius Caesar** (29 B.C.) is its podium. Under its green metal roof is the rocky mound where Caesar's funeral pyre burned for 7 days in 44 B.C. Near here, the picturesque *tria columna* of the **7F** ★★ **Temple of Castor and Pollux** have helped centuries of poets imagine the splendor of Rome in its heyday. A curved grouping of smaller columns in this area is

the ruins of the **7G** ★ **Temple of Vesta,** where the six Vestal Virgins tended the eternal flame of Rome. Opposite, the hexastyle **7H** ★★ **Temple of Antoninus and Faustina** (A.D. 141) survives because it was reconsecrated as a church in the medieval period. The three soaring vaults of the spectacular, 4th-century-A.D. **7I** ★★★ **Basilica of Maxentius** represent only one-third of the law court's original size. Sculptural reliefs on the **7J** ★★ **Arch of Titus** (A.D. 81) glorify the sack of Jerusalem. Reopened to the public in 2010 after a 26-year restoration the **7K** **Temple of Venus and Roma** was the largest in ancient Rome. ⏱ *1 hr. Apr–Oct, go after 2pm to avoid crowds. Largo Romolo e Remo.* ☎ *06-39967700. 12€ (includes Colosseum and Palatine). Daily 9am–1 hr. before sunset. Metro: Colosseo. Bus: 60, 75, 85, 87, 95, or 175.*

❽ ★★ Palatine Hill. Back in 753 B.C., Romulus killed Remus and founded Roma on the Palatine. Later, emperors and other ancient bigwigs built their palaces and private entertainment facilities here. Nowadays, it's a sprawling, crowd-free archaeological garden, with plenty of shady spots good for picnicking and cooling off in summer. Be sure to check out the House of Augustus, which was opened to the public in 2008. The Palatine's extensive ruins are time-consuming to explore and not very well marked, which is fascinating for some but frustrating for those in a hurry. ⏱ *45 min. Entrances near Arch of Titus and at Via di San Gregorio 30.* ☎ *06-39967700. 12€ (includes Roman Forum, and Colosseum). Daily 9am–1 hr. before sunset. Metro: Colosseo. Bus: 60, 75, 85, 87, 95, or 175. Tram: 3.*

❾ ★ Arch of Constantine. Decorated largely with sculpture looted from earlier emperors' monuments, this arch was dedicated in

Steep stairs ascend into the Colosseum.

A.D. 315 to commemorate the Battle of the Milvian Bridge (A.D. 312), in which Constantine defeated his co-emperor, Maxentius, after having a vision of the Christian cross. The superstitious Constantine legalized Christianity in A.D. 313 with the Edict of Milan, ending centuries of persecution.

❿ ★★★ Colosseum. Occupying the masses' free time with escapist, high-testosterone spectacles, the games at the Flavian amphitheater were the NASCAR of antiquity. Inaugurated in A.D. 80 over the site of Nero's lake, the Colosseum hosted 65,000 fans every other day with its gory contests between men and animals. The enormous scale and masterful architecture of the amphitheater, supported entirely on radial and lateral arches, can be appreciated well enough from the outside, but inside, a modern catwalk allows visitors to stand at the same level where gladiators and hippos once fought to the death. Below, an ingenious system of 32 elevator shafts and trapdoors kept the action constant, replenishing the arena with new combatants and props when one fight ended. In A.D. 523, well after the rise of Christianity, the fights ended for good. Over the years, earthquakes, popes, barbarians, and the environment have all played a role in the Colosseum's decay. The pockmarks that riddle the travertine walls indicate where metal-hungry Lombards gouged into the stone in the 9th century to extract the lead fasteners between the blocks. ⏱ *45 min.; crowded until late afternoon—buy tickets at the Roman Forum or Palatine Hill to skip the queue. Piazza del Colosseo.* ☎ *06-39967700. 12€ (includes Roman Forum and Palatine). Daily 9am–1 hr. before sunset. Metro:*

held fans—300,000 of them—most in thrall. The Circo Massimo is now just a grassy cavity, but its long racetrack shape remains, and with the evocative brick ruins of the Palatine towering above, it's still a powerful place. *Metro: Circo Massimo. Bus: 30, 60, 75, or 95. Tram: 3.*

⓬ ★★ Terme di Caracalla. Luxurious bathing complexes, like those built by Caracalla in A.D. 212 below the Aventine Hill, were a sort of country club in ancient times, but open to rich and poor and as integral to the Romans' daily life as shuffling through the Forum on business or watching gladiators slug it out in the Colosseum. ⏱ *45 min. Viale delle Terme di Caracalla 52.* ☎ *06-39967700. 6€ (valid for 7 days; includes Villa dei Quintili and Mausoleum of Cecilia Metella). Audioguide 4€. Tues–Sun 9am–1 hr. before sunset; Mon 9am–2pm. Metro: Circo Massimo. Bus:118. Tram: 3.*

Taking a break at Circus Maximus, with a view of the Palatine.

Colosseo. Bus: 60, 75, 85, 87, 95, or 175. Tram: 3.

⓫ ★ Circo Massimo. Before there was Russell Crowe in *Gladiator*, there was Charlton Heston in *Ben-Hur*. In the world of ancient Roman sports, it was the chariot races at the Circus Maximus that

The baths of Caracalla.

The Best Museums

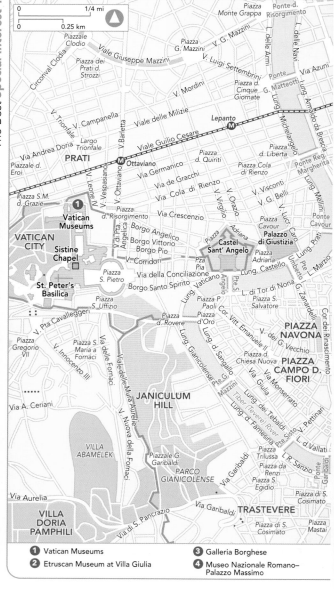

1. Vatican Museums
2. Etruscan Museum at Villa Giulia
3. Galleria Borghese
4. Museo Nazionale Romano–Palazzo Massimo

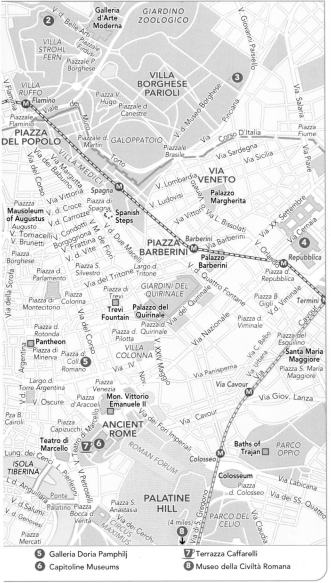

5 Galleria Doria Pamphilj

6 Capitoline Museums

7 Terrazza Caffarelli

8 Museo della Civiltà Romana

Of the more than 150 museums in Rome, those listed here are my favorites for all-around interest, from intimate family collections to Fascist-era didactic museums. START: Take bus 23, 49, or 492 to the entrance of the Vatican Museums, or take tram 19 to Piazza Risorgimento, or take Metro Line A to Ottaviano-San Pietro or Cipro-Musei Vaticani, and walk.

❶ ★★★ Vatican Museums.
From mummies to moon rocks, the papal collections have the best of everything. See p 49, ❻.

❷ ★★ Etruscan Museum at Villa Giulia.
Pope Julius III's gorgeous Mannerist villa houses priceless artifacts including intricate gold jewelry and a charming his-and-hers sarcophagus from the civilization that ruled Italy before the Romans. ⏱ 45 min. Piazza Villa Giulia (at Viale delle Belle Arti). ☎ 06-3226571. 8€. Tues–Sun 8:30am–7:30pm. Tram: 2, 3, or 19.

❸ ★★★ Galleria Borghese.
Immensely entertaining and mercifully manageable in size,

Agesander, Athenodoros, and Polydorus' Laocoön and His Sons at the Vatican Museums.

the collection at this 17th-century garden estate is museum perfection. Ancient Roman mosaics in the entrance salon depict gory scenes between gladiators and wild animals. In Room 1, Canova's Pauline Bonaparte (1805–08) lies, topless, on a marble divan. Bernini's staggeringly skillful sculptures of David, Apollo and Daphne and Rape of Persephone (1621–24), in rooms 2 to 4, are so realistically rendered that their subjects seem to be breathing. The paintings by Caravaggio in Room 8 range in tone from luscious (Boy with a Basket of Fruit, 1594) to strident and grisly (David and Goliath, 1610). Renaissance masterpieces like Raphael's Deposition (1507) and Titian's Sacred and Profane Love (1514) hang casually upstairs in the pinacoteca. ⏱ 1 hr. Piazzale Museo Borghese. ☎ 06-32810. www.galleriaborghese. it. Reservations required. 11€. Tues–Sun 8:30am–7:30pm. Bus: 116 or 910.

❹ ★★ Museo Nazionale Romano—Palazzo Massimo.
An embarrassment of ancient riches—paintings, mosaics, statues, and inscriptions—is displayed at this recently restored, bright, and airy palazzo near the train station. Frescoes teeming with delightful animal and vegetable motifs, rescued from the bedrooms and dining rooms of Roman villas, are the highlight here and totally unique among Rome's museums. ⏱ 1 hr. Largo di Villa Peretti 1 (at Via Giolitti). ☎ 06-39967700. 7€. Tues–Sun 9am–7:45pm. Metro: Termini. Bus: C2, H, 36, 38, 40, 64, 86, 90, 92, 105, 170, 175, 217, 310, 360, 714, or 910.

Emperor Constantine, the Capitoline Museums.

sculptures in the world. The Palazzo dei Conservatori houses the 5th-century-B.C. bronze Capitoline Wolf, mascot of Rome, in Room 4, and the photogenic fragments of the colossal statue of *Constantine* in the courtyard. The *pinacoteca* has a number of fine works by Caravaggio, Titian, Tintoretto, and Guido Reni. Across the square in the Palazzo Nuovo are the majestic 2nd-century-A.D. bronze of *Marcus Aurelius*, haunting busts of emperors and philosophers in rooms 4 and 5, and myriad marble fauns and satyrs throughout. Not to be missed, the ponderous tufa blocks of the *tabularium* (Roman archive hall, 78 B.C.) connect the two wings of the museums and offer dramatic views over the Forum. ⏱ *1½ hr. Best in late afternoon. Piazza del Campidoglio 1.* ☎ *06-67102071. 9.50€. Tues–Sun 9am–8pm. Bus: 40, 44, 62, 63, 64, 70, 81, 87, 95, 170, 204, 628, 640, 715, 716, 780, 810, 850, or 492.*

The Capitoline Museum's café **7** ★ **Terrazza Caffarelli** has fresh sandwiches and drinks—and a commanding view of the centro storico. Non-museumgoers can access the cafe from the northern wall of Palazzo dei Conservatori. *$–$$.*

⑤ ★★ **Galleria Doria Pamphilj.** The patinated halls of this noble palace still smell like the 17th century. Masterpieces collected by the Doria Pamphilj family—one of the most influential in Roman history—include works by Caravaggio, Guercino, Raphael, and Titian, and Velázquez's famous portrait of Pope Innocent X Pamphilj. Admission includes the highly entertaining audio tour, narrated by the living princes themselves. ⏱ *1 hr. Via del Corso 305.* ☎ *06-6797323. 11€. Mon–Sun 10am–5pm. Bus: 30, 40, 62, 64, 85, 87, 95, 170, or 492.*

⑥ ★★★ **Capitoline Museums (Musei Capitolini).** In the Michelangelo-designed buildings of Piazza del Campidoglio are some of the most important Roman

⑧ ★★ **Museo della Civiltà Romana.** It's worth the subway ride to Mussolini's fantasyland—EUR—to see the enormous, 1:250-scale plastic model of ancient Rome. The rest of the museum is filled with reproductions of ancient structures (the aqueducts) and fascinating engineering feats (construction of the Colosseum). *Piazza Agnelli 10.* ☎ *06-5926135. 8.50€. Tues–Sun 9am–2pm. Metro: Fermi.*

Baroque Rome

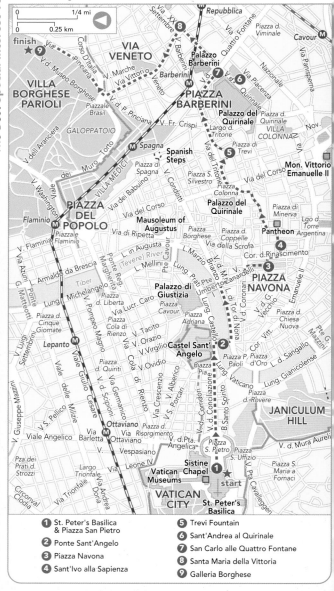

1. St. Peter's Basilica & Piazza San Pietro
2. Ponte Sant'Angelo
3. Piazza Navona
4. Sant'Ivo alla Sapienza
5. Trevi Fountain
6. Sant'Andrea al Quirinale
7. San Carlo alle Quattro Fontane
8. Santa Maria della Vittoria
9. Galleria Borghese

Straight lines and right angles? Ugh—so 1500s! The 17th century in Rome saw a boom in artistic patronage—the biggest in the city since the days of the Caesars—that heralded the arrival of a new style, called *barocco* ("irregular pearl"), in which sculptors and architects traded the balance and symmetry of the Renaissance for dynamism and theatrical flourish. The two greatest exponents of Roman baroque were Francesco Borromini and Gian Lorenzo Bernini, who left their respective curricula vitae virtually strewn about the city. Occasionally over-the-top, but always fun, the baroque style is what gave Rome its signature sinuous building facades and its myriad playful fountains. It's what makes an aimless stroll through the *centro storico* so rewarding. START: **Take bus 23, 40, 62, or 64 to Piazza Pia/Via della Conciliazione.**

❶ ★★★ St. Peter's Basilica & Piazza San Pietro. Reaching out from either side of the church, the curving, colonnaded arms of Piazza San Pietro were designed by Bernini in the 1650s to mimic a gigantic human embrace, clutching visitors, caliper-like, inexorably toward the bosom of St. Peter's Basilica. Under the dome, Bernini's

Bernini angel, Ponte Sant'Angelo.

corkscrew-legged bronze Baldacchino is flecked with tiny bumblebees, the symbol of his—and the baroque's—greatest patron, Pope Urban VIII Barberini. *See p 48,* ❶ *and* ❷.

❷ ★★ **Ponte Sant'Angelo.**
The angels studding this bridge to Castel Sant'Angelo are copies of original sculptures by Bernini. Each figure holds an instrument of the passion of Christ; their masterfully rendered emotions run the gamut from introverted sorrow to wrenching pain to that Bernini warhorse, the parted-lips swoon. ⏱ *15 min. Best at night. Between Castel Sant' Angelo and Lungotevere Sant'Angelo. Bus: 34, 40, 49, 62, 64, or 280.*

❸ ★★★ **Piazza Navona.**
Rome's grandest baroque square is the stage for an architectural smack-down between Borromini and Bernini. Weighing in on the western side of the oblong piazza is Borromini's **Sant'Agnese in Agone** (1653–57), a small church whose

proud bearing is enhanced by its telescoping bell towers, oversized dome, and concave facade—a popular baroque feature, designed to draw in passersby. A bare basin for centuries, the **Fountain of Neptune** was only given its namesake figure and fanciful decoration in the 1800s. In the center, Neptune engages an octopus in fierce battle as unfazed duos of sea horses, nymphs, and aquatic cherubs cavort around the fountain's edge. In the center of the square, Bernini's action-packed, obelisk-crowned **Fountain of the Four Rivers** (1651; see photo below) is a feisty competitor, with four reclining figures representing the Danube, Plata, Ganges, and Nile. The fountain's base is a mass of travertine, hewn in the pre-weathered, organic style so favored in the 17th and 18th centuries. And any baroque sculptor worth his salt would sooner be caught dead than design a fountain that didn't include cavorting animals—today, overheated tourists and mentally unstable locals splash

Fountain of the Four Rivers, Piazza Navona.

(illegally) alongside Bernini's "hippopotamus" (which is just a horse wading) and river serpents. Between Borromini and Bernini, who wins? After 350 years, the jury is still out—but if you look up at the left bell tower of the church, a devastatingly *superb* statue of St. Agnes, placed there after the fountain's completion, seems to have the last laugh. *See also p 54,* ❻.

❹ ★ **Sant'Ivo alla Sapienza.** Borromini always created drama in his architecture by employing elements of curvaceous tension; here, an upside-down marble tornado of a dome crowns a dizzying, star-shaped church. ⏱ *15 min. Corso Rinascimento 40. Interior open only Sun 9am–noon. Bus: 34, 40, 62, 64, 70, 87, 116, or 492.*

❺ ★★★ **Trevi Fountain.** The tourist swarms are annoying, but Nicola Salvi's fountain (1732–62) is a monumental feast for the eyes that never fails to delight—and to surprise, given its hidden location. An ingeniously sculpted base of faux boulders and "fallen" building cornices gives rise to a dynamic pageant of mythological figures, over which thousands of gallons of water per minute thunder to the inviting blue pool below. You know the drill: A coin tossed backwards over your left shoulder as you stand facing away from the fountain is said to ensure your return trip to Rome (someday). ⏱ *30 min. Piazza di Trevi. Crowded from 10am–midnight. Bus: 62, 95, 116, 175, or 492.*

❻ ★ **Sant'Andrea al Quirinale.** The smallest church Bernini designed, known as the "pearl of the baroque," is understated only in size. Amid a rich dessert of pink marble and gilded stucco, a plaster St. Andrew steals the show, rising to the heavens past the broken pediment above the altar. ⏱ *15 min. Via del Quirinale 29. Daily 9am–noon, 4–7pm. Metro: Barberini. Bus: 40, 64, 70, 170, or H.*

❼ ★★ **San Carlo alle Quattro Fontane.** It feels almost like being trapped inside an elaborate crystal in Borromini's tiny church (his favorite). "San Carlino" is an oppressive, colorless frenzy of concave chapels, jutting cornices, intricate coffers, and tricks of light. ⏱ *15 min. Via del Quirinale 23. Mon–Fri 10am–1pm and 3–6pm, Sat and Sun 10am–1pm. Metro: Barberini. Bus: 40, 62, 64, 70, 95, 116, 170, 175, or 492.*

❽ ★★ **Santa Maria della Vittoria.** Still risqué after all these years, Bernini's *Ecstasy of St. Teresa* (in the Cornaro Chapel, to the left of the altar) captures the mystical saint in a moment of spiritual rapture that looks for all the world like another kind of climax. From their "box seat" to the side, the animated Cornaro family members react to the ambiguously scandalous spectacle. ⏱ *15 min. Via XX Settembre 17. Daily 8:30am–noon and 3:30–6pm. Metro: Repubblica. Bus: 60, 62, or 910.*

❾ ★★★ **Galleria Borghese.** The word "incredible" is often used lightly, but Bernini's chisel wizardry here truly confounds belief. In his sculptures of *Apollo and Daphne, Rape of Persephone,* and *David,* he defies the physical properties of marble, involving us emotionally with his subjects and reverentially with his skill. The museum's strict reservations policy keeps crowds to a blessed minimum; be sure to book at least a few days in advance. *See p 30,* ❸.

Rome's Best Piazzas

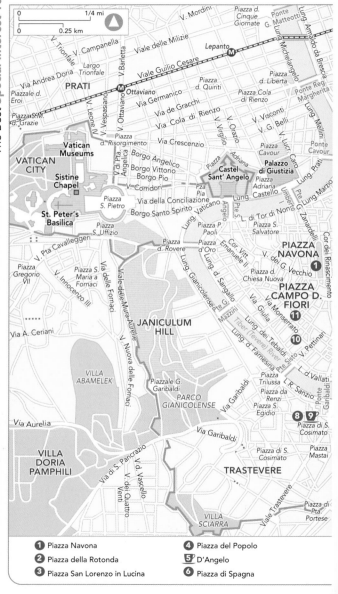

1 Piazza Navona

2 Piazza della Rotonda

3 Piazza San Lorenzo in Lucina

4 Piazza del Popolo

5 D'Angelo

6 Piazza di Spagna

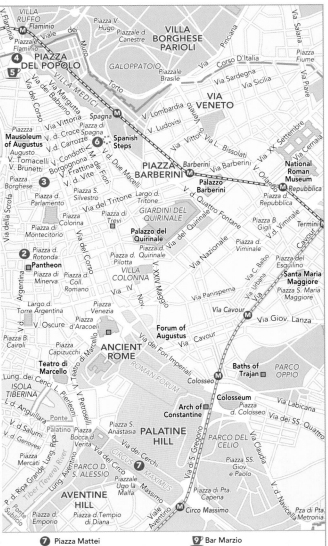

7 Piazza Mattei

8 Piazza Santa Maria in Trastevere

9 Bar Marzio

10 Piazza Farnese

11 Campo de' Fiori

Giving every city neighborhood its own alfresco salon, with newsstands, cafes, and room to breathe, the piazza is one of the great Italian urban inventions. In Rome, some are grandiose gifts to the city from politically minded popes; others are the incidental result of streets meeting at odd angles; but the best piazzas are those where Romans act out their daily pageants, fully aware of their dramatic backdrops. START: Take bus 30, 40, 62, 64, 70, 87, 116, or 492 to Corso Vittorio Emanuele or Corso Rinascimento.

❶ ★★★ Piazza Navona. This theatrical baroque platter retains the shape of the ancient stadium over which it was built. Vying for your attention at the center of the oval are Bernini's dynamic Fountain of the Four Rivers and Borromini's haughty Church of Sant'Agnese in Agone. Cafes and restaurants abound on the square, but you'll never find locals dining here. Piazza Navona is at its best before 10am, when the tourist hordes and trinket sellers start to descend, so come for a morning cappuccino to enjoy an unspoiled view. See p 54, ❻. *Bus: 34, 40, 62, 64, 70, 87, 116, or 492.*

❷ ★★★ Piazza della Rotonda. Despite a 9m (30-ft.) rise from the surrounding ground level, the 2nd-century-A.D. Pantheon still stands, awesomely imposing, at the southern end of this square; the fountain is from the 18th century.

Stop by in the late evening for a drink, when the atmosphere is more intimate and tourist-free. *Bus: 34, 40, 62, 64, 70, 85, 87, 95, 116, or 175. Tram: 8.*

❸ ★ Piazza San Lorenzo in Lucina. Tourists have taken over Piazza di Spagna, but well-heeled locals in the Tridente shopping district still have this wedge-shaped square when they want to sit down for Campari and sandwiches. The two cafes here—Ciampini and Teichner—are almost identical, and great for watching big-spending Romans on parade. *Metro: Spagna. Bus: 62, 85, 95, 175, or 492.*

❹ ★★ Piazza del Popolo. A 4,000-year-old pink granite obelisk with wonderful hieroglyphics presides over this grand, pedestrianized expanse at the top of the Tridente. On the north side of the

Piazza del Popolo.

Mornings bustle at the marketplace of Campo de'Fiori.

piazza, Santa Maria del Popolo (p 61, ❷) is a trove of art treasures. *Metro: Flaminio.*

5 ★ **D'Angelo** is an old-fashioned coffee bar offering pastries and light snacks; it has an elegant feel and parlor-style seating (which costs a bit more than counter service). *Via della Croce 30.* ☎ *06-6782556. $–$$.*

6 ★★ **Piazza di Spagna.** Sure, it's a zoo, but the thousands of tourists and flashy locals who flood this gorgeous square—framed by the Spanish Steps, palm trees, brightly colored *palazzi*, and designer shops galore—must be onto something, right? *Metro: Spagna.*

7 ★ **Piazza Mattei.** A scrappy little square in the old Jewish Ghetto charms all with its endearing Fontana delle Tartarughe (Fountain of the Tortoises), begun in 1588 by Giacomo della Porta and Taddeo Landini and given its namesake amphibians by Bernini in 1638. *Bus: 23, 34, 40, 62, 63, 64, 70, 87, 170, 280, or 492. Tram: 8.*

8 ★★ **Piazza Santa Maria in Trastevere.** The crossroads of daily life in village-y Trastevere meet all criteria: a sprinkling of cafes and restaurants, children with *nonna* in tow, a graceful fountain,

and a big church. *Bus: H, 23, 280, or 780. Tram: 8.*

The outdoor tables here at **9** ★ **Bar Marzio** offer a prime view across the square to the splendid facade of Santa Maria in Trastevere. *Piazza Santa Maria in Trastevere 15.* ☎ *06-5816095. $*

10 ★★ **Piazza Farnese.** Just steps away from the buzz of the Campo, Piazza Farnese is elegant, sedate, and open, graced on its west side by the stately Palazzo Farnese, designed in part by Michelangelo and now home to the French Embassy. The fountains here are granite bathtubs filched from the Baths of Caracalla in the 1500s and topped by the Farnese family emblem, the iris. *Bus: 23, 34, 40, 62, 64, 70, 87, 116, 280, or 492. Tram: 8.*

11 ★★★ **Campo de' Fiori.** With a pricey produce market in the morning and a booming social scene at its many bars in the evening, this former "field of flowers" is the liveliest square in the *centro storico*. The Campo may lack the architectural refinement of other Roman piazzas, but its round-the-clock utility and heavy traffic of locals are tough to beat. *Bus: 34, 40, 62, 64, 70, 87, 116, or 492. Tram: 8.*

Rome's Best Churches

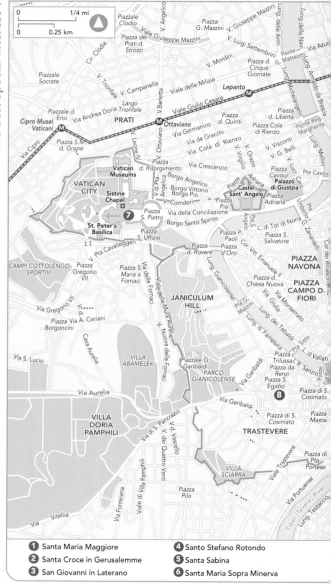

1. Santa Maria Maggiore
2. Santa Croce in Gerusalemme
3. San Giovanni in Laterano
4. Santo Stefano Rotondo
5. Santa Sabina
6. Santa Maria Sopra Minerva

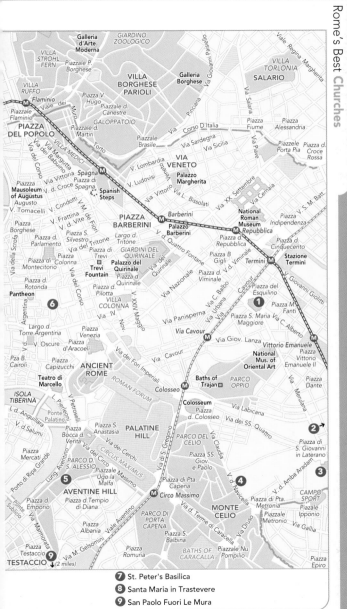

7 St. Peter's Basilica

8 Santa Maria in Trastevere

9 San Paolo Fuori Le Mura

The city's best all-around churches have artistic treasures, relics, and fascinating histories, as well as architecture—humbling or haunting—that reinforce the religious function of the space. All churches in Rome are free of charge and refreshingly cool in summer, but opening hours are notoriously subject to change. START: Take bus 70 or 75 to Piazza Santa Maria Maggiore, or take Metro Line A or B, or bus 40, 64, 170, 175, 492, or H to Stazione Termini, and walk.

❶ ★★ Santa Maria Maggiore. In this perfect example of the prototypical basilica, the main nave, flanked by two lower and narrower side aisles, terminates in a curved apse, which is decorated with dazzling polychrome and gold mosaics. Near the right side of the main altar, a modest marble slab marks the tomb of baroque superstar Gian Lorenzo Bernini; the epitaph, inlaid in bronze, is a pithy summary of his life: "He decorated the city." *Piazza di Santa Maria Maggiore.* ☎ 06-69886800. *Daily 7am–6:45pm. Metro: Termini. Bus: 70, 75, 649, or 714.*

❷ ★ Santa Croce in Gerusalemme. The mother lode of relics here includes a piece of the True Cross, remnants of the Crown of Thorns, and the finger of doubting St. Thomas. (Photos aren't allowed, but postcards of all can be purchased at the church gift shop.) *Piazza di Santa Croce in Gerusalemme 12.* ☎ 06-70613053. *Daily 7am–2:45pm and 3:30pm–7:30pm.*

Metro: Manzoni. Bus: 81 or 649. Tram: 3.

❸ ★★ San Giovanni in Laterano. The cathedral of Rome and mother church of the world is not St. Peter's in the Vatican, but this church dedicated to St. John. The spare, slightly grave interior is by Borromini (1646); the facade, with its chorus line of saints, dates from 1735. In a separate building across the piazza are the Scala Santa (holy stairs, supposedly the very set that Jesus climbed in Pontius Pilate's barracks, and which the faithful climb on their knees) and the Sancta Sanctorum ("holy of holies"), boasting rare 13th-century frescoes by Cimabue and relics of furniture from the Last Supper. *Piazza San Giovanni in Laterano.* ☎ 06-69886433. *Free admission to church and Scala Santa; 3€ Sancta Sanctorum. Church daily 7am–6:45pm. Scala Santa* ☎ 06-7726641. *Daily 6:30am–noon and 3:30–6pm. Sancta Sanctorum Mon, Tues, Thurs, Fri, Sat*

San Giovanni in Laterano.

Vicolo del Piede, in Trastevere.

10:30–11:30am and 3:30–4:30pm; Wed 3:30–4:30pm. Metro: San Giovanni. Bus: 85, 87, or 117. Tram: 3.

❹ ★ **Santo Stefano Rotondo.** Deep in the rustic Celio Hill, this ancient church is reminiscent of a railway roundhouse. The walls of the ambulatory are frescoed with R-rated scenes of gruesome martyrdoms. *Via di Santo Stefano Rotondo 7.* ☎ *06-421199. Nov–Mar Tues–Sat 9:30am–12:30pm and 2–5pm, Sun 9:30am–12:30pm; Apr–Oct Tues–Sat 9:30am–12:30pm and 3–6pm, Sun 9:30am–12:30pm. Closed Mon. Bus: 81.*

❺ ★★ **Santa Sabina.** Built in the 5th century on the site of the martyred saint's home and widely recognized as Rome's best early Christian architecture, this church stands perched on the Aventine Hill, providing awesome views of the city from the adjacent orange grove. *Piazza Pietro d'Illiria.* ☎ *06-5743573. Daily 8:15am–12:30pm and 3:30–6pm. Bus: 23 or 280.*

❻ ★★ **Santa Maria Sopra Minerva.** The only Gothic church in the city is a soothing contrast to the sometimes-gaudy baroque interiors of many Roman churches. Pointy medieval arches create soaring vaults that are decorated with a cool, blue, starry sky motif. *Piazza della Minerva 42.* ☎ *06-6793926. Mon–Sat 7am–7pm, Sun 8am–noon and 2–7pm Bus: 30, 40, 62, 64, 70, 87, 116, or 492.*

❼ ★★★ **St. Peter's Basilica.** The facade is the pompous result of too many architects' tinkerings, but the sublime interior of St. Peter's (built 1506–1626) is astounding, visit after visit. The church is, quite simply, huge. Its vastness plays out in the building's every feature, from the 2m-tall (6-ft.) Latin inscription to the 45-story-high dome, designed by Michelangelo to "crown" the Roman skyline. *See p 48,* ❷.

Dress Code

St. Peter's has a hard-and-fast dress code that makes no exceptions to the rule: Men and women in shorts, above-the-knee skirts, or bare shoulders will not be admitted to the Vatican City basilica. Period.

❽ ★★ **Santa Maria in Traste-vere.** It's best to visit just after Mass has let out, when the basilica is still fragrant with incense. *See p 58,* ❻.

❾ ★★ **San Paolo Fuori Le Mura.** The immense basilica of St. Paul "Outside the Walls" (one of the Vatican's four patriarchal churches) was built over the site of Paul's tomb in A.D. 324 but heavily damaged by fire in the 19th century. It has since been painstakingly restored. The stunning interior features acres of marble paving, endless colonnades, and mosaic portraits of all the popes from Peter to Benedict XVI—and space is running out. *Via Ostiense 186.* ☎ *06-69880800. Daily 7am–6:30pm. Metro: Basilica San Paolo. Bus: 23 or 271.*

Romantic Rome

1. Laghetto di Villa Borghese
2. Casina Valadier
3. Pincio
4. Roof Bar at Raphael Hotel
5. Ponte Sant'Angelo
6. Gianicolo
7. Ponte Sisto
8. Campidoglio

Between gorgeous lookouts, intimate piazzas, and the general ardor of the natives, Rome is one sprawling romantic setting. The itinerary below will have you waxing sappy and gushing *"Ti amo"* from dusk till dawn. START: **Take bus 490 or 495 to Villa Borghese/Viale Fiorello La Guardia, or tram 3 or 19 to Villa Borghese/Viale delle Belle Arti, or bus 52, 53, or 116 to Via Veneto/Piazza San Paolo del Brasile.**

❶ ★ Laghetto di Villa Borghese. Take your lover for a gentle row around Villa Borghese's idyllic lake. Boats can be rented daily from 9:30am to sunset. *Bus: 88, 116, 490, 495, or 926. Tram: 3 or 19.*

Toast the sweetness of life at **❷ ★★ Casina Valadier,** the garden cafe/bar of the fancy Casina Valadier restaurant. *Piazza Bucarest.* ☎ *06-69922090. Metro: Spagna. $$–$$$.*

❸ ★★★ Pincio. The utterly tryst-worthy Pincio gardens are recommended during the lingering glow after sunset, or in the full dark of night. *Metro: Flaminio.*

Stroll over to the **❹ ★★ Roof Bar at Raphael Hotel** for a pre-dinner aperitivo or post-meal digestivo. *Largo Febo 2.* ☎ *06-682831. Bus: 23, 70, 87, 116, or 492. $$$.*

❺ ★★★ Ponte Sant'Angelo. The bridge, lined with Bernini angels, is especially bewitching by night. *Bus: 23, 34, 40, 49, 62, 64, 280, or 571.*

❻ ★★ Gianicolo. No romantic Roman itinerary is complete without the city's make-out point par excellence, the Janiculum Hill. The tree-lined ridge above Trastevere is perfect for a lovers' stroll. *Piazza Garibaldi/Passeggiata del Gianicolo. Bus: 115 or 870.*

❼ ★★★ Ponte Sisto. The "kissing bridge" is characteristic because of its central *oculus* (Latin for "eye") and sensual humped footpath. It connects two fashionable nightlife areas, Campo de' Fiori and Trastevere, and provides the perfect sunset backdrop— dome of St. Peter's aglow in the distance—for romance. *Piazza Trilussa/Via dei Pettinari. Bus: 23, 271, or 280.*

❽ ★★★ Campidoglio. The sublime, deserted piazza is a fine place to be at night, but the evening view from the Campidoglio terraces over the Roman Forum is quite possibly the most rapturous sight in the world. *Bus: 40, 62, 63, 64, 70, 85, 87, 95, 170, 810, or 850.*

Lovers on the Laghetto di Villa Borghese.

Underground Rome

1 Catacombs of San Callisto and San Sebastiano
2 San Clemente
3 Amarcord
4 Case Romane di Santi Giovanni e Paolo
5 Mamertine Prison
6 Crypt of the Capuchin Monks
7 Stadium of Domitian
8 Necropolis of St. Peter's

In a city whose street level has risen about 9m (30 ft.)—due to flooding of the Tiber—since the days of the Caesars, it's only natural that a whole other Rome should exist hidden away beneath the modern buildings. The catacombs have been drawing visitors underground for centuries, but there are also plenty of places (some newly opened) within the city center that permit visitors a fascinating descent into the bowels of history. START: **Take bus 118 or a taxi to the Catacombs of San Callisto or San Sebastiano, on the Via Appia Antica.**

1 ★★ **Catacombs of San Callisto and San Sebastiano.** Rome's most famous underground tourist attractions, the catacombs, are outside the city walls, as ancient Roman law forbade burials within the sacred *pomerium*, or city boundary. Of Rome's 65 known catacombs—networks of hand-dug tunnels that became massive "dormitories" for the dead—only a handful are open to the public. The catacombs of San Callisto are the largest, with 500,000 burial niches (*loculi*). Nearby, the catacombs of San Sebastiano are more intimate. *See p 95.*

2 ★★ **San Clemente.** This "lasagna of churches" is the best

place in Rome to understand the city's archaeological evolution. Descend 18m (60 ft.) through medieval and paleo-Christian layers to the lowest level, where adherents of the ancient cult of Mithras met and performed grisly rituals in the long, rectangular *mithraeum*. ⏱ *30 min. Via Labicana 95.* ☎ *06-7740021. 6€. Mon–Sat 9am–12:30pm and 3–6pm; Sun 10am–12:30pm and 3–6pm. Metro: Colosseo. Bus: 60, 75, 85, 87, 95, 175, or 850. Tram: 3.*

Pick up a custom-made piadina (flatbread sandwich, a specialty of Fellini's native Rimini) and soft drink or beer at 3P ★ **Amarcord;** this casual lunch spot is frequented by local students and office workers. *Via di San Giovanni in Laterano 164.* ☎ *347-7679342. Closed Sun. $–$$.*

④ ★ **Case Romane di Santi Giovanni e Paolo.** Recent excavations beneath this Romanesque church on the Celio Hill revealed 1st-century-A.D. Roman houses with splendid wall frescoes. ⏱ *45 min. Piazza Santi Giovanni e Paolo 13.* ☎ *06-70454544. www.caseromane. it. 6€. Thurs–Mon 10am–1pm and 3–6pm. Metro: Colosseo. Bus: 60, 75, 81, 117, 118, 175, 628, or 673. Tram: 3.*

⑤ ★ **Mamertine Prison.** Dank and oppressive, these black-rock chambers are said to be where saints Peter and Paul were imprisoned before their martyrdoms. Claustrophobes steer clear. ⏱ *45 min. Clivo Argentario 1.* ☎ *06-698961. 1€–2€ donation expected. Daily 9am–5pm; 9am–7pm in summer. Bus: 60, 81, 87, 95, or 175.*

⑥ ★★★ **Crypt of the Capuchin Monks.** Macabre yet oddly

Skull "art" at the Capuchin crypt.

pleasing, this must-see church crypt is decorated with thousands of artfully arranged monks' bones and skulls. Each chapel is a bizarre diorama where propped-up monks, still in their desiccated skin and cassocks, strike cautionary poses. ⏱ *20 min. Via Veneto 27.* ☎ *06-4871185. 1€–2€ donation expected. Fri–Wed 9am–noon, 3–6pm. Metro: Barberini. Bus: 62, 95, 116, 175, or 492.*

⑦ ★★ **Stadium of Domitian.** At the northern end of Piazza Navona, explore the fascinating remains of the 1st-century-A.D. athletic venue that gave the square its oblong shape. ⏱ *45 min. Piazza di Tor Sanguigna 13.* ☎ *06-67103819. 6€. Sat–Sun 10am–1pm by appointment only. Bus: 70, 87, 116, or 492.*

⑧ ★★ **Necropolis of St. Peter's.** Positively chill-inducing, these humble, narrow tunnels beneath the immense Vatican basilica make for an unforgettable descent into the bowels of early Christian history. *See p 49,* ④.

Vatican City

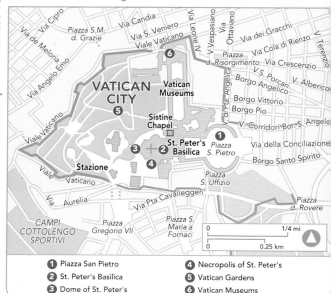

1. Piazza San Pietro
2. St. Peter's Basilica
3. Dome of St. Peter's
4. Necropolis of St. Peter's
5. Vatican Gardens
6. Vatican Museums

Welcome to Popeland, the sovereign state of visual delights. From the star-studded halls of the Vatican Museums to the gargantuan volume of St. Peter's Basilica, the Holy See is brimming with things for the tourist to see and do. Allow about 4 hours to take it in. START: **Take bus 23, 49, or 492 to Viale Vaticano/ Viale dei Bastioni di Michelangelo, or take Metro Line A to Ottaviano-San Pietro or Cipro-Musei Vaticani, and walk.**

❶ ★★★ Piazza San Pietro.

Designed in the 1650s by Bernini to mimic a human embrace, this sweeping colonnade is the gateway to the largest church in the world. In the center stands an Egyptian obelisk that once marked the center of Nero's Circus, where St. Peter was martyred in A.D. 64. Along the south wall of the square are official Vatican souvenir- and book-shops and a branch of the Vatican post office. ⏱ *30 min. Free admission.*

❷ ★★★ St. Peter's Basilica.

Everything in St. Peter's is made of marble, bronze, or gold, and what appear to be altar paintings are actually mosaics with minuscule tesserae. The outstanding artworks in the basilica include Michelangelo's intensely moving *Pietà* (1499) and Bernini's spiral-legged bronze Baldacchino (1633). ⏱ *45 min. Free admission. Daily 7am–7pm; can vary with papal appearances and religious holidays.*

Piazza San Pietro and the basilica.

3 ★ Dome of St. Peter's. Recommended for those who can't visit a European city without climbing a dome—its perspective on the Vatican is impressive, but its general city view is overrated. (For that, you're much better off at the Vittoriano, p 11.) There is a coffee bar at the dome's midway point, but it doesn't have views of the skyline. ○ *45 min. Queue is shortest in early morning or late afternoon. Piazza San Pietro. 7€ (elevator, then 320 stairs); 5€ (all 551 stairs). Daily 8am–5pm in winter; 8am–6pm in summer.*

4 ★★★ Necropolis of St. Peter's. A haunting descent beneath the basilica takes you into the ancient level where bones believed to be St. Peter's were found in the 1940s. See also p 47. ○ *90 min. Ufficio Scavi. ☎ 06-69885318. Fax 06-69873017. 13€. Tours Mon–Sat 9am–3:30pm. Book at least 1 month in advance.*

5 ★★ Vatican Gardens. An oasis of manicured lawns, quaint fountains, and the occasional nun-driven Vespa exists behind the imposing Vatican fortification walls. ○ *2 hr. ☎ 06-69883145 or 06-69884676. Fax 06-69873250. 32€. Children 6–18 and students 24€; includes Vatican Museums and Sistine Chapel. Tours Tues and Thurs–Sat 10am only. Book at least 1 week in advance.*

Book Online & Skip the Line

Book online for the Museums and Sistine Chapel to avoid the line. The Vatican Museums and Sistine Chapel are flooded with up to 30,000 visitors per day, which can mean waiting up to 2 hours, but if you book your tickets online (biglietteriamusei.vatican.va) you can request a precise entry time and skip the line entirely. The 4€ service fee is money well spent. Online booking is also mandatory for the special evening openings of the Museums and chapel (Fri in May, June, July, Sept, and Oct).

6 ★★★ Vatican Museums. The richest museum in the world is enthralling in its quantity and quality, aggravating in its utter lack of explanatory signage. As a rule, the important stuff is where the crowds are, but try to resist the riptide of tour groups that washes headlong toward the Sistine Chapel, skipping a ton of fabulous art along the way. The museum guidebook—or, better yet, the audioguide—can make your meander through these masterpiece-packed halls vastly more meaningful.

Start your tour of the Museums in the ★★ **Pinacoteca** (picture gallery), home to Raphael's *Transfiguration* (1520; his last painting), in Room 8; Leonardo's enigmatic *St. Jerome* (1482), in Room 9; and Caravaggio's

Enjoying some gelato on the go in Vatican City.

eerie, green-fleshed *Deposition* (1604), in Room 12. In the Octagonal Courtyard, the exquisite marble ★★ **Apollo Belvedere** (a 2nd-c.-A.D. copy of a 5th-c.-B.C. original) is a paragon of classical composure. In radical stylistic contrast, the stunning 1st-century-A.D. ★★★ *Laocoon* (Lay-*ah*-koh-on) sculpture depicts the fate of a Trojan priest who was suspicious of the Trojan horse and asked his people to "beware of Greeks bearing gifts." The Greek-favoring gods, angered, sentenced him to death by sea serpents. The expressive, though fragmentary, ★ **Belvedere Torso** inspired Michelangelo's rendering of Christ in the *Last Judgment,* in the Sistine Chapel. Upstairs, the ★ **Etruscan Museum** has knockout gold breastplates from a 2,500-year-old tomb. From here, the Vatican Museums morph into fresco heaven.

The brightly colored frescoes in the ★ **Gallery of the Maps** are a wonderfully detailed cartographical record of 16th-century Italy. Pink-tinged frescoes by Giulio Romano in the ★ **Hall of Constantine** (1522–25) are a tribute to Christianity toppling paganism. In the famed and splendidly restored ★★★ **Raphael Rooms** (1506–17), exquisite frescoes like *School of Athens* and *Liberation of St. Peter* display

the harmony of color and balance of composition that were the hallmark of High Renaissance classicism and Raphael's mastery.

After the Raphael Rooms, a wrong turn and confusing signs can take you downstairs to the Vatican's dreadful modern art collection; stay to the left for the direct route to the ★★★ **Sistine Chapel,** where Michelangelo's spectacular frescoes very much live up to the hype. On the ceiling (1508–12), the stories of creation, Adam and Eve, and Noah are told in nine frames, surrounded by faux architectural elements and medallions. On the altar wall, the swirling *Last Judgment* (1535–41) is much more fire-and-brimstone, reflecting the anger and disappointment of Michelangelo's later years. Exit the Museums via the right rear door of the Sistine Chapel to go straight to St. Peter's or the left door to return any rented audioguides. ⏱ *2 hr. Reservations recommended. Viale Vaticano.* ☎ *06-69884676 or 06-69883145. http://mv.vatican.va. 16€ adults, 8€ students. Audioguide 7€. Mon–Sat 9am–4pm (exit by 6pm). Last Sun of month open 9am– 12:30pm (exit by 2pm). May–July and Sept–Oct also open Fri 7–11pm, reservations required. Closed Catholic holidays; check website for most up-to-date schedule.* ●

Piazza Navona & the Pantheon

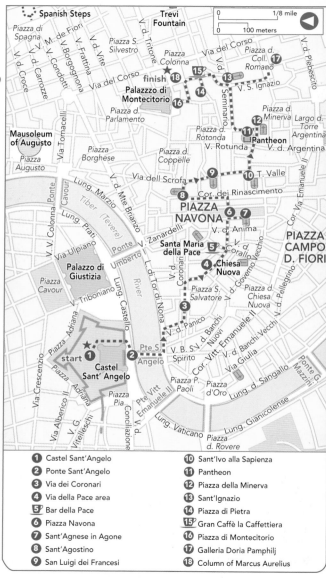

1 Castel Sant'Angelo
2 Ponte Sant'Angelo
3 Via dei Coronari
4 Via della Pace area
5 Bar della Pace
6 Piazza Navona
7 Sant'Agnese in Agone
8 Sant'Agostino
9 San Luigi dei Francesi
10 Sant'Ivo alla Sapienza
11 Pantheon
12 Piazza della Minerva
13 Sant'Ignazio
14 Piazza di Pietra
15 Gran Caffè la Caffettiera
16 Piazza di Montecitorio
17 Galleria Doria Pamphilj
18 Column of Marcus Aurelius

Previous page: Bernini's Fontana dei Quattro Fiumi, designed for Pope Innocent X.

Prepare to switch sightseeing gears quickly in the most central part of the old city—quiet, labyrinth-like alleys abruptly give way to imposing monuments and knockout postcard panoramas, and a slew of nonchalant-looking churches stash away some of the city's most celebrated works of art. START: **Take bus 40, 62, or 74 to Castel Sant'Angelo/Piazza Pia.**

Accordion player on Piazza Navona.

❶ ★★★ Castel Sant'Angelo. Rome's hamburger of history started out as Hadrian's mausoleum in the 2nd century A.D. and was converted in the Middle Ages into a fortress for the popes, who then gave themselves apartments here in the Renaissance. Its final incarnation, as a prison, lasted through the end of the 19th century, long enough to inspire Puccini's *Tosca*. Be sure to climb all the way up to the highest terrace—looking straight down over the Tiber is as soaring and dramatic as an operatic finale. ⏱ *1 hr. Lungotevere Castello 50.* ☎ *06-6819111. castelsantangelo.beniculturali.it. 7€. Tues–Sun 9am–7pm.*

❷ ★★ Ponte Sant'Angelo. *See p 34,* ❷.

❸ ★ Via dei Coronari. This charming little street was formerly a pilgrim route to the Vatican; today,

it's lined with antiquarians' shops and intersected by dozens of quaint alleys, with hidden *trattorie* and artists' studios.

❹ ★ Via della Pace area. Via della Pace bisects the web of streets, known as the "triangle of fun," between Via dei Coronari and Via del Governo Vecchio. By day, motorcycle mechanics rub shoulders with Roman nobility; by night, Roman hipsters flock to the area's countless eateries and *boîtes*.

The chic and the restless flutter in and out of the eternally fashionable **❺ ★ Bar della Pace** from morning to night, but I recommend you stay awhile—it's a prime spot for reading, postcard-writing, and ogling the lovely Santa Maria della Pace, just down the street. *Via della Pace 3–7.* ☎ *06-6861216. $$.*

6 ★★★ Piazza Navona. Nine meters (30 ft.) below the baroque fountains and churches located here is the site where the ancient *agones* (athletic competitions) were held in the Stadium of Domitian (p 47, **7**). In the medieval period, the Romans called this space *platea in agona* ("place of competition"), which later evolved into the modern appellation, Piazza Navona. See p 34, **3**.

7 ★ Sant'Agnese in Agone. Borromini's broad, flamboyant facade belies this church's rather small interior. Through a door marked SACRA TESTIA, to the left of the altar, there's a reliquary holding the chimpanzee-sized skull of St. Agnes, martyred here in the 4th century A.D. ① *15 min. Piazza Navona.* ☎ *06-68192134. Free admission. Tues–Sun 9am–noon, 4–7pm.*

8 ★ Sant'Agostino. On the left wall, Caravaggio's *Madonna dei Pellegrini* (1604) shocked contemporaries with its frank depiction of dirty-footed pilgrims. On a pillar nearby, Raphael's meaty *Isaiah* (1512) recalls the frescoes of the Sistine Chapel. ① *20 min. Piazza Sant'Agostino.* ☎ *06-68801962. Free admission.. Daily 8am–noon and 4–6:30pm.*

9 ★★ San Luigi dei Francesi. Revolutionary for their high-keyed emotions and contrived play of light, Caravaggio's three *Life of St. Matthew* altarpieces (1603), displayed here, are some of his greatest masterpieces. ① *20 min. Piazza San Luigi dei Francesi.* ☎ *06-688271. Free admission. Fri–Wed 10am–12:30pm and 4–7pm; Thurs 10am–noon.*

10 ★★ Sant'Ivo alla Sapienza. See p 35, **4**.

11 ★★★ Pantheon. Hands-down the most masterful architectural feat of ancient Rome, the Pantheon is almost perfectly preserved. The porch consists of 16 monolithic Egyptian granite columns, weighing 74 metric tons (82 tons) each. Inside, the 44m-wide (143-ft.) dome—poured in concrete in the 120s A.D. and never structurally modified—is pierced by a 9m-wide (30-ft.) *oculus*, open to the sky. While most ancient buildings lost their marbles to the popes, the Pantheon's brick walls retain their rich revetment of yellow marble and purple porphyry. The tombs of Raphael and the Savoia monarchs are also here. ① *30 min. Best in early morning or late afternoon, and in the rain. Piazza della Rotonda.* ☎ *06-68300230. Free admission. Daily 8:30am–7:30pm; Sun 9am–6pm.*

12 ★★ Piazza della Minerva. In front of the Gothic church Santa Maria Sopra Minerva (p 43, **6**), an Egyptian obelisk—1 of 13 in Rome—is supported on the back of a plucky elephant, sculpted by Bernini. The

The interior of the Pantheon features an oculus, which opens to the sky.

Piazza di Montecitorio.

neighborhood is also home to most of Rome's religious outfitters, with their fabulous window displays of gem-encrusted chalices and the latest in liturgical couture.

⑬ ★ **Sant'Ignazio.** The focal point of this tight and tidy baroque square is the Jesuit Church of St. Ignatius, famous for its illusionist-style "dome," frescoed on the church's flat roof by Andrea Pozzo in 1626. ⏱ *15 min. Piazza di Sant'Ignazio.* ☎ *06-6794406. Free admission. Daily 7:30am–12:20pm and 3–7:20pm.*

⑭ ★★ **Piazza di Pietra.** The impressive row of columns here were the north wall of the 2nd-century-A.D. Temple of Hadrian, a plastic model of which can be seen in a showcase window across the square.

The elegant coffee and snack bar (and outré Internet hotspot) ⑮ ★ **Gran Caffè La Caffettiera** is especially cozy in winter. *Piazza di Pietra 65.* ☎ *06-6798147. $–$$.*

⑯ ★ **Piazza di Montecitorio.** On this sloping square in front of the Bernini-designed lower house of Parliament, dapper *carabinieri* (army police) survey the scene for terrorists—and eligible foreign women. The 2,600-year-old obelisk, moved here in 1751, was the shadow-casting gnomon of Augustus's sundial (9 B.C.), an approximation of which is inlaid in bronze over the square.

⑰ ★★ **Galleria Doria Pamphilj.** This collection, whose audioguide is read (in English) by a living Pamphilj prince, has an enviable array of 16th- and 17th-century canvases, as well as Velázquez's famously soul-exposing portrait of Pope Innocent X Pamphilj. *Via del Corso 305.* ☎ *06-6797323. www.doriapamphilj.it. 11€. Daily 10am–5pm.*

⑱ ★ **Column of Marcus Aurelius.** Dismissed by some art historians as a cheap imitation of Trajan's Column (p 24, ⑤), this 30m-high (100-ft.) marble shaft (180–96 A.D.) depicts Marcus Aurelius's military exploits in Germany. *Piazza Colonna.*

Campo de' Fiori

1. Campo de' Fiori
2. Craftsmen's Streets
3. Piazza Farnese
4. Via Giulia
5. Galleria Spada
6. Via dei Giubbonari
7. Antico Forno Rosioli
8. Via di Grotta Pinta
9. Sant'Andrea della Valle
10. Area Sacra di Largo Argentina

Unpretentious, workaday, and totally picturesque, the area around Campo de' Fiori is the best place in the *centro storico* to see Roman daily life at its most authentic. Locals far outnumber tourists, and you can't walk a few steps without coming across a coffee bar, wine shop, or neighborhood trattoria. START: **Take bus 30, 40, 62, 64, 70, 87, 116, 492, 571, or 628 to Corso Vittorio Emanuele, or tram 8 to Largo Argentina, and then walk.**

---

① ★★★ Campo de' Fiori. Bustling with energy night and day, Campo de' Fiori is the beating heart of the *centro storico*. In the morning, the stalls of the city's most charming fruit and vegetable market sell produce to top chefs and local housewives. At night, all and sundry descend on the piazza's cafes and wine bars for the evening *aperitivo*.

② ★★ Craftsmen's Streets. Many of the streets in the *centro*

storico are named for the crafts practiced by artisans there throughout the ages; the best examples of these lie north of the Campo. On Via dei Cappellari, medieval hat-makers have been replaced by furniture workshops, and Arco degli Acetari (vinegar-makers' arch) is an ochre-drenched courtyard that appears on many a Roman postcard.

③ ★★ Piazza Farnese. Serene Piazza Farnese enjoys the same

Quiet moment in bustling Campo de' Fiori.

Renaissance harmony as its namesake architectural feature, the dignified and imposing 16th-century Palazzo Farnese. The square and its immediate vicinity have recently become some of the most sought-after real estate in the city.

④ ★★ **Via Giulia.** The dead-straight path of Via Giulia—for many, the most beautiful street in Rome—was cleared by Pope Julius II in the 1500s to give pilgrims safe passage to the Vatican. The picturesque ivy-covered arch that spans the street was to be part of a private bridge—never completed—for the Farnese family, connecting Palazzo Farnese with the Villa Farnesina.

⑤ ★ **Galleria Spada.** Works by Titian and other Renaissance masters are almost a dime a dozen in Rome; what makes the Spada especially worth a visit is the uncannily deceptive Borromini Corridor, which is only 9m (30 ft.) long but appears to be three times that. ⏱ *30 min. Piazza Capo di Ferro 13.* ☎ *06-6874896. 5€. Tues–Sun 9am–7pm. Bus: 23, 30, 40, 62, 64, 70, 87, 116, 280, or 492. Tram: 8.*

⑥ ★ **Via dei Giubbonari.** This narrow, cobblestone thoroughfare is bursting with up-and-coming fashion boutiques, gourmet food stores, and street vendors.

Three-generation family owned ⑦ ★★★ **Antico Forno Roscioli** bakes crisp pizza, breads, and pastries, and serves a few cooked items such as pasta, roasted meats, and fritters daily 7am to 8pm. *Via dei Chiavari 34.* ☎ *06-6864045. www.anticofornoroscioli.com. $–$$.*

⑧ **Via di Grotta Pinta.** The inward curve of this hidden road, named for the underlying "painted grotto" of the 55-B.C. Theater of Pompey, corresponds with the *cavea* (seating area) of the ancient theater.

⑨ ★ **Sant'Andrea della Valle.** The second-highest dome in Rome—after St. Peter's—rests atop this excellent 16th-century basilica. ⏱ *15 min. Corso Vittorio Emanuele II at Piazza Vidoni 6.* ☎ *06-6861339. Free admission. Daily 8am–noon and 4:30–7:30pm.*

⑩ ★ **Area Sacra di Largo Argentina.** During the excavation fever of the 1930s, Mussolini evicted hundreds of Romans and ordered archaeologists to dig. What you see today, 9m (30 ft.) below street level, are four Republican temple foundations and a fragment of the Senate house *(Curia Pompei)* where Julius Caesar was stabbed on the Ides of March, 44 B.C. *Ruins generally closed to the public, but visible from street level outlook.*

Trastevere

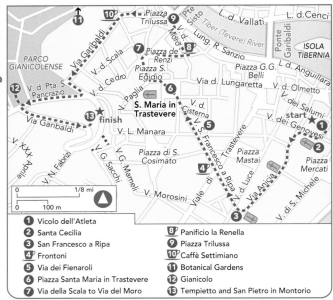

① Vicolo dell'Atleta
② Santa Cecilia
③ San Francesco a Ripa
④ Frontoni
⑤ Via dei Fienaroli
⑥ Piazza Santa Maria in Trastevere
⑦ Via della Scala to Via del Moro
⑧ Panificio la Renella
⑨ Piazza Trilussa
⑩ Caffè Settimiano
⑪ Botanical Gardens
⑫ Gianicolo
⑬ Tempietto and San Pietro in Montorio

Picturesque Trastevere developed its own identity in ancient times, when it was dubbed *Trans Tiberim* ("across the Tiber"). Although expatriates have relocated here in droves, the district maintains its insular character and village-y appeal. START: **Take bus 23, 271, 280, 780, or H, or tram 8 to Piazza G. G. Belli (Lungotevere degli Anguillara/Viale Trastevere).**

① ★ **Vicolo dell'Atleta.** The "alley of the athlete"—as tiny as streets get in Rome—has a facade of a 13th-century synagogue, now the restaurant Spirito di Vino (p 116).

② ★★ **Santa Cecilia.** See p 15, ①.

③ ★ **San Francesco a Ripa.** Home to Bernini's overtly sexual *Beata Ludovica Albertoni* (1674). ⏱ 15 min. Piazza San Francesco d'Assisi 88. ☎ 06-5819020. Free admission. Daily 7am–noon and 4–7:30pm.

Fuel up at ④ ★★ **Frontoni** on pizza-bread sandwiches stuffed with deli meats, cheeses, or roasted vegetables. *Viale Trastevere 52.* ☎ *06-5812436. $–$$.*

⑤ **Via dei Fienaroli.** Dense ivy blankets the walls of this pretty street, hiding numerous interesting bookshops and cafes.

⑥ ★★ **Piazza & Basilica Santa Maria in Trastevere.** The hub of daily life in Trastevere is graced by the magnificent church of Santa Maria. Legend has it the church was built over the spot where a fountain of oil miraculously bubbled up in 38 B.C., apparently heralding the coming of Christ. *See p 39,* ⑧, *and p 43,* ⑧.

⑦ ★ **Via della Scala to Via del Moro.** This warren of gnarled streets is the most charming part of old Trastevere, where clotheslines are strung over narrow alleys, parking jobs reach new heights of ingenuity, and neighbors chat animatedly.

Purveyor of pane to all restaurants and households in the vicinity, the bread bakery ⑧ ★★ **Panificio la Renella** also has excellent pizza by the slice, bar stools to sit on, and a community message board. *Vicolo della Renella 15–16.* ☎ *06-5817265. $.*

⑨ **Piazza Trilussa.** This is the point of egress for all the tiny streets in the area, and where pedestrian Ponte Sisto leads across the Tiber toward Campo de' Fiori.

In the shadow of the old Septimian Gate (part of the 3rd-c.-A.D. Aurelian Walls), ⑩ ★ **Caffè Settimiano** is a wonderful place to rest your feet, read the paper, and watch trasteverini go by. *Via di Porta Settimiana.* ☎ *06-5810468. $.*

⑪ ★★★ **Botanical Gardens.** The turn of the 20th-century country-club-style park covers 12 sloping acres of tropical jungles, thick pine forests, gravel paths, ponds, and rolling hillsides amid the collection of 3,500-plus species of rare plants, trees, and exquisite flowers. ⏲ *2 hr. Largo Cristina di Svezia 24.* ☎ *06-6864193. 8€. Mon–Sat 9am–5:30pm (6:30pm in summer).*

⑫ ★★★ **Gianicolo.** The hike to the top of Janiculum Hill is well worth the spectacular views, tree-lined promenades, clear air, and the fabulously inviting 17th-century Fontanone dell'Acqua Paola. ⏲ *30 min. Take Via Garibaldi to Via di Porta San Pancrazio and climb the steps to the Passeggiata del Gianicolo.*

⑬ ★ **Tempietto and San Pietro in Montorio.** In the courtyard of this church is Donato Bramante's round, classically inspired Tempietto (1508). ⏲ *15 min. Piazza San Pietro in Montorio 2.* ☎ *06-5813940. Free admission. Open daily 8:30am–noon; Mon–Fri 3–4pm. Bus: 44, 75, 115, and Roma Cristiana double-decker.*

Scenic Trastevere retains its neighborhood feel.

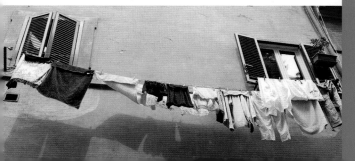

Tridente

1 Piazza del Popolo

2 Santa Maria del Popolo

3 Via del Corso

4 Ara Pacis

5 Mausoleum of Augustus

6 Largo della Fontanella Borghese

7 Streets from Piazza Borghese to Piazza del Parlamento

8 Piazza San Lorenzo in Lucina

9 Caffè Teichner

10 Via Condotti

11 Piazza di Spagna

12 Via Margutta

Named for the three-pronged splay of streets (Via Ripetta, Via del Corso, and Via del Babuino) south of Piazza del Popolo, the Tridente is the toniest part of town, where wealthy neighborhood co-ops keep their cobblestone streets swept clean and lined with potted plants. The area east of Via del Corso is a shopper's paradise; to the west, it's darker and quieter, with dog-legged alleys that evoke the 16th century. Relieved on both sides by open spaces (the Tiber and the Villa Borghese), the air here is jaunty and glamorous. Note that "Tridente" is a term largely made up for the convenience of guidebook writers; locals usually refer to this neighborhood by its principal streets or squares (Piazza di Spagna and Piazza del Popolo). START: **Take Metro Line A to Flaminio, or take bus 62, 85, 95, 116, 175, or 492 to Largo Chigi, and walk.**

Shoppers on the Via Condotti.

① ★★★ **Piazza del Popolo.** In the tradition of the grandest Roman piazzas, the vertex of the Tridente is vast, sun-drenched, and obelisked. It was given its present oval shape by neoclassical architect Giuseppe Valadier in 1818 and made traffic-free in 1998. The piazza is bounded to the east by the glorious green terraces of the Pincio gardens, one of the most romantic spots in the city. *See p 38,* **④**.

② ★★ **Santa Maria del Popolo.** In 1099, a church was built on this spot to "expel the demons"—tradition holds that the

detested emperor Nero was secretly buried here by his mistress, Poppaea Sabina, in 68 A.D. The low-ceilinged interior is at first unremarkable, but look closely and you'll find works by Bramante, Pinturicchio, Raphael, and Bernini, as well as two masterpieces by Caravaggio—the tipsy *Martyrdom of St. Peter* (1600) and *Conversion of St. Paul* (1601), with its prominent horse's butt. ① *30 min. Piazza del Popolo 12.* ☎ *06-3610836. www. santamariadelpopolo.it. Mon–Sat 7am–noon and 4–7pm; Sun 8am–1pm and 4:30–7:30pm.*

3 Via del Corso. Named for the barbaric riderless horse races (course) that took place here during Carnevale, Via del Corso is the main north–south thoroughfare in the *centro storico* and packed with midrange boutiques. The pedestrianized northern half is the favored stamping ground of obnoxious Roman teens and best avoided if you're looking for a pleasant place to stroll.

4 ★★ Ara Pacis. Housed in a strikingly modern, Richard Meier–designed pavilion along the riverbank, this 9 B.C. "altar of peace" is one of the most important works of Roman relief sculpture in the world. The marble panels making up the square altar depict Emperor Augustus and his entourage and mythological scenes of the deities that supposedly protected Rome and fostered peace within it; the Ara Pacis was commissioned when Augustus returned triumphant from his military endeavors in Gaul and Spain. The museum structure, opened in 2006, is the first work of new architecture in the *centro storico* since the Fascist period.
🕐 *30 min. Lungotevere in Augusta.* ☎ *06-82059127. 8€, higher during special exhibitions Tues–Sun 9am–7pm.*

5 ★ Mausoleum of Augustus. This crumbling though still massive brick cylinder, the 28 B.C. tomb of the first Roman emperor, was once clad with marble and planted with elegant rings of cypress trees. Mussolini had designs on making the mausoleum his own family tomb, so he built the surrounding iceberg-like travertine buildings to give the area an appropriately harsh Fascist aesthetic. In fact, the Duce had plans to enshrine all the ruins of Rome with such austere honorific architecture; had he remained in power longer, similarly stark facades would appear all over the *centro* today. *Piazza Augusto Imperatore.*

6 Largo della Fontanella Borghese. Home to the Mercato delle Stampe antique books market. *See p 86.*

7 ★ Streets from Piazza Borghese to Piazza del Parlamento. These dark and narrow alleys seem to breathe ancient intrigue. Indeed, Vicolo del Divino Amore is where the short-tempered painter Caravaggio threw rocks at his landlord's window after a rent dispute. Nearby, Palazzo Firenze is home to the Società Dante Alighieri, the city's most venerable school of Italian for foreigners. *www.dantealighieri-roma.it.*

The Piazza de Spagna, named after the Spanish Embassy to the Holy See.

Barcaccia fountain, Piazza di Spagna.

⑧ ★ Piazza San Lorenzo in Lucina. This cafe-equipped refuge for weary shoppers is home of the eponymous church, where the very grill on which St. Lawrence was barbecued is kept in a side chapel. ⏱ *15 min. Church open daily 8am–8pm.*

Coffee, beer, and light sandwiches are served at ⑨ **Caffè Teichner**. Caffè Ciampini, adjacent, is its virtual twin. *Piazza San Lorenzo in Lucina 17.* ☎ *06-6871683. $–$$.*

⑩ Via Condotti. Aided by its deputies—Via Borgognona, Via Bocca di Leone, Via Mario de' Fiori, and Via Belsiana—high-end retail artery Via Condotti spearheads an effort to bring financial ruin on all who dare to carry a credit card near the Spanish Steps.

⑪ ★★★ Piazza di Spagna. It's de rigueur on any tourist's itinerary, but prepare to contend with perpetual mobs of gelato-wielding tourists and Casanovas trawling the square for naive foreign females. Luckily, neither taints the overall beauty of the glamorously upsweeping Spanish Steps (which were actually designed and funded by the French). At the base of the 18th-century stairs, the sunken *Barcaccia* ("bad boat") fountain is by Pietro Bernini (Gian Lorenzo's father) and fed by the ancient Aqua Virgo. It's reputed to have the sweetest water in Rome. At no. 26 on the piazza is the Keats-Shelley House where Keats died of tuberculosis at the age of 25. Crowning the top of the stairs is the graceful Trinità dei Monti Church. ⏱ *20 min. Piazza di Spagna. Best in early morning or late evening.*

⑫ ★★ Via Margutta. This impossibly gorgeous lane, nestled between the Pincio and Via del Babuino and lined with artists' ateliers, has sparked many a visitor's fantasy about dropping everything and moving to Rome.

Monti

1. Piazza Madonna dei Monti
2. La Bottega del Caffè
3. Santa Maria dei Monti
4. Ancient Wall along Via Tor de' Conti
5. Totti Mural
6. Via degli Zingari and Via Leonina
7. Mia Market
8. Streets between Via Urbana and Via Panisperna
9. Urbana 47

What was once the **red-light district of ancient Rome** and the poorest part of the city in the Renaissance, Monti is now one of the hippest, most authentic, and least-touristed quarters of Rome's historic core. Century-old butcher shops are adjacent to progressive boutiques and salons, and ethnic eating and classic *enoteche* (wine cellars) abound. START: **Take Metro Line B to Cavour, and then walk.**

La Bottega del Caffè, Piazza Madonna dei Monti.

1 ★★ **Piazza Madonna dei Monti.** Start your walking tour at Monti's hub of social life and foot and motor traffic. The 16th-century fountain here is rather unassuming for Rome, which indicates the level of poverty in this area at the time of its construction.

When visiting Piazza Madonna dei Monti, do as the locals do and stop for a cappuccino—or a beer, depending on the time of day—at

the vibrant hive of local color 2
★★ **La Bottega del Caffè.** *Piazza Madonna dei Monti 5.* $–$$.

③ **Santa Maria dei Monti.**
Across Via dei Serpenti is the piazza's namesake, a church dedicated to Mary and designed in 1580 by Giacomo della Porta, who also designed the more famous Gesù, just west of Piazza Venezia. *Via Madonna dei Monti 14.*

④ ★★ **Ancient Wall along Via Tor de' Conti.** The massive grey tufa wall running along the south side of the street was erected in 2 B.C. as a firewall and visual barrier between the Suburra (Monti's old moniker) and the glorious Imperial Forums, the ruins of which are visible through breaks in the wall. The Suburra was the ancient city's red-light district and general bad neighborhood—if you've seen HBO's *Rome,* you may have some sense of how rough it was. Unfortunately, the firewall proved ineffectual during the infamous conflagration of A.D. 64, which started in the Suburra and raged for 7 days, destroying two-thirds of the city.

⑤ ★ **Totti Mural.** You won't find it marked on most maps, but tiny Via del Pozzo dead-ends with a vivid, red-and-yellow mural of homegrown soccer hero Francesco Totti (the captain of A.S. Roma and member of the Italian national team). The iconic image, which depicts Totti kissing his finger and raising it to the sky, was painted on the occasion of *La Roma*'s championship title in 2001.

⑥ ★ **Via degli Zingari and Via Leonina.** Stroll these narrow streets and browse the cutting-edge boutiques that have cropped up in the neighborhood in recent years and that account for much of its renaissance. Image-conscious

Totti mural, Via del Pozzo

women can stop in for an 18€ *piega* (blow-out) at cool Contesta Rock Hair, *Via degli Zingari 9.*

⑦ ★★ **Mia Market** is a small neighborhood produce shop whose shelves overflow with canned goods, olive oils, and other pantry basics, exclusively from the Lazio region, plus baskets and crates of fresh fruit and vegetables. Sit for lunch at the mismatched chairs and tables. *Via Panisperna 225.* ☎ 06-47824611. $–$$.

⑧ ★ **Streets between Via Urbana and Via Panisperna.** These stepped backstreets—from Via Ciancaleoni to Via Capocci— will make you forget you're in a world capital. Cats sleep on the sidewalk, and women dry their laundry on lines outside their cramped *palazzi.* It's what Trastevere used to look like before the rents went up.

Wind up your tour at ⑨ **Urbana 47;** this modern bohemian cafe serves light fare and potent caffeinated beverages at all hours. *Via Urbana 47.* ☎ 06-47884006. $$.

Jewish Ghetto & Tiber Island

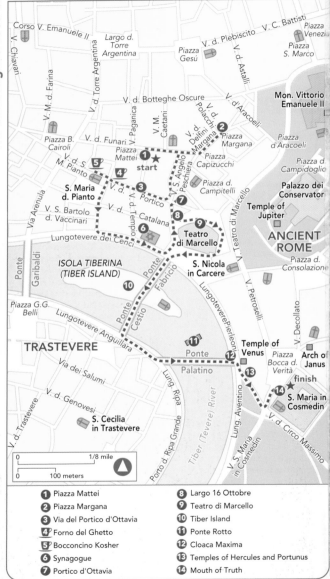

1. Piazza Mattei
2. Piazza Margana
3. Via del Portico d'Ottavia
4. Forno del Ghetto
5. Bocconcino Kosher
6. Synagogue
7. Portico d'Ottavia
8. Largo 16 Ottobre
9. Teatro di Marcello
10. Tiber Island
11. Ponte Rotto
12. Cloaca Maxima
13. Temples of Hercules and Portunus
14. Mouth of Truth

Packed with monuments from every era of Roman history, the Jewish Ghetto has left its dark days behind and become a vibrant, rewarding place to explore. Tiber Island and the riverbank here offer rustic charm and some of the city's most interesting, unsung sights. START: Take bus 30, 40, 62, 64, 70, 87, 116, 492, 571, or 628, or tram 8 to Largo Argentina.

① ★★ Piazza Mattei. One of Rome's most prized possessions, the Fontana delle Tartarughe (Tortoise Fountain) lies tucked away in this gem of a square, where you'll often find film crews shooting and art students sketching its picturesquely patinated centerpiece.

② ★ Piazza Margana. This textbook example of a charming Italian square is complete with geraniums spilling out of window boxes, a pretty alfresco cafe/restaurant, and, if you look carefully down tiny Via di Tor Margana, a gun-barrel view of Trajan's Column, .5km (⅓ mile) away.

③ ★ Via del Portico d'Ottavia. Formerly the eastern boundary of the Jewish Ghetto, this bumpy, busy street is now the principal thoroughfare of the modern neighborhood, with shop signs in Hebrew alluding to the community's heritage.

It's hard to resist the sweet smells of almonds, cinnamon, and ricotta emanating from the **④ ★ Forno del Ghetto,** run by three gruff matrons. Cookies and candied cakes are sold by the kilo and are best eaten fresh out of the oven. *Via del Portico d'Ottavia 1.* ☎ 06-6878637. $.

Delicious—and kosher—pizza by the slice is served at **⑤ ★ Bocconcino Kosher,** and there are a few stools to sit on while you scarf it down. *Via Santa Maria del Pianto 64.* ☎ 06-68192968. $.

⑥ ★★ Synagogue. Rome's gorgeous, palm-treed Sinagoga is a

The historic Jewish Ghetto.

particularly triumphant edifice in this part of town. It was built in the 1890s over land that was once the most squalid part of the Ghetto, shortly after the decree that ended the Jewish segregation. Inside the temple is the Museo d'Arte Ebraica, with vivid exhibits documenting the persecution of the Jews in Rome from 1555—when the papal bull, *Cum nimis absurdum*, established the Ghetto laws—through the Nazi occupation of the 1940s. ⓒ *30 min. Lungotevere Cenci 15.* ☎ *06-68400661. 10€, includes Museo Ebraico. Sun–Thurs 10am–4pm; Fri 9am–1:30pm.*

⑦ ★ Portico d'Ottavia. Poking up from the ancient level at the end of Via del Portico d'Ottavia are the impressive remains of a propylaeum (gate to a temple precinct), built by Augustus, and named for his sister, in 23 B.C. Today the portico is the monumental entry to the modest medieval Church of

Upwards toward the cupola of the Sinagoga.

Sant'Angelo in Pescheria, where Jews were forced to attend Catholic Mass during the Ghetto period. The pavement outside was for centuries the site of Rome's fish market *(pescheria)*, hence the name of the church. ⓒ *15 min. Free admission. Excavations daily 9am–5pm.*

⑧ ★ Largo 16 Ottobre. In front of the Portico d'Ottavia ruins, a plaque on the wall commemorates the place where, on the night of October 16, 1943, Roman Jews were rounded up by Nazi troops and deported to the concentration camps of Auschwitz and Birkenau. Of the 3,091 men, women, and children deported, only 15 survived.

⑨ ★★ Teatro di Marcello (Theater of Marcellus). With a 15,000-spectator capacity, this 13-B.C. theater was the main ancient Roman venue for plays, concerts, and the occasional public execution. In the 1300s, the Savelli family built a fortress on top of the ponderous ruins, which they then converted into a palace during the Renaissance. Above the ancient travertine arches, the apartments are still inhabited by modern princes and *contessas.* ⓒ *15 min. Free admission. Excavations daily 9am–5pm.*

⑩ ★★ Tiber Island. In 391 B.C., a snake slithered onto the shores of Tiber Island; at the same time, a decade-long plague in Rome ended. Ever since, the river island has been a sanctuary of medicine, with the Fatebenefratelli Hospital today occupying the majority of the real estate. The ancient Romans, in a moment of fancy, sculpted the island to look like a ship; part of the "hull" (a fragment of carved travertine) can still be seen on the lower esplanade, a favorite sunning spot of Romans on their lunch breaks. Stairs to the lower esplanade are

Tiber Island after dark.

located west of the main entrance to the hospital. ⏱ *30 min.*

⓫ ★ **Ponte Rotto.** Stranded in the middle of the river below Tiber Island is the single arch of the 142-B.C. Ponte Rotto, or "broken bridge," which fell and was rebuilt so many times that the city finally abandoned it when it collapsed in 1598. From the neighboring modern bridge, Ponte Palatino, wheel ruts can still be seen on the Ponte Rotto's roadway. *No access.*

⓬ **Cloaca Maxima.** A gaping arch in the riverbank walls, under the eastern end of the Ponte Palatino, is the mouth of the 6th-century-B.C. "great sewer," constructed to drain the moisture from the swampy valley of the Roman Forum. According to some archaeologists, the underground waterway is still navigable, with secret access hatches in unlikely parts of the city. *No access.*

⓭ ★ **Temples of Hercules and Portunus.** In a beautiful setting, among oleanders and fountains on a grassy rise near the riverbank, these two Republican-era temples survive because of their reconsecration as churches. For centuries, the round temple (of Hercules) was known as the Temple of Vesta because the only other known round temple was that of Vesta in the Roman Forum. The rectangular temple was dedicated to Portunus, god of port activity; in antiquity, the most important cargo coming to Rome, like columns for the Forum or lions for the Colosseum, was unloaded from river barges here. *No access to temples' interiors*

⓮ ★ **Mouth of Truth.** Propped up at the end of the portico of the Church of Santa Maria in Cosmedin (which has a fantastic Romanesque bell tower and unusual Greek Orthodox interior) is an ancient sewer cover known as the Bocca della Verità (Mouth of Truth), which is supposed to bite off the hands of liars. All day, tourists line up to take pictures of themselves with their hands in the mouth slot—cheesy, but a Roman rite of passage. ⏱ *15 min. Queue shortest before 1pm. Piazza della Bocca della Verità.* ☎ *06-6781419. Free admission. Daily 9am–5pm.*

Pigneto

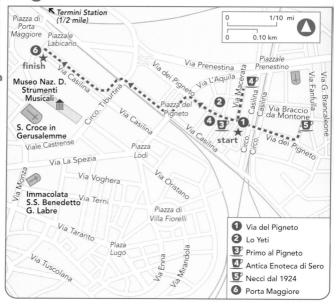

Piazza di Porta Maggiore

Termini Station (1/2 mile)

Piazzale Labicano

6 finish

Via Casilina

Museo Naz. D. Strumenti Musicali

S. Croce in Gerusalemme

Viale Castrense

Circo. Tiburtina

Via Casilina

Via Prenestina

Via dei Pigneto

Via L'Aquila

Via Macerata

Piazzale Prenestino

Via Fanfulla

Via G. Brancaleone

4

Casilina

Piazza del Pigneto

Via Casilina

2

4 **3** **1**

start

Circo.

Circo.

Via Braccio da Montone

Via del Pigneto

5

Via La Spezia

Via Voghera

Piazza Lodi

Via Oristano

Via Monza

Immacolata S.S. Benedetto G. Labre

Via Terni

Piazza di Villa Fiorelli

Via Taranto

Plaza Lugo

Via Enna

Via Mirandola

Via Tuscolana

1	Via del Pigneto
2	Lo Yeti
3	Primo al Pigneto
4	Antica Enoteca di Sero
5	Necci dal 1924
6	Porta Maggiore

0   1/10 mi
0   0.10 km

If you want to check out what's going on in modern Rome, far from the tourist hordes, take a short bus ride east of Termini to Pigneto, which for the past several years has been the "it" neighborhood for the arbiters of Rome's contemporary culture. Via del Pigneto is the pedestrian-only main strip of this trendily gritty quarter, where Pasolini filmed *Accattone* and Rossellini filmed *Roma Città Aperta*. Nowadays, stylish bars and edgy jewelry shops sit adjacent to the old mom-and-pop hardware stores that sell dust brooms to local housewives. Don't think of this as a tour of "sights"—it's more about being with multiple generations of real Romans doing their thing, far from the chaos of the Spanish Steps and Vatican. START: Take bus 81 or 105 or tram 5, 14, or 19. Day to avoid: Monday, when almost everything's closed.

1 ★★ **Via del Pigneto.** The .8km-long (½-mile) main drag of Pigneto, closed to automobile traffic, is where you'll find most of the area's bars, shops, and restaurants. For the best people-watching, come on a late Sunday afternoon, when

you can join tons of locals out for a *passeggiata* (stroll) and an *aperitivo*.

2 ★ **Lo Yeti.** This low-key cafe/bookshop is a good place to sample the Pigneto vibe and find out what's on, events-wise. They host or sponsor a lot of cultural happenings, from Roman folk-music concerts to avant-garde film screenings. There's also an Internet point. *Via Perugia 4.* ☎ *06-7025633. Closed Mon.*

The premier "cool restaurant" of Pigneto, ③ ★★ **Primo al Pigneto,** serves beautifully presented modern Italian cuisine. Chef/owner Marco Gallotta's creations have received tons of positive press among local food critics. Come for a full meal or just a snack and drink. *Via del Pigneto 46.* ☎ *06-7013827. Closed Mon. $$–$$$.*

Most Pigneto boites don't open until 6pm, but wine bar ④ ★ **Antica Enoteca di Sero** serves from 8am (though note they close from 2:30–4:30pm), with a huge selection of wines by the bottle or glass and yummy bar snacks like cheese and meat plates. It's a neighborhood institution that feels like a time-warp back to 1962, the year it opened. *Via Macerata 58b.* ☎ *06-70300111. Daily 8am–2:30pm, 4:30–9pm.*

Retro-chic bar/restaurant ⑤ ★★ **Necci dal 1924**—a favorite of film types since the '50s—is a great casual hangout any time of day. Grab a table inside and admire the movie memorabilia, or sit outside,

shaded by trees in the front garden, and watch local life roll by on this secluded side street. Feel free to bring a book or laptop to go along with your Campari and soda. *Via Fanfulla da Lodi 68.* ☎ *06-97601552. Daily 8am–1am. $–$$.*

⑥ ★★ **Porta Maggiore.** Not part of Pigneto proper, but within reasonable walking distance, this travertine gateway was first built by emperor Claudius in A.D. 52 as a monument to mark the point of entry into the city of the Aqua Claudia and Aqua Anio Novus aqueducts. Look at the top of the monument and you'll see the hollow channels where the water flowed. (The Latin inscription congratulates Claudius, as well as later emperors Vespasian and Titus, for their contributions to city waterworks.) Two centuries later, the free-standing gateway was incorporated into Rome's Aurelian Walls. Immediately southeast of Porta Maggiore is the one-of-a-kind **Tomb of Eurysaces**—look for the white structure with uniform round holes along the sides. Eurysaces was a freedman and baker in 1st-century-B.C. Rome, and the cylinders have been interpreted as models of grain measures or vessels for mixing dough. Some friezes with scenes of the baking life are preserved at the top of the tomb. *Tram 3 or 19.*

The Boho scene at Necci dal 1924.

Testaccio

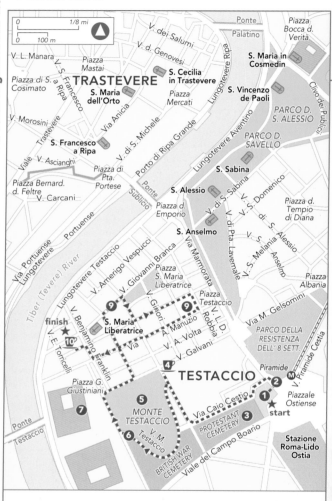

0 1/8 mi
0 100 m

Ponte
Palatino

Piazza
Bocca d.
Verità

V. dei Salumi

V. L. Manara

V. d. Genovesi

Piazza
Mastai

S. Cecilia
in Trastevere

S. Maria in
Cosmedin

Piazza di S.
Cosimato

TRASTEVERE

S. Maria
dell'Orto

Piazza
Mercati

S. Vincenzo
de Paoli

Lungotevere Ripa

Clivo dei Publici

V. Morosini

S. Francesco
a Ripa

Via Anicia

V. di S. Michele

Porto di Ripa Grande

*PARCO D.
S. ALESSIO*

Viale Trastevere

V. di S. Francesco a Ripa

V. Ascianghi

Piazza di
Pta.
Portese

Lungotevere Aventino

*PARCO D.
SAVELLO*

S. Sabina

Piazza Bernard.
d. Feltre

V. Carcani

Ponte
Sublicio

Piazza d.
Emporio

S. Alessio

V. di S. Sabina

V. di S. Domenico

Piazza d.
Tempio
di Diana

Via Portuense

Portuense

S. Anselmo

Via Marmorata

V. di Pta. Lavernale

V. di S. Alessio

V. di S. Melania

V. di S. Anselmo

Piazza
Albania

Via Portuense

Lungotevere

Tiber (Tevere) River

Lungotevere Testaccio

V. Amerigo Vespucci

V. Giovanni Branca

Piazza
S. Maria
Liberatrice

Piazza
Testaccio

Via M. Gelsomini

9

V. Ginori

9

V. L. D.
Robbia

*PARCO DELLA
RESISTENZA
DELL' 8 SETT.*

finish

V. Benjamino Franklin

**S. Maria
Liberatrice**

A. Manuzio

V. A. Volta

V. Galvani

V. Piramide Cestia

10

V. E. Torricelli

Via

4

TESTACCIO

Piramide

M

2

Piazza G.
Giustiniani

5

*MONTE
TESTACCIO*

Via Caio Cestio

3

Piazzale
Ostiense

start

1

Ponte
Testaccio

7

6

V. M.
Testaccio

*PROTESTANT
CEMETERY*

Viale del Campo Boario

*BRITISH WAR
CEMETERY*

Stazione
Roma-Lido
Ostia

① Pyramid of Gaius Cestius
② Porta San Paolo
③ Protestant Cemetery
④ Il Seme e la Foglia
⑤ Monte Testaccio

⑥ Via di Monte Testaccio
⑦ Mattatoio
⑧ 00100 Pizza
⑨ Mercato di Testaccio
⑩ Sora Rosa

Testaccio, whose most salient physical features are a defunct slaughterhouse, an ancient rubbish heap, and a slew of night-clubs, has long been a working-class bastion of real Romans and average architecture. Although it's become one of Rome's shabby-chic "in" neighborhoods, Testaccio's salt-of-the-earth flavor remains. START: **Take Metro Line B, bus 23, 30, 170, 271, or 280, or tram 3 to Piramide/Piazzale Ostiense.**

① ★ Pyramid of Gaius Cestius. Egyptomania was all the rage in 1st-century-B.C. Rome, and though none would mistake this rather incongruous spike of white marble for the pyramids of Giza, the Roman magistrate who had it built as his tomb probably intended to have it taken just as seriously. *Open by appointment only.* ☎ *06-39967700.*

② ★ Porta San Paolo. One of the best-preserved gateways from the 3rd-century-A.D. Aurelian Walls, this is home to the small Museo di Via Ostiense, with interesting artifacts relating to Roman roads. ⏱ *20 min. Piazzale Ostiense/Via R. Persichetti 3.* ☎ *06-5743193. Free admission. Opening hours vary.*

③ ★ Protestant Cemetery. Just beyond a ruined stretch of the Aurelian Walls, the charming *Cimitero Acattolico* complies with the ancient mandate that all burials be outside the city limits. Its peaceful, totally unexpected grounds are home to the graves of Percy Bysshe Shelley, who drowned off the Italian Riviera in 1822 before his 30th birthday; John Keats; and Antonio Gramsci, founder of the Italian Communist Party, among others. *Via Caio Cestio 6.* ☎ *06-5741900. Donation expected. Tues–Sun 9am–5pm; Sun 9am–1pm.*

Opposite Monte Testaccio, **④** ★ **Il Seme e la Foglia** offers monstrous salads, beers on tap, and great local flavor. *Via Galvani 18.* ☎ *06-5743008. $–$$.*

Pyramid of Gaius Cestius, near the Porta San Paolo.

⑤ ★★ Monte Testaccio. One of the ancient Romans' most remarkable creations, the "Monte dei Cocci" (hill of shards) is an artificial mountain, 30m high (100 ft.), made entirely of broken amphorae (slender vessels used to transport oil and wine) that were discarded here over centuries of importation. There's a good view of the red clay shards through the gates at the corner of Via Galvani and Via Zabaglia, and through the back walls of many of the clubs and bars built against the hill. *Via Zabaglia 24. Open by appointment only.* ☎ *06-0608. 3€, does not include guided tour.*

⑥ ★ Via di Monte Testaccio. Only in Rome: By night, this is disco central; by day, livestock bleat happily in their pens on the hillside, directly above the shuttered nightclubs where techno beats blared hours earlier.

⑦ ★ Il Mattatoio. Rome's decommissioned abattoir—still recognizable by the statue of a naked hero slaughtering a hapless ox atop its neoclassical facade—is now an exhibition space for a variety of contemporary cultural endeavors, under the aegis of MACRO (Museo d'Arte Contemporanea di Roma). *Piazza O. Giustiniani 4.* ☎ *06-0608. http://www.macro.roma.museum. Hours and prices depend on exhibition.*

Popular pizzeria named for the 00 grade of semolina flour and Rome's postal code, **⑧ 00100 Pizza** specializes in "trappizzini"—triangular pieces of pillowy pizza bianca, filled with stewed oxtail, meatballs, tripe, and other savory Roman stuffings, for only 3€. *Via Giovanni Branca 88.* ☎ *06-43419624. $.*

⑨ ★★ Mercato di Testaccio. Mingle with local matrons decked out in their finest housedresses and bedroom slippers at the lively covered market at Piazza Testaccio. Then take a walk on Via di Monte Testaccio (⑥ in this tour), the circular road that skirts the base of the "mountain made of pottery." *Mon–Sat 7am–1pm.*

Don't leave Testaccio without having smiling Sandro make you a sandwich at his delightful throwback of a snack bar **⑩ ★ Sora Rosa.** Join little old men sipping wine (poured from a spigot in the marble wall) and eating generously stuffed panini that won't cost you more than 2€. *Via Galileo Ferraris 7. Closed Sun. $.* ●

Market-fresh fish, Mercato di Testaccio.

Shopping Best Bets

Best **Multi-Label Boutique**
★★ Gente, *Via del Babuino 81* (p 82)

Best **Stylish & Affordable Shoes**
★★★ Danielle, *Piazza Risorgimento 38* (p 87); and ★★ Posto Italiano, *Via dei Giubbonari 37A* (p 88); and ★★ Ibiz, *Via dei Chiavari 39* (p 88)

Best **Wine Shop**
★★★ Trimani, *Via Goito 20* (p 86)

Best **Street for Contemporary Fashion**
Via dei Giubbonari (off Campo de' Fiori)

Best **Accessories at Good Prices**
★ COIN, *Via Cola di Rienzo 173* (p 84)

Best **Museum Store**
★★ Capitoline Museums, *Piazza del Campidoglio* (p 31)

Best **Teen Threads**
★ Brandy Melville, *Via Cola di Rienzo 136* (p 81); and ★ Energie, *Via del Corso 408–409* (p 81)

Best **Toys and Children's Books**
★★ Città del Sole, *Via della Scrofa 65* (p 88)

Best **Papal Vestments**
★★ Ghezzi, *Via de' Cestari 32–33* (p 87)

Best **Gourmet Foods**
★★★ Franchi, *Via Cola di Rienzo 204* (p 86); and ★★★ Volpetti, *Via Marmorata 47* (p 86)

Best **Local Market**
★★★ Piazza Testaccio (p 87)

Best **Gifts**
★★★ Modigliani, *Via Condotti 24* (p 85)

Previous page: Keeping up a bella figura in the stylish streets of Rome. Above: Shopping at the market.

Centro Storico Shopping

Ai Monasteri 2	Feltrinelli Libre e Musica 7	Nuyorica 18
Al Sogno 3		People 16
Campo de' Fiori market 17	Ghezzi 5	Posto Italiano 12
Città del Sole 4	Ibiz 15	Prototype 13
Davide Cenci 1	L.E.I. 10	Roscioli 14
Ditta G. Poggi 6	Limoni 9	Sole 19
Ethic 11	Loco 20	Spazio Sette 8

Rome Shopping

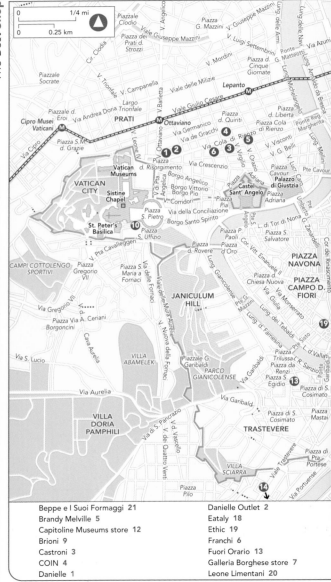

Beppe e I Suoi Formaggi 21
Brandy Melville 5
Capitoline Museums store 12
Brioni 9
Castroni 3
COIN 4
Danielle 1

Danielle Outlet 2
Eataly 18
Ethic 19
Franchi 6
Fuori Orario 13
Galleria Borghese store 7
Leone Limentani 20

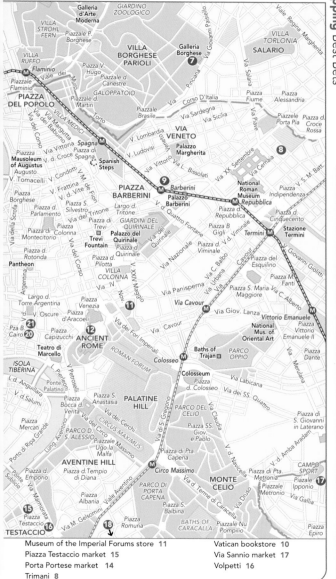

Museum of the Imperial Forums store 11
Piazza Testaccio market 15
Porta Portese market 14
Trimani 8

Vatican bookstore 10
Via Sannio market 17
Volpetti 16

Spanish Steps Shopping

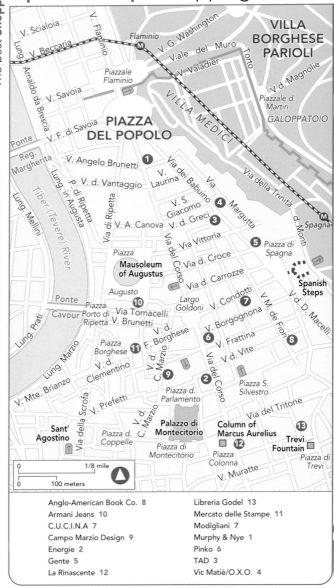

Anglo-American Book Co. 8
Armani Jeans 10
C.U.C.I.N.A 7
Campo Marzio Design 9
Energie 2
Gente 5
La Rinascente 12

Libreria Godel 13
Mercato delle Stampe 11
Modigliani 7
Murphy & Nye 1
Pinko 6
TAD 3
Vic Matiè/O.X.O. 4

Rome Shopping A to Z

High-end shops on Via Condotti.

striped T-shirts, tanks, leggings, and underwear. A must for the young fashionista on your shopping list. *Via Cola di Rienzo 136 (at Via Orazio).* ☎ *06-32609878. AE, MC, V. Metro: Ottaviano. Bus: 70 or 81. Map p 81.*

★★ **Brioni** PIAZZA BARBERINI You're in excellent (if expensive) hands at this custom men's clothier—the same sartorial masters who have tailored the suits of every dashing 007 from Connery to Craig. *Via Barberini 79–81 (at Piazza Barberini).* ☎ *06-485855. AE, MC, V. Metro: Barberini. Map p 78.*

★★ **Davide Cenci** PANTHEON At this Roman emporium of classic and ultra-chic men's and women's wear, country clubbers feel right at home with labels like Fay, Belvest, Loro Piana, and Cenci's own brand. *Via Campo Marzio 1–7 (at Via Uffici del Vicario).* ☎ *06-6990681. AE, MC, V. Bus: 62, 85, 95, 175, or 492. Map p 77.*

★ **Energie** PIAZZA DEL POPOLO The brash and bright fashions here are meant for teens, but you'll find many a Roman mom squeezing herself into jeans while out ostensibly shopping for cool tees for her 15-year-old son. *Via del*

Apparel & Accessories

★ **Armani Jeans** SPANISH STEPS Armani for the rest of us: fun, well-cut clothes in cotton and denim for men and women at humane prices. *Via Tomacelli 137 (at Largo degli Schiavoni).* ☎ *06-68193040. www.armani. com. AE, MC, V. Metro: Spagna. Bus: 492 or 628. Map p 80.*

★ **Brandy Melville** VATICAN Sort of like Abercrombie meets Urban Outfitters, this Italian label is where Rome's privileged teens go for boho and preppy staples like

VAT Refund

If you're a non-E.U. citizen and spend 151€ or more at any one retailer, the VAT refund knocks 11% to 13% off your bill. In order to get your refund, you must 1) obtain a completed tax-free form from the store, and 2) present your unused purchases for inspection at the airport (in Rome or your last European port). The inspector will stamp your form, which then enables you to pick up a **cash refund** at the airport, or to file for a **credit card adjustment.**

De rigeur styles at Brandy Melville.

Corso 179. ☎ 06-6781045. AE, MC, V. Metro: Flaminio. Map p 80.

★ **Ethic** VATICAN   A favorite of 20- and 30-something Roman women, with reasonably priced boho-chic pieces in retro designs and adherent cuts. *Via Cola di Rienzo 265A.* ☎ *06-3224621. (Branch at Piazza Cairoli 11–12, at Via dei Giubbonari.* ☎ *06-68301063.) www.3ndlab.com. AE, MC, V. Bus: 30, 40, 62, 64, 70, 85, 87, 95, 116, 175, or 492. Map p 77.*

★ **Fuori Orario** TRASTEVERE This tiny corner shop has a kaleidoscopic array of leather jackets, plus inexpensive, trendy apparel by French designers. Discounts for

Energie, Via del Corso.

cash payment are often available. *Via del Moro 29 (at Via della Pellic-cia).* ☎ *06-5817181. MC, V. Bus: 23, 271, or 280. Map p 78.*

★★ **Gente** SPANISH STEPS   A microcosm of the Via Condotti boutiques, with more affordable denim and accessories. *Via del Babuino 81 (at Piazza di Spagna).* ☎ *06-3207671. AE, MC, V. Metro: Spagna. (Branch at Via Cola di Rienzo 277, Vatican area.) Map p 80.*

★★ **L.E.I.** CAMPO DE' FIORI   Should one of Rome's remaining princes invite you to the ball, come here first for a feast of frocks in all shapes and all price ranges. *Via dei Giubbonari 103 (at Via dei Chiavari).* ☎ *06-6875432. AE, MC, V. Bus: 34, 40, 62, 64, 70, 87, or 492. (Branch at Via Nazionale 88.) Map p 77.*

★ **Murphy & Nye** PIAZZA DEL POPOLO   Roman men love to dress as if they're on a backup crew for a major regatta. Join 'em with threads from this trendy, nautical-inspired sportswear boutique. *Via del Corso 26–27 (near Piazza del Popolo).* ☎ *06-36004461. AE, MC, V. Metro: Flaminio. Map p 80.*

★★ **Nuyorica** CAMPO DE' FIORI   With carefully selected clothes, bags, and shoes by such A-list designers as Marni and Balen-ciaga, this startlingly hip boutique shows just how far the Campo de' Fiori area has come from its humble roots. *Piazza Pollarola 36–37 (at Via del Biscione).* ☎ *06-68891243. www. nuyorica.it. AE, MC, V. Bus: 34, 40, 62, 64, 70, 87, or 492. Map p 77.*

★★ **People** CAMPO DE' FIORI By far the best vintage clothing store in town. The boutique also sells new clothing with retro styling (think dresses that look like 1960s Pucci). *Piazza Teatro di Pompeo 4A (at Via dei Chiavari).* ☎ *06-6874040. AE, MC, V. Bus: 30, 40, 62, 64, 70, 87, 116, or 492. Map p 77.*

★★ **Pinko** SPANISH STEPS Embellished knits, deconstructed denim, and great pants in mineral tones are the hallmark of this Northern Italian women's label—but you'd better be skinny. *Via Frattina 101– 102.* ☎ *06-69294666. www.pinko.it. AE, DC, MC, V. Bus: 30, 40, 62, 64, 70, 87, or 492. Map p 80.*

★ **Prototype** CAMPO DE' FIORI The owners of this unisex boutique scour the land to bring hip and colorful casual wear and sneakers to Roman 20- and 30-somethings. *Via Giubbonari 50 (at Campo de' Fiori).* ☎ *06-6800330. AE, MC, V. Bus: 30, 40, 62, 64, 70, 87, or 492. Tram: 8. Map p 77.*

★ **Sole** CAMPO DE' FIORI Glam women's accessories and clothing with Italian attitude—think sassy, bejeweled handbags and snug-fitting, fur-trimmed trenches—make

Classy threads and kicks at Nuyorica.

for fabulous I-picked-this-up-in-Rome purchases. *Via dei Baullari 21 (at Piazza della Cancelleria).* ☎ *06-68806987. AE, MC, V. Bus: 30, 40, 62, 64, 70, 87, 116, or 492. Map p 77.*

★★ **TAD** SPANISH STEPS Everything in this lifestyle "concept" boutique, which looks like a lush, glossy magazine spread, is for sale, from the Lucite pumps to the bamboo trees. *Via del Babuino 155A (at Via dei Greci).* ☎ *06-96842086. www. wetad.it. AE, MC, V. Metro: Spagna. Map p 80.*

Books
★★ **Anglo-American Book Co.** SPANISH STEPS English-language titles of all kinds are sold here, but the selection is particularly strong on art and architecture. *Via della Vite 102 (at Via Mario de' Fiori).* ☎ *06-6795222. AE, MC, V. Metro:*

Sale Season

If you come to Rome in late January or late July, you might not find the best weather, but if you're a shopper, your timing is perfect. All stores in Italy have two annual liquidation periods *(saldi)*. Discounts start at 30% (though most are 50%) and can go as deep as 75% off regular retail. I've made off with Dolce & Gabbana pumps, Pucci sandals, and Max Mara jackets for proverbial pennies.

COIN, basics in a range of prices.

Spagna. Bus: 52, 53, 61, 62, 63, 71, 85, 116, or 117. Map p 80.

★ **Feltrinelli Libri e Musica** PANTHEON With bar-code-scanning CD-listening stations and a great travel section, Rome has its answer to Barnes & Noble in this renovated branch of a national book chain, many with an in-store cafe. *Largo di Torre Argentina 11 (at Corso Vittorio Emanuele II).* ☎ 06-68663001. AE, MC, V. Bus: 30, 40, 62, 64, 70, 87, or 492. Map p 77.

★ **Libreria Godel** TREVI FOUNTAIN New and used books for tourists and scholars, plus Vespa clocks, Fiat 500 models, and vintage Italian graphic design gifts.

Come here for fun, no-brainer souvenirs. *Via Poli 45 (at Piazza Poli).* ☎ 06-6798716. www.libreriagodel. it. AE, MC, V. Bus: 62, 63, 85, 95, 175, or 492. Map p 80.

Department Stores
★ **COIN** VATICAN It's underwhelming if you're used to the U.S. or U.K. department store standard, but COIN does have some great finds in its accessories section, where the latest looks in handbags and belts are very budget-friendly. *Via Cola di Rienzo 173 (at Via Paolo Emilio).* ☎ 06-36004298. AE, MC, V. Metro: Ottaviano. Map p 78.

★ **La Rinascente** VIA DEL CORSO Similar to COIN but larger and more central, La Rinascente is a good bet when you need to buy a last-minute leather wallet or silk scarf for someone back home. No need to go upstairs unless you're seeking a frumpy blouse. *Galleria Alberto Sordi (at Piazza Colonna).* ☎ 06-6784209. AE, MC, V. Bus: 62, 63, 85, 95, 175, or 492. Map p 80.

Design & Home Furnishings
★★ **C.U.C.I.N.A.** SPANISH STEPS At this shrine to

High-Fashion Boutiques

All roads lead to Rome. The roads around the Spanish Steps lead to credit card debt. Leading the luxury retail pack is Via Condotti, which boasts the boutiques of **Alberta Ferretti, Armani, Dior, Dolce & Gabbana, Ferragamo, Gucci, Hermès, La Perla, Louis Vuitton, Max Mara, Prada, Valentino, YSL,** and the massive **Fendi** flagship, anchoring the western end of the street. Piazza di Spagna weighs in with **Roberto Cavalli, D&G, Escada, Frette, Missoni,** and **Sergio Rossi;** while Via Babuino has **Chanel, Etro, Giuseppe Zanotti,** and **Prada Sport.** Nearby Via Borgognona is graced by the doors of **Givenchy, Loro Piana, Tod's,** and **Versace;** and Via Belsiana features **Moschino.**

Museum Stores

When it comes to only-in-Rome gifts and souvenirs, steer clear of the tchotchke street vendors and head to one of the city's excellent museum bookshops. Some of the best are at the **Capitoline Museums** (p 31), the new **Museum of the Imperial Forums at Trajan's Markets** (p 24), and the **Galleria Borghese** (p 30). The Vatican bookstore, on the south side of St. Peter's Square, has a dizzying array of art books, religious tomes, rosaries, and "pope-phernalia."

stainless-steel cookware and kitchen gadgets, you can pick up authentic Bialetti stove-top coffeemakers, mini-parmigiano graters, and all gauges of ravioli-cutters. *Via Mario de' Fiori 65 (at Via delle Carrozze).* ☎ 06-6791275. www.cucinastore.com. AE, MC, V. Metro: Spagna. Map p 80.

★★ **Leone Limentani** JEWISH GHETTO Explore the vast maze of 19th-century underground corridors, losing all sense of direction among rows of gold-encrusted dinner plates. Selling everything from modern kitchen gadgets to classic Italian pottery. *Via Portico d'Ottavia 47 (at Largo 16 Ottobre).* ☎ 06-68806949. www.leonelimentani.it. AE, MC, V. Bus: 87 or 119. Tram: 8. Map p 78.

★★★ **Modigliani** SPANISH STEPS From Murano wineglasses to hand-painted Tuscan platters, the

The highly coveted Prada brand.

fine (but not fussy) merchandise at this four-story tabletop-goods store makes great gifts that can be shipped anywhere in the world. *Via Condotti 24 (at Via Bocca di Leone).* ☎ 06-6785653. www.modigliani.it. AE, MC, V. Metro: Spagna. Map p 80.

★★ **Spazio Sette** CAMPO DE' FIORI The hottest Italian design, in everything from sofas to picture frames, reigns supreme at this three-floor housewares emporium. *Via dei Barbieri 7 (at Largo Argentina).* ☎ 06-6869708. AE, MC, V. Bus: 30, 40, 62, 64, 70, 87, or 492. Map p 77.

Food & Wine

★★ **Beppe e I Suoi Formaggi** CAMPO DE' FIORI Dairy farmer Beppe Giovale opened this cheese shrine in 2010, and his "droolsome" organic formaggi, Alpine butters, cured meats, pasta, and elegant wine selection have a strong focus on his native Piedmont. *Via Santa Maria del Pianto 9 (at Via Portico d'Ottavia).* ☎ 06-68192210. AE, MC, V. Bus: 30, 40, 62, 64, 70, 87, or 492. Tram: 8. Map p 78.

★★ **Castroni** VATICAN This coffee bar extraordinaire has bulk candy, caviar, fine wines, and all manner of oils and vinegars. A godsend for many expats, Castroni also stocks hard-to-get foreign foodstuffs like Bisquick and Vegemite.

Via Cola di Rienzo 196–198 (at Via Terenzio). ☎ 06-6874383. www. castronicoladirienzo.com. *AE, MC, V. Metro: Ottaviano. Map p 78.*

★★★ **Eataly** SOUTHERN SUBURBS An impressive marriage of artisanal Italian food and the big-box concept, the largest outlet of the Eataly chain opened here in June 2012, with 170,000 square feet of retail and dining space on four floors. Though you don't get the same fuzzy feeling here as at Franchi and Volpetti, foodies will want to make a pilgrimage here. It's located in the revamped glass-and-steel "Air Terminal" building attached to the Piramide metro station. *Via 12 Ottobre, 1492 (off Via Ostiense).* ☎ 06-90279201. *AE, MC, V. Metro: Piramide or Garbatella. Bus: 30, 80, 175, 280, Tram: 3. Map p 78.*

★★★ **Franchi** VATICAN One of the top two gourmet delis in town (Volpetti is the other), Franchi has every cheese and cured meat under the sun. At lunch, hot prepared food (including heavenly *suppli*) is available to go. *Via Cola di Rienzo 204 (at Via Terenzio).* ☎ 06-6874651. *AE, MC, V. Metro: Ottaviano. Map p 78.*

★★ **Roscioli** CAMPO DE' FIORI Calling itself a *salumeria con cucina*, beloved Roscioli is a compact destination with a spectacular

Foot traffic on Via Condotti.

selection of charcuterie and cheese and other gourmet groceries, as well as quality wines. You can also eat here, hence the cucina part of the name. *Via dei Giubbonari 21 (at Via dei Chiavari).* ☎ 06-6875287). *AE, MC, V. Bus 30, 40, 62, 64, 70, 87, or 492. Tram: 8. Map p 77.*

★★★ **Trimani** TERMINI Founded in 1821 and still run by the same family, this is Rome's best wine shop. The knowledgeable owners can help you navigate the overwhelming selection. *Via Goito 20 (at Via Cernaia).* ☎ 06-4469661. *AE, MC, V. Metro: Castro Pretorio. Bus: 60, 75, or 492. Map p 78.*

★★★ **Volpetti** TESTACCIO The aromas of cheese and cured meat beckon more wildly than at any other deli in Rome. The enthusiastic staff will let you taste everything from the amazing selection of honeys, vinegars, Italian spirits, pâtés, preserves, infused oils, and truffled items. *Via Marmorata 47 (at Via Alessandro Volta).* ☎ 06-5742352. *AE, MC, V. Metro: Piramide. Bus: 23, 30, 75, 95, 271, or 280. Tram: 3. Map p 78.*

Markets

★★ **Campo de' Fiori** This historic produce market is still a Roman institution, though kitschy souvenir aprons and all manner of kitchen tools have begun to take over what used to be the city's most authentic fruit-and-veg bazaar. *Mon–Sat 7am–2pm. No credit cards. Bus: 30, 40, 62, 64, 70, 87, or 492. Map p 77.*

★★ **Mercato delle Stampe** PIAZZA DEL POPOLO Here you'll find wonderfully worn antique books, old engravings, vintage magazines, and their loving dealers. To get the best price, feign some sort of expertise in the print market. *Largo della Fontanella Borghese. No credit cards. Metro: Spagna. Bus: 81. Map p 80.*

★★★ **Piazza Testaccio** In salt-of-the-earth Testaccio, this covered market is the real deal. Women in housedresses greet everyone by name as they shuffle from butchers' stalls to produce stands, where their inevitable laments over the rising cost of zucchini blossoms are pure theater. *Mon–Sat 7am–1pm. No credit cards. Metro: Piramide. Bus: 23, 75, or 170. Tram: 3. Map p 78.*

★ **Porta Portese** TRASTEVERE Unless you're in the market for a Turkish casino ashtray or a dot-matrix printer, you'll find Rome's biggest flea market more spectacle than practical shopping experience. *Via Portuense (from Piazza Porta Portese to Via Ettore Rolli). Sun only 7am–2pm. No credit cards. Bus: 23, 271, or 280. Tram: 3 or 8. Map p 78.*

★ **Via Sannio** SAN GIOVANNI Good for new and used clothes, leather jackets, shoes, military camo apparel, and cashmere deals. *Via Sannio. Mon–Sat 10am–2pm. No credit cards. Metro: San Giovanni. Map p 78.*

Perfumery/Personal Care
★★ **Ai Monasteri** PIAZZA NAVONA In a space that recalls a medieval apothecary, choose from potions, elixirs, candles, and sweets—all made by Italian monks. *Corso Rinascimento 72 (at Piazza Cinque Lune).* ☎ *06-68802783. www.aimonasteri.it. AE, MC, V. Bus: 30, 70, 87, 492, or 628. Map p 77.*

★ **Limoni** PIAZZA VENEZIA/PANTHEON This national chain carries basic toiletries that also make for easy souvenirs; people back home always get a kick out of Italian Aquafresh. *Corso Vittorio Emanuele 91 (near Via di Torre Argentina).* ☎ *06-68210952. www.limoni.it. AE, MC, V. Bus: 30, 40, 70, 87, 492, 571, or 628. Map p 77.*

Tea towels are among the wares at Campo de'Fiori.

Religious Goods
★★ **Ghezzi** PANTHEON Couture cassocks, fab fonts, and marvelous monstrances. Unlike other liturgical outfitters on this street, Ghezzi welcomes even lay people to scope (but not buy) its glorious inventory of all things relating to Catholic ceremony. *Via de' Cestari 32–33 (at Via dell'Arco della Ciambella).* ☎ *06-6869744. www.arredisacri.it. Bus: 30, 40, 62, 64, 70, 87, 116, or 492. Map p 77.*

Shoes
★ **Danielle Outlet** VATICAN This miniscule shop has of-the-moment pairs for under 30€—just don't expect the shoes to last much longer than the trend. *Piazza Risorgimento 40 (at Via Ottaviano).* ☎ *06-39744675. www.danielle-shoes.com. AE, MC, V. Bus: 23, 81, 271, or 492. Tram: 19. Map p 78.*

★★ **Loco** CAMPO DE' FIORI If Dorothy lived in Rome, she might well find her ruby slippers at this wild and wonderful (and pricey) shoe boutique. Classy, unique men's styles are available, too. *Via dei Baullari 22 (at Campo de' Fiori).* ☎ *06-68808216. AE, MC, V. Bus: 30, 40, 62, 64, 70, 87, 116, 492, or 571. Map p 77.*

★★★ **Danielle** VATICAN The shoe store formerly known as Martina Novelli has changed names and expanded into two shopfronts.

Pick your poison from Ai Monasteri.

Delightfully opinionated shopgirls help women choose the right pair (or handbag) across a range of price points. *Piazza Risorgimento 38 (at Via Ottaviano).* ☎ *06-39737247. AE, MC, V. Bus: 23, 81, 271, or 492. Tram: 19. Map p 78.*

★★ **Ibiz** CAMPO DE' FIORI Shoes and bags are made by hand in the on-site workshop: You can relax in a comfy armchair while choosing between custom-made sandals, handbags, briefcases, and leather accessories. *Via dei Chiavari 39 (at Via dei Giubbonari).* ☎ *06-68307297. AE, MC, V. Bus: 30, 40, 62, 64, 70, 87, or 116. Map p 77.*

★★ **Posto Italiano** CAMPO DE' FIORI This friendly "Italian place" stocks well-priced and current shoes and boots for men and women. *Via Giubbonari 37A (off Campo de' Fiori).* ☎ *06-6869373. (Branch: Viale Trastevere 111.* ☎ *06-58334820.) www.posto italiano.com. AE, MC, V. Bus: 30, 40, 62, 64, 70, 87, or 492. Map p 78.*

★★ **Vic Matiè/O.X.O.** SPANISH STEPS Edgy, wearable shoes and boots for men and women. Most pairs under 200€. *Via del Babuino 59 (at Via dei Greci).* ☎ *06-6790168. (Branch: Via Giubbonari 53.* ☎ *06-64760231.) www.vicmatie.it. AE, MC, V. Metro: Spagna. Map p 80.*

Stationers

★ **Campo Marzio Design** PAN-THEON These colorful leather-bound notebooks and pens worthy of Dante himself might just inspire you to keep a journal of your visit to Rome. *Via Campo Marzio 41 (at Piazza San Lorenzo in Lucina).* ☎ *06-68807877. www.campomarzio design.it. AE, MC, V. Bus: 62, 63, 85, 116, or 492. Map p 80.*

★★ **Ditta G. Poggi** PANTHEON Amid tubes of oil paint and stencils at this 180-year-old art-supplies store, you might stumble across charming 1950s composition books (at 1950s prices) and the odd Italian BEWARE OF DOG sign. *Via del Gesù 74–75 (at Via Pie' di Marmo).* ☎ *06-6793674. www. poggi1825.it. AE, MC, V. Bus: 30, 40, 62, 64, 70, 87, or 492. Map p 77.*

Toys

★★ **Al Sogno** PIAZZA NAVONA What Santa's workshop must have looked like 50 years ago. This fantastic high-end toyshop amazes young and old alike with its collectible gnomes, life-sized stuffed animals, and themed chess sets. *Piazza Navona 53 (at north end).* ☎ *06-6864198. www.alsogno. com. AE, MC, V. Bus: 30, 70, 87, 492, or 628. Map p 77.*

★★ **Città del Sole** PANTHEON Italy's excellent educational toy and children's books chain invites even adults to spend hours browsing its wonderful merchandise. Translated versions of Dr. Seuss and *Where the Wild Things Are. Via della Scrofa 65.* ☎ *06-68803805. (Branch: Piazza San Cosimato 39.* ☎ *06-58310429.) www. cittadelsole.it. AE, MC, V. Bus: 30, 70, 87, 492, or 628. Map p 77.* ●

Villa Borghese

0 — 1/8 mile
0 — 100 meters

Piazza Monte Grappa
Ponte d. Risorgimento
Piazzale d. Belle Arti
Viale della Belle Arti
Viale Bruno Buozzi
V. d. Villa Giulla
Museo di Villa Giulia
V. G. Mazzini
Via G. Nicotera
Lungotevere delle Armi
Lung. delle Navi
V. Gravina
V. Filangieri
Via di S. Eugenio
V. L. Settembrini
Ponte G. Matteotti
V. Dom A. Azuni
V. S. Mancini
V. Scialoia
V. Beccaria
Piazza d. Cinque Giornate
Lung. A. da Brescia
V. Flaminia
Flaminio
V. G. Washington
Lepanto
Michelangelo
V. Savoia
Piazzale Flaminio
S. Maria del Popolo
11
V. Marcant. Colonna
V. Pompeo Magno
Via dei Gracchi
Ponte Reg. Margherita
Piazza d. Liberta
PIAZZA DEL POPOLO
V. Brunetti
V. d. Vantaggio
V. d. Babuino
Piazza Cola di Rienzo
V. Valadier
V. Visconti
V. G. Belli
Lungotevere Mellini
Tiber (Tevere) River
Lung. in Augusta
P. di Ripetta
Via di Ripetta
del Corso
Via Lucr. Caro
Via Cicerone
Via Tacito
Via Orazio
V. Cossa
V. Dionigi
V. Colonna
V. Ulpiano
Piazza Cavour
Piazza Adriana
Castel Sant' Angelo
Palazzo di Giustizia
Lung. Prati
Lung. Marzio
Ponte Cavour
Augusto
Mausoleum of Augustus
Piazza
SS. Ambrosio e Carlo al Corso
V. Tomacelli
V. Font Borghese

1 Porta Pinciana
2 Viale del Museo Borghese
3 Bioparco
4 Piazza di Siena
5 Laghetto
6 Temple of Aesculapius
7 Caffè delle Arti

Previous page: The Appian Way.

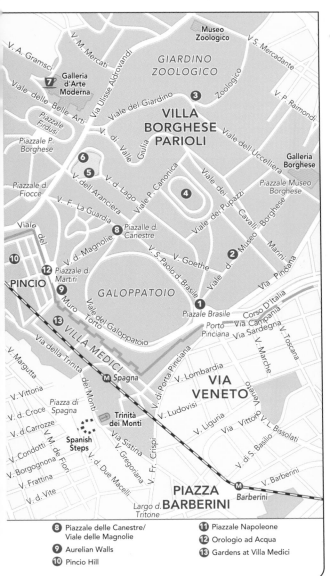

8 Piazzale delle Canestre/
Viale delle Magnolie

9 Aurelian Walls

10 Pincio Hill

11 Piazzale Napoleone

12 Orologio ad Acqua

13 Gardens at Villa Medici

Other Roman parks are larger, wilder, and less crowded, but none is as treasured by the city as the gorgeous, glamorous Villa Borghese. Gracing the higher ground directly above the *centro storico*, the Villa Borghese became public property in 1901, when the once-powerful Borghese family ran into financial trouble and sold their estate, complete with its museums, fountains, and faux temples, to the city. The park offers myriad recreation opportunities, with shady lanes, open fields, a lake, a zoo; and bikes, *risciò* (rickshaws that you pedal), in-line skates, and rowboats that can be rented at several facilities in the park. Bordering some of the city's wealthiest neighborhoods, the Villa Borghese is also the preferred jogging ground—groomed and level—of Rome's rich and famous. **Daily 6am–sunset. Bus: 116 or 490.**

Bikers in Villa Borghese.

❶ Porta Pinciana. Enter the park here, at the top of Via Veneto, just beyond the ancient walls.

Shady, hedge-lined **❷ Viale del Museo Borghese** leads to the Galleria Borghese (p 30). When the Borghese family sold their estate to the city, they insisted on a proviso that would preserve the integrity of their magnificent collection of baroque and ancient art in the galleria. On either side of the road are grassy fields, popular with picnickers, sunbathers, and lovers.

Swing by the **❸ Bioparco** biodiversity and wildlife park, with moats and ravines instead of bars and cages, complete with perfectly reproduced animal environment ambience and a unique zoology/natural history museum.

Head back west down Viale Canonica past the elegant **❹ Piazza di Siena,** where joggers plod (and, in May, horses jump) around a track rimmed with umbrella pines.

Turn right, and go north to the man-made **⑤ Laghetto,** whose northern shore is graced by the picturesque 17th-century **⑥ Temple of Aesculapius,** the pagan god of medicine. Rent a boat (daily 9am–sunset; 3€ per person for 20 min.), and enjoy a relaxing row around the lake.

☕ ⑦ Caffè delle Arti is surrounded by trees and the white marble of the modern art gallery, with alfresco tables perfect for a romantic interlude. There's a lunch buffet with light and savory fare. Stop in any time for a coffee, beer, or cocktail. *Via Gramsci 73–75 (at Viale delle Belle Arti). Closed Mon. $$.*

After your snack, retrace your steps past the *laghetto* to **⑧ Piazzale delle Canestre** and **Viale delle Magnolie,** a favorite haunt of strolling Roman families and their cuter-than-thou bambinos. This pedestrianized avenue is often tricked out with low-lying obstacle courses for skaters and bladers, so be careful of soda-can slaloms underfoot.

Continue to the bridge that crosses Viale del Muro Torto ("street of the crooked wall") and its namesake, the 3rd-century-A.D. **⑨ Aurelian Walls,** behind which lies **⑩ Pincio Hill,** whose primary attraction is the knockout vista at **⑪ Piazzale Napoleone.** Gaze past the terrace parapets to the ocher rooftops of Rome and the dome of St. Peter's. *See p 43, ⑦.*

The 80-hectare (148-acre) Villa Borghese.

While on the Pincio, don't miss the recently restored **⑫ Orologio ad Acqua,** a whimsical 19th-century water clock in a delightful little pond.

Tuesday to Sunday (10am–2pm), the Renaissance **⑬ Gardens at Villa Medici** comprise the open-air home of priceless works of ancient sculpture. In his *Italian Hours,* Henry James called the exclusive gardens "the most enchanting place." Walk back to Porta Pinciana.

Appia Antica (Appian Way)

1. Porta San Sebastiano
2. Museo delle Mura
3. Catacombs of San Callisto
4. Catacombs of San Sebastiano
5. Jewish Catacombs
6. Hostaria Antica Roma
7. Villa and Circus of Maxentius
8. Mausoleum of Cecilia Metella
9. Bar Caffè dell'Appia Antica
10. Via Appia Antica
11. Cavalieri dell'Appia Antica

The most important of Rome's famous ancient roads, the rustic Appian Way (Via Appia Antica) is home to most of the city's catacombs and a world away from the bustle of the *centro*. Visit the catacombs for a fascinating descent into the ancient tufa tunnels where Roman Christians were buried, then continue south to the Circus of Maxentius and Tomb of Cecilia Metella, where a landscape steeped in antiquity should leave you spellbound. **Bus: 118 (from Metro Circo Massimo or Metro Piramide) to the Porta San Sebastiano stop. Or, if you start at the catacombs, take bus 118 to either the Catacombe San Callisto (see ③) or Basilica San Sebastiano (see ④). Or take a taxi (10–15 min. from the city center; 15€–20€). Allow 3 to 4 hours for the whole trip.**

The massive ① **Porta San Sebastiano,** a brick gateway left over from Rome's 3rd-century-A.D. fortification, marks the start of Via Appia Antica's southbound route. Inside the gateway is the ② **Museo delle Mura** ("museum of the walls"), which has neat exhibits on ancient Roman defense systems. Restoration permitting, you can also walk on top of a stretch of wall here for an impressive view of the countryside. *Via di Porta di San Sebastiano 18.* ☎ *06-70475284. Tues–Sun 9am–2pm. Admission 5€.*

The next mile of the Appia is visually underwhelming and plagued with traffic; take bus no. 118 five stops (about 1.6km/1 mile) south to the catacombs, where the landscape is greener and quieter.

Enjoy Rome offers a 3-hour bus and walking tour of the Appia Antica, including the stupendous aqueduct park off Via Appia Nuova, otherwise hard to reach. *Call for tour times.* ☎ *06-4451843. www.enjoyrome.com.*

Skip the package-tour-infested catacombs of Domitilla and make for San Callisto or San Sebastiano instead (below). Admission to each catacomb (8€ adults, 5€ ages 5–15)

includes a 35-minute guided tour, offered in English every 15 minutes or so. The tours can be quite large and guides' accents difficult to understand, so try to stay close to the front of the group.

③ **Catacombs of San Callisto.** Once home to 500,000 tombs, these are by far the most impressive and extensive of Rome's catacombs. *Via Appia Antica 110–126. Thurs–Tues 9am–noon and 2:30–5pm. Closed Feb.*

④ **Catacombs of San Sebastiano.** A 5-minute walk from San Callisto (and more intimate, with better-preserved tomb decorations), this cluster of pagan tombs offers a fascinating look at the typically Roman practice of layering architectures and faiths. *Via Appia Antica 136. Mon–Sat 9am–noon and 2:30–5pm. Closed mid-Nov to mid-Dec. www.catacombe.org.*

While catacombs are most often associated with Christianity, the Jews of ancient Rome also buried their dead in the same kinds of underground networks. The ⑤ **Jewish Catacombs** at Via Appia Antica 119A can be visited only with prior permission from the Cultural Heritage Department. ☎ *06-67103819. Fax 06-6892115.*

Visiting the Catacombs

Ancient Roman law forbade burials, regardless of religion, inside the city walls. Of the more than 60 catacombs that have been discovered on the roads leading out of Rome, the most famous are San Callisto and San Sebastiano on the Appian Way (see ❸ and ❹, above). On your guided visit, you'll descend through multiple levels of 1,900-year-old hand-dug corridors, past a mind-boggling number of tomb niches. (To protect them from looters, the bones have been removed.) Christian-themed inscriptions and frescoes, often endearingly simplistic but carrying strong messages of faith, are everywhere in the catacombs.

After the catacombs, enjoy a relaxed and rustic meal as you sit in the shade of trees, umbrellas, and a 1st-century-B.C. columbarium (funerary monument with niches for the deceased's ashes). Wonderful Roman atmosphere and hospitality abound at ❻ **Hostaria Antica Roma**. *Via Appia Antica 87.* ☎ *06-5132888. www.anticaroma.it. Closed Mon. $$–$$$.*

❼ **Villa and Circus of Maxentius.** A 5-minute walk south of San Sebastiano, the ruins of a

4th-century imperial country estate (poorly preserved) and circus (chariot racetrack, which held 10,000 spectators) lie in a field on the east side of the ancient road. Pay the small entrance fee here for awe-inspiring views of Cecilia Metella among the umbrella pines, and for a closer look at the circus's construction. *Via Appia Antica 153. Tues–Sun 10am–4pm. Admission 5€.*

❽ **Mausoleum of Cecilia Metella.** The best view of this cylindrical tomb of a 1st-century-B.C. socialite is from the middle of the Circus of Maxentius (above) or the

Circus of Maxentius, Appian Way.

History meets modernity on the Appian Way.

road. (The entrance fee here does not gain you access to the tomb's interior but to a courtyard cluttered with ancient marble pieces.) The Appian Way was the Rodeo Drive of tombs in antiquity, and Cecilia Metella's was only one of hundreds of marble-clad sepulchers that used to crowd the roadside. The other tombs, dismantled by the popes and barbarians in the Middle Ages for their valuable materials, are now little more than brick stumps. *Via Appia Antica 161. Tues–Sun 9am–4:30pm before sunset. Admission 7€.*

A bike ride can be a very pleasant way to see the Appia Antica, provided you start at 🚲 **Bar Caffè dell'Appia Antica** and ride south, where vehicle traffic is light to nonexistent. This informal coffee bar rents bikes by the hour. The Appian Way's flagstones can get very uneven at times, meaning you'll have to get off and walk a bit, but you can travel as far as 3km (2 miles) on the ancient road, viewing ruins and rural life, and not worry about getting lost—the Appia's path is due south and dead-straight. *Via Appia Antica 175. $.*

🔟 **Via Appia Antica.** The leafy, 3km (2-mile) segment beginning at Cecilia Metella is the Appia at its most evocative. Here, the road is 4m (14 ft.) wide (the Roman standard), with ancient basalt flagstones still in place. Private villas on either side of the road eventually give way to ruins-strewn fields and the occasional flock of sheep. You'll need to walk for at least 500m (⅓ mile) to appreciate the change of scenery; beyond that, it's somewhat repetitive—umbrella pines, tomb stumps—but still wonderfully soaked in history. *Public transportation is spotty at the southern end of the road; return by foot or bike to* 🔟. *From there, catch bus no. 660 to Metro San Giovanni, or call a taxi (📞 06-3570) from the bar.*

⓫ **Cavalieri dell'Appia Antica.** If you really want to do as the Romans did on the "Queen of Roads," get a horse. This small, friendly stable offers an alternative to biking and walking on the Appia Antica. Scenic rides (for all skill levels) take you past the most important ruins. *Via dei Cercenii 15. 📞 06-7801214, 328-2085787, or 329-1025360. Owners speak almost no English, so have your hotel make reservations for you. Tues–Sun 9am–6pm (7pm in summer). 25€ per 1-hr. ride. Bus: 118.*

Other Rome **Parks to Explore**

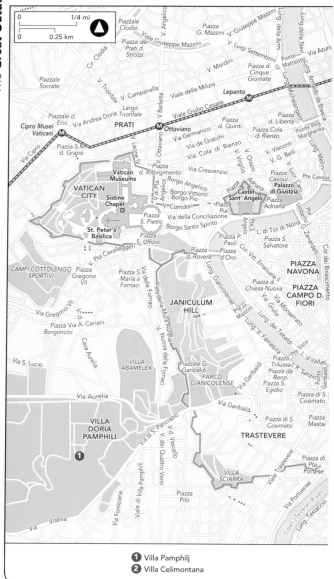

1 Villa Pamphilj
2 Villa Celimontana

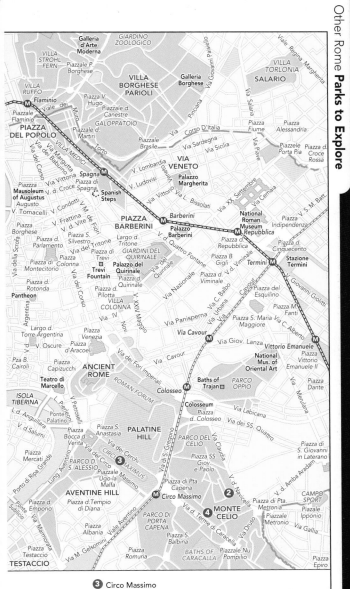

3 Circo Massimo

4 Terme di Caracalla Greenbelt

In addition to the parks and green areas I've mentioned so far in this chapter, other parks I love are Villa Pamphilj, a tourist-free and gargantuan sprawl of woods, lawns, and manicured gardens west of Trastevere; and Villa Celimontana, a beautiful hilltop park a stone's throw from the Colosseum. Circo Massimo and the Terme di Caracalla greenbelt offer runners the chance to work out alongside majestic ruins.

The chariot racetrack of Circus Maximus.

❶ Villa Pamphilj. This huge swath of green (184 hectares/455 acres) is where Romans come when they don't want to slum it with tourists at Villa Borghese. Its hilly topography is best suited for serious joggers, but Villa Pamphilj has no shortage of scenic trails for walkers in search of *bel respiro* ("good breathing," the original name of the 17th-c. park). Locals love to bring full-spread picnics here on weekends. A delightful pond teeming with turtles awaits the leftovers. *Bus: 44, 870, or 984.*

❷ Villa Celimontana. Perched atop Celio Hill, just a 5-minute walk south of the Colosseum, the Villa Celimontana park has a bustling kids' play area, limited jogging paths, and a fabulous nighttime jazz festival in summer, where the setting is straight out of *La Dolce Vita*. *Via della Navicella 12.* **Metro:** *Colosseo.* **Bus:** *60, 75, 81, 175, or 271.* **Tram:** *3.*

❸ Circo Massimo. Many ridicule the derelict state of the Circus Maximus, Rome's erstwhile racetrack, but there's still something glorious about treading the same earth where chariots once thundered to the deafening cheers of 300,000 Roman spectators. Palatine Hill is where the emperors lived, and the slope you see from here is the spot from which the emperors watched the races. See how fast you can complete 7 laps (one lap is 1,200m/¾ mile), the standard distance for all ancient races. There's no shade, however, and you'll need to watch out for broken beer bottles. *Metro: Circo Massimo. Bus: 30, 60, 75, 118, 170, 175, or 271. Tram: 3.*

❹ Terme di Caracalla Greenbelt. "Real" Roman runners eschew the Circus Maximus, but you will find them treading the shaded paths just to the south, near the 3rd-century ruins of the Baths of Caracalla. ●

Dining Best Bets

Zucchini flowers stuffed with cheese and fried are a local delicacy.

Best **All-Around Cucina Romana Experience**
★★ Perilli $$ *Via Marmorata 39* (p 113)

Best **Understatedly Cool, Insider Spots**
★★ Settembrini $$ *Via Settembrini 27* (p 116); and ★★ Fiaschetteria Beltramme $$ *Via della Croce 39* (p 110)

Best **Boisterous Lunch**
★★ Enoteca Corsi $ *Via del Gesù 87* (p 109)

Best **Pizzeria**
★★ La Montecarlo $ *Vicolo Savelli 11* (p 111); and ★ Remo $ *Piazza di Santa Maria Liberatrice 44* (p 116)

Best **Outdoor Tables**
★★ Antica Pesa $$$ *Via Garibaldi 18* (p 107); and ★★ La Veranda $$$ *Borgo Santo Spirito 73* (p 112)

Best **For Serious Oenophiles and Food Snobs**
★★ Casa Bleve $$ *Via del Teatro Pace 48–49* (p 108); and ★★ Enoteca Cavour 313 $$ *Via Cavour 313* (p 109)

Best **Bragging-Rights Splurge**
★★★ La Pergola $$$$ *Via Cadlolo 101* (p 112)

Best **Paparazzi Haunt**
★★ Due Ladroni $$$ *Piazza Nicosia 24* (p 109)

Best **Quick Lunch Near the Ruins**
★ La Bottega del Caffè $ *Piazza Madonna dei Monti 5* (p 111)

Best **Coffee**
★★★ Bar Sant'Eustachio $ *Piazza di Sant'Eustachio 82* (p 107)

Best **Seafood**
★★★ Quinzi e Gabrieli $$$$ *Via delle Coppelle 5* (p 116); and ★★★ La Gensola $$$ *Piazza della Gensola 15* (p 111)

Previous page: Dining al fresco is a Roman standard.

Centro Storico Dining

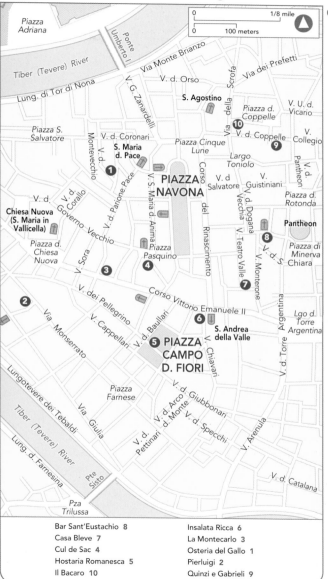

Bar Sant'Eustachio 8

Casa Bleve 7

Cul de Sac 4

Hostaria Romanesca 5

Il Bacaro 10

Insalata Ricca 6

La Montecarlo 3

Osteria del Gallo 1

Pierluigi 2

Quinzi e Gabrieli 9

Rome Dining

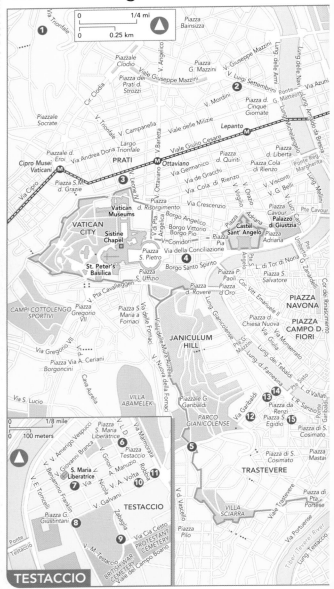

0   1/4 mi

0   0.25 km

Via Trionfale

Piazza
Bainsizza

Piazzale
Clodio

Piazza dei
Prati d.
Strozzi

Piazza
G. Mazzini

V. Giuseppe Mazzini

Viale Giuseppe Mazzini

V. Angelico

V. Luigi Settembrini

Lungo. delle Navi

Lung. delle Armi

Lungo Ponte P. G. Matteotti

Via Azuni

V. Mordini

Piazza d.
Cinque
Giornate

Lung Arnaldo da Brescia

Cir. Clodia

V. Trionfale

V. Campanella

Viale delle Milizie

Lepanto

M

Piazzale
Socrate

Piazzale d.
Eroi

Largo
Trionfale

Via Andrea Doria

Viale Giulio Cesare

Piazza
d. Quiriti

Piazza
d. Liberta

Lung.Michelangelo

Ponte Reg.
Margherita

Cipro Musei
Vaticani

M

Piazza S.M.
d. Grazie

PRATI

M

Ottaviano

Via Germanico

Piazza Cola
di Rienzo

V. Visconti

Via Cipro

V. Leone

V. Ottaviano

Via di Gracchi

V. Orazio

V. G. Belli

Lung. Mellini

Via Crescenzio

Via Cola di Rienzo

V. Virgilio

Piazza
d. Risorgimento

Vatican
Museums

Via Crescenzio

Piazza
Cavour

Palazzo
di Giustizia

Pte Cavour

VATICAN
CITY

Sistine
Chapel

Borgo Angelico

Borgo Vittorio

Borgo Pio

Castel
Sant' Angelo

Piazza
Adriana

Pte Umberto G. Zanardelli

St. Peter's
Basilica

V=Corridori

Piazza
Pia

Piazza
S. Pietro

Via della Conciliazione

Piazza
Adriana

Piazza
S. Uffizio

Borgo Santo Spirito

L. di Tor di Nona

Piazza P.
Paoli

Piazza S.
Salvatore

Cor. dei Rinascimento

CAMPI COTTOLENGO
SPORTIVI

Piazza
Gregorio
VII

Piazza S.
Maria a
Fornaci

Piazza
d. Rovere

Piazza
d'Oro

Lung. Giancolense

Cor. Vitt Emanuele II

PIAZZA
NAVONA

Via Gregorio VII

Piazza Via A. Ceriani
Borgoncini

JANICULUM
HILL

Piazza d.
Chiesa Nuova

Lung. dei Tebaldi

PIAZZA
CAMPO D.
FIORI

Via Aurelia

Via d. Mura Aurelie della Fornaci

Lung. d. Farnesina

Pte S.

Via S. Lucio

VILLA
ABAMELEK

Piazzale G.
Garibaldi

Via Garibaldi

L.R. Sanzio

Piazza da
Renzi

Piazza di S.
Cosimato

0   1/8 mile

0   100 meters

Piazza
S. Maria
Liberatrice

PARCO
GIANICOLENSE

Piazza S.
Egidio

Piazza da
Renzi

Piazza di S.
Cosimato

Piazza di S.
Mastai

Piazza
Testaccio

S. Maria
Liberatrice

TRASTEVERE

Piazza di
Pta.
Portese

V. Amerigo Vespucci

V.L.D

Via Mamorata

A. Manuzio

V. Nicola A. Volta

Robba

V. Giovanni Branca

TESTACCIO

VILLA
SCIARRA

Viale Trastevere

V. Benjamin Franklin

V. Galvani

Piazza G.
Giustintani

V. E. Torricelli

Zabaglia

Via Cia Cesto

Piazza
Pilo

Ponte
Testaccio

V.- M.-Testaccio

PROTESTANT
CEMETERY

Viale del Campo Boario

Via Portuense

Tiber (Tevere) River

Lung. Testaccio

TESTACCIO

BRITISH WAR
CEMETERY

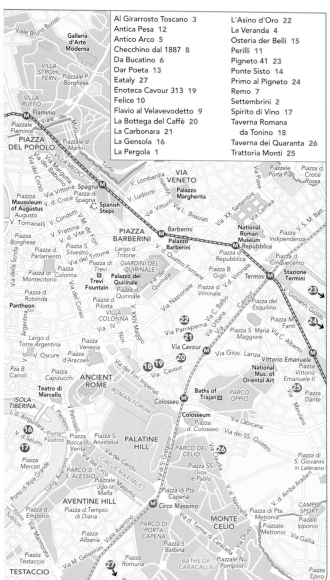

Al Girarrosto Toscano 3
Antica Pesa 12
Antico Arco 5
Checchino dal 1887 8
Da Bucatino 6
Dar Poeta 13
Eataly 27
Enoteca Cavour 313 19
Felice 10
Flavio al Velavevodetto 9
La Bottega del Caffè 20
La Carbonara 21
La Gensola 16
La Pergola 1

L'Asino d'Oro 22
La Veranda 4
Osteria der Belli 15
Perilli 11
Pigneto 41 23
Ponte Sisto 14
Primo al Pigneto 24
Remo 7
Settembrini 2
Spirito di Vino 17
Taverna Romana
da Tonino 18
Taverna dei Quaranta 26
Trattoria Monti 25

Tridente/Via Veneto Dining

Due Ladroni 4

Enoteca Antica di Via
della Croce 2

Enoteca Corsi 5

Fiaschetteria Beltramme 3

'Gusto 1

Il Margutta 6

Pastificio 7

Rome Restaurants **A** to **Z**

★★ **Al Girarrosto Toscano**
VATICAN *GRILL* Carnivores go wild for the succulent perfection of these Tuscan-style grilled meats. *Via Germanico 58–60 (at Via Vespasiano).* ☎ 06-39725717. *Entrees 12€–20€. AE, MC, V. Tues–Sun lunch and dinner. Metro: Ottaviano. Bus: 23 or 492. Tram: 19. Map p 104.*

★★ **Antica Pesa** TRASTEVERE
ROMAN Refined *signori e signore* trek halfway up the Gianicolo Hill to this charmer with a reliable, traditional menu and lovely interior garden (a converted bocce court.) *Via Garibaldi 18 (at Via del Mattonato).* ☎ 06-5809236. *Entrees 12€–20€. AE, MC, V. Mon–Sat dinner. Bus: 23, 271, or 280. Map p 104.*

★★★ **Antico Arco** TRASTEVERE
CREATIVE This stylish and well-known address for upscale new Italian consistently delivers mouth-watering dishes made with the finest local and seasonal ingredients. Creative and artistic plates like carbonara with black truffle or tartare of amberjack with ginger and lime, are accompanied by excellent wine and top-notch service. While a full meal here is a guaranteed special night out (and reservations are essential), you can also just come to the wine bar side of the establishment; a few glasses of vino here pair nicely with the rapturous centro storico views from the nearby terraces of the Janiculum Hill. *Piazzale Aurelio 7 (at Via San Pancrazio).* ☎ 06-5815274. www.anticoarco.it. *Entrees 15€–35€. AE, MC, V. Mon–Sat dinner. Bus: 115, 710, or 870. Map p 104.*

★★★ **Bar Sant'Eustachio** PANTHEON *COFFEE* Its blue-script neon sign is a beacon for coffee snobs in search of the richest,

Dining Tips

In this chapter, I've given you my top recommendations for different cuisine types, price ranges, and levels of formality. However, should you strike out on your own, keep these guidelines in mind:

1. Don't eat at any restaurant where the menu is translated into five languages (or, worse yet, where the menu is simply photographs of spaghetti drowning in red sauce).
2. Avoid restaurants where the waitstaff is overly solicitous of passersby. If their restaurant is so great, why do they need to hustle you in off the street?
3. Most restaurants located right on the main piazzas are big-time tourist traps. Stick to the smaller squares and side streets.
4. Do as the Romans do. If you follow the locals (they're the ones who go out after 8pm), you'll be in good shape.
5. Never order priced-by-weight seafood without first confirming what it will actually cost. That baked turbot might come back to haunt you once you see the insane 100€ charge for it on your bill.

Pasta, the classic Italian staple.

creamiest brew in the city. The *gran caffè* is the specialty. *Piazza Sant'Eustachio 82 (south side of square).* ☎ *06-68802048. Coffee 1.60€–4€. No credit cards. Daily breakfast, lunch, and dinner. Bus: 30, 40, 62, 64, 70, 87, 116, or 492. Map p 103.*

★★ **Casa Bleve** PANTHEON *WINE BAR* Lavish spreads of cheeses, meats, olives, and other delicacies at this ambitious *enoteche (wine cellar)*-and-more resemble a Renaissance feast. *Via del Teatro Valle 48–49 (off Corso Vittorio Emanuele II).* ☎ *06-6865970. www.casableve.it. Entrees 8€–18€. AE, MC, V. Tues–Sat lunch and dinner. Bus: 30, 40, 62, 64, 70, 87, 116, or 492. Tram: 8. Map p 103.*

★★ **Checchino dal 1887** TESTACCIO *ROMAN* Often mischaracterized as an offal-only joint, this establishment, opened in 1887 across from Rome's now-defunct abattoir, is a special-night-out type of place, serving wonderful *bucatini all'amatriciana* and veal saltimbocca—as well as hearty plates of, er, heart and other slaughterhouse castoffs. Tasting menus from 42€. *Via di Monte Testaccio 30 (at Via Galvani).* ☎ *06-5746316. www.checchino-dal-1887.com. Entrees 16€–30€. AE, MC, V. Tues–Sat dinner. Metro: Piramide. Bus: 23, 95, 170, or 280. Tram: 3. Map p 104.*

★ **Cul de Sac** PIAZZA NAVONA *WINE BAR* Cozy and lively, this popular *enoteca* has a mind-boggling selection of cheeses and cold cuts, savory Mediterranean salads and hors d'oeuvres, and wines by the glass or bottle. *Piazza Pasquino 73 (at Via del Governo Vecchio).* ☎ *06-68801094. www.enotecaculdesac.com. Entrees 8€–15€. MC, V. Tues–Sun lunch, daily dinner. Bus: 40, 62, 64, 70, 87, or 492. Map p 103.*

★★ **Da Bucatino** TESTACCIO *ROMAN* The best place in Testaccio for a casual Roman meal, this authentic *hostaria* treats you like family, and you'll get to watch the antics of the many local families that eat here regularly. *Via Luca della Robbia 84–86 (at Via Bodoni).* ☎ *06-5746886. www.bucatino.com. Entrees 8€–16€. AE, MC, V. Tues–Sun lunch and dinner. Bus: 23, 75, 271, or 280. Tram 3. Map p 104.*

★★ **Dar Poeta** TRASTEVERE *PIZZA* Throw carb-caution to the wind at this hard-to-find, eternally packed pizzeria. Expect a wait, then gorge yourself on flavor-filled *bruschette* and pizzas, but save room for the heavenly Nutella-and-ricotta dessert calzone. *Vicolo del Bologna 45 (at Piazza della Scala).* ☎ *06-5880516. www.darpoeta.com. Pizzas 6€–12€. AE, MC, V. Daily lunch and dinner. Bus: 23, 271, or 280. Map p 104.*

★★ **Due Ladroni** PIAZZA DEL POPOLO *ITALIAN* Italian gossip mags always feature a few grainy photos of celebs dining at this classy but unpretentious restaurant, where standard fare is solid, and waiters treat you as if you might be famous. *Piazza Nicosia 24 (off Via di Ripetta).* ☎ 06-6896299. www.dueladroni.com. *Entrees 14€–26€. AE, MC, V. Mon–Fri lunch and dinner; Sat lunch only. Bus: 87, 280, 492, or 628. Map p 106.*

★★ **Eataly** SOUTHERN SUBURBS *ITALIAN* With more than 18 restaurants on four floors, this is a bonafide foodie mothership. Each eatery specializes in something different—pizza, fried items, sandwiches, handmade pasta, normal pasta, regional breads, meat, fish, vegetables, chocolate, cheese, salumi, wine, you name it—and has its own chef. The atmosphere is Italian mall-ish, so I wouldn't go for dinner, but lunch on a weekday? Definitely. *Via 12 Ottobre, 1492 (off Via Ostiense).* ☎ 06-90279201. *Entrees from 8€. AE, MC, V. Metro: Piramide or Garbatella. Bus: 30, 80, 175, 280, Tram: 3. Map p 104.*

★ **Enoteca Antica di Via della Croce** SPANISH STEPS *WINE BAR* A prime spot to rest your feet after shopping. There's a long bar, as well as table service in back and outside, great antipasti, and dozens of wines by the glass. *Via della Croce 76b (at Via Bocca di Leone).* ☎ 06-6790896. www.antica enoteca.com. *Entrees 10€–16€. AE, MC, V. Daily lunch and dinner. Metro: Spagna. Map p 106.*

★★ **Enoteca Cavour 313** MONTI *WINE BAR* Serious foodies stop into this handsome gem near the Forum for plates of the highest-quality prosciutto, carpaccio, cheese, vegetable dishes, and, of course, wine. *Via Cavour 313 (at Via dell'Agnello).* ☎ 06-6785496. www.cavour313.it. *Entrees 10€–18€. AE, MC, V. Daily lunch and dinner. Closed Sun June–Aug. Metro: Cavour or Colosseo. Bus: 75, 85, 87, 117, 175, 571. Map p 104.*

★★ **Enoteca Corsi** PANTHEON *ROMAN* At this terrific remnant of early-20th-century Rome, office workers settle into cramped tables to eat hearty, messy plates like *amatriciana,* which sloshes dangerously close to their Zegna ties and Armani shirts. The loud and lively scene—and the prices—are a time warp

Felice restaurant, a Testaccio institution since 1936.

A classic trattoria scene.

back to more carefree days. *Via del Gesù 87 (near Via del Plebiscito).* ☎ *06-6790821. Entrees 7€–12€. MC, V. Mon–Sat lunch only. Bus: 30, 40, 62, 64, 87, 492, or 571. Map p 106.*

★★★ Felice TESTACCIO
ROMAN   Long gone are the days when old Felice would shun away customers based on first impressions. Testaccio's most famed *cucina romana* restaurant now welcomes patrons in droves, and still serves the planet's best *tonnarelli cacio e pepe*—seasoned and tossed at the table. *Via Mastro Giorgio 29 (at Via Galvani).* ☎ *06-5746800. www.feliceatestaccio.com. Entrees 9€–15€. AE, MC, V. Mon–Sat lunch and dinner. Bus: 23, 75, 95, 170, or 280. Tram: 3. Map p 104.*

★★ Fiaschetteria Beltramme
SPANISH STEPS ROMAN   Chic locals, expats, and visitors in-the-know brave the no-phone, no-reservations policy at this homey spot, run by cool women, for one of the most satisfying casual-dining experiences in the *centro*. The menu offers a nice mix of cold, lighter plates and traditional Roman dishes. Their carbonara is outstanding. *Via della Croce 39 (at Via Belsiana). No phone. Entrees 12€–22€. No credit cards. Mon–Sat lunch and dinner. Metro: Spagna. Map p 106.*

★ Flavio al Velavevodetto
TESTACCIO ROMAN   Secret little trattoria with inner courtyard seating, where locals line up for the terrific seafood, traditional *cucina romana*, rich pizzas, and the signature *ravioli alla Velavevodetto* (perfect pasta pockets stuffed with ricotta and spinach, served dipped in tomato sauce with Roman herbs). *Via di Monte Testaccio 97 (at Via Nicola Zabaglia).* ☎ *06-5744194. Entrees 12€–25€. Daily lunch and dinner. Bus: 23, 75, 95, 170, or 280. Tram: 3. Map p 104.*

★ 'Gusto PIAZZA DEL POPOLO
CREATIVE ITALIAN/PIZZA   This conglomerate of hip, modern restaurants has several locations on a Fascist-era piazza. The pizzeria (at no. 9) is buzzy and kid-friendly; the "fish and vegetables" restaurant (at no. 28) is fresh and airy, with two whitewashed dining levels and interesting pastas. One of few places in Rome besides McDonald's where you can have a sit-down meal any time of day. *Piazza Augusto Imperatore 7, 9, and 28, Via della Frezza 16.* ☎ *06-3226273. www.gusto.it. Entrees 10€–25€. AE, MC, V. Daily; hours vary by location. Metro: Flaminio or Spagna. Bus: 913. Map p 106.*

Hostaria Romanesca CAMPO DE' FIORI *ROMAN* Recommended mostly for its ringside seats on the piazza, Romanesca does dependable Roman fare at low prices, including a gloriously juicy *pollo ai peperoni* (stewed chicken with peppers) for 8€. *Campo de' Fiori 40 (east side of square).* ☎ *06-6864024. Entrees 8€–14€. No credit cards. Tues–Sun lunch and dinner. Bus: 30, 40, 62, 64, 70, 87, 116, 492, or 571. Tram: 8. Map p 103.*

★★ **Il Bacaro** PANTHEON *ITALIAN* This romantic and low-key spot on a hidden back street offers respite from the traffic and tourist crush. Insanely delicious *primi* and *secondi* (like *tortelli* with *taleggio* and pumpkin, or grouper with porcini mushrooms) are a welcome departure from the usual Roman fare. *Via degli Spagnoli 27 (off Via della Scrofa).* ☎ *06-6872554. www.ilbacaro.com. Entrees 12€–21€. AE, MC, V. Mon–Sat lunch and dinner. Bus: 30, 62, 70, 81, 87, 116, or 492. Map p 103.*

★★ **Il Margutta** PIAZZA DEL POPOLO *VEGETARIAN* Rome's trendiest vegetarian restaurant blends Mediterranean flavors with classic Italian cuisine, sourcing only the finest seasonal ingredients. Candlelit tables, sophisticated jazz muzak, and contemporary art displays. *Via Margutta 118 (off Via del Babuino).* ☎ *06-32650577. www. ilmarguttavegetariano.it. Entrees 10€–25€. AE, MC, V. Daily lunch and dinner. Metro: Flaminio. Map p 106.*

★ **Insalata Ricca** CAMPO DE' FIORI *SALADS* The "rich salads" at this wildly popular lunch spot are laden with everything from lobster meat to hearts of palm to fresh mozzarella. Other branches around town are no match for the original. *Largo Chiavari 85 (at Corso Vittorio Emanuele II).* ☎ *06-68803656. www. linsalataricca.it. Entrees 9€–16€. AE,* *MC, V. Daily lunch and dinner. Bus: 30, 40, 62, 64, 70, 87, 116, 492, or 571. Tram: 8. Map p 103.*

★ **La Bottega del Caffè** MONTI *LIGHT FARE/PIZZA* The social epicenter of newly hip Monti has tons of outdoor tables and a laid-back vibe—no one cares whether you order a full meal or just a cappuccino. Perfect for lunch between tours of ruins, or for a late-night bite after hitting the bars. *Piazza Madonna dei Monti 5 (at Via dei Serpenti).* ☎ *06–4741578 or 393-9311013. Entrees 7€–14€. AE, MC, V. Daily breakfast, lunch, and dinner. Metro: Cavour. Bus: 60, 75, 85, 87, or 175. Map p 104.*

★★ **La Carbonara** MONTI *ROMAN/PIZZA* Not to be confused with the touristy La Carbonara on Campo de' Fiori, this hip and buzzy trattoria (with exposed brick vaults and white walls patrons are welcome to write on) has a sprawling menu of all things Roman—all prepared with love and aplomb by *mamma* Teresa. Extensive, well-priced wine list. *Via Panisperna 214 (near Via Cimarra).* ☎ *06-4825176. www.lacarbonara.it. Entrees 10€–16€. AE, MC, V. Mon–Sat lunch and dinner. Metro: Cavour. Bus: 40, 60, 62, 64, or 75. Map p 104.*

★★★ **La Gensola** TRASTEVERE *ROMAN* Irene and Claudio Dordei greet you like family, serving up smiles, warm cozy ambiance, and classic Roman dishes, as well as über-fresh seafood, prepared with hard-to-find artisanal ingredients like saba, a sweet grape-must reduction. *Piazza della Gensola 15 (off Via della Lungaretta).* ☎ *06-5816312. www. osterialagensola.it. Entrees 10€–18€. AE, MC, V. Daily lunch and dinner. Bus: 23, 271, or 280. Map p 104.*

★★ **La Montecarlo** PIAZZA NAVONA *PIZZA* Dirt-cheap and immensely popular among Romans,

Three types of gelato.

Montecarlo feels like a big party: Efficient, flirtatious servers sling piping-hot, thin-crusted pies, and the wine and beer flow freely. *Vicolo Savelli 11 (at Corso Vittorio Emanuele II).* ☎ 06-6861877. Pizzas 6€–10€. AE, MC, V. Tues–Sun lunch and dinner. Bus: 40, 64, or 571. Map p 103.

★★★ **La Pergola** MONTE MARIO/WESTERN SUBURBS *MEDITERRANEAN* Celebrity chef Heinz Beck's always-perfect, creative cuisine employs the full bounty of the region, from seasonal vegetables to rare game. Backed by dramatic views, good-looking staff, and two Michelin stars, this is one of the best meals you'll have in your life—priced accordingly. Jacket required. *Via Cadlolo 101 (at the Cavalieri Hilton).* ☎ 06-35092152. Reserve at least 1 month in advance. 130€ and up per person. AE, MC, V. Tues–Sat dinner only; closed part of Jan and Aug. Map p 104.

★★ **L'Asino d'Oro** MONTI *CREATIVE ITALIAN* Come for the amazingly affordable lunch priced at 12€, which includes a starter, pasta, entree, water, and a glass of wine. *Merenda* (afternoon snack) is served from 5 to 7:30pm, when wine or beer comes with 3€ tasty treats. *Via del Boschetto 73 (at Via del Viminale).* ☎ 06-48913832. Entrees: 8€–15€. AE, MC, V. Daily lunch and

dinner. Metro: Cavour. Bus: 60, 75, 85, 87, or 175. Map p 104.

★★ **La Veranda** VATICAN *CREATIVE ITALIAN* A gorgeous frescoed hall gives way to leafy terraces at this wonderfully patinated place, a favorite of the Vatican press corps and visiting cardinals with the ol' archdiocese Amex. Look for inventive dishes like *tonnarelli* with ricotta and cinnamon. *Borgo Santo Spirito 73 (at the Hotel Columbus).* ☎ 06-6872973. www.laveranda.net. Entrees 18€–36€. AE, MC, V. Tues–Sun lunch and dinner. Bus: 23, 40, 62, 64, or 271. Map p 104.

★ **Osteria del Gallo** PIAZZA NAVONA *ITALIAN* This lovely little trat, on a quiet *centro storico* alley, was made for languorous lunching. Menu standouts include the pecorino cheese plate with fig marmalade, and ravioli with porcini. *Vicolo di Montevecchio 27 (at Via della Pace).* ☎ 06-6873781. www.osteria delgalloroma.it. Entrees 10€–18€. AE, MC, V. Wed–Mon lunch and dinner. Bus: 30, 70, 87, or 492. Map p 103.

★ **Osteria der Belli** TRASTEVERE *SARDINIAN/SEAFOOD* Proprietor Leo keeps locals and visitors alike happy with a knockout sauté of clams and mussels, *spaghetti alla pescatora*, and grilled swordfish. The energetic indoor-outdoor spot gets especially lively on Friday nights, when boozy old-timers settle in for their fish fix. *Piazza Sant'Apollonia 9–11 (at Via della Lungaretta).* ☎ 06-5803782. Entrees 10€–18€. AE, MC, V. Tues–Sun lunch and dinner. Bus: 23, 271, 280, 780, or H. Tram: 8. Map p 104.

★★★ **Pastificio** TRIDENTE *ROMAN* A pasta factory most of the day, but come 1pm, the inconspicuous mom and pop store is one of the best secret lunch finds in Rome. Elbow room is scarce, but for 4€ patrons can indulge in the day's choice of two or three freshly made pasta dishes, free water, and house wine. *Via della Croce 8 (at Via Mario de' Fiori).* ☎ 06-6793102. No credit cards. Daily lunch. Metro: Spagna. Map p 106.

★★ **Perilli** TESTACCIO *ROMAN* Enjoy the old-school atmosphere at this beloved institution of Roman *ristorazione*. With zero pretense, Perilli's formally attired waitstaff serve you unadulterated renditions of Roman classics. Perilli is like a play with many acts, so get the *antipasto*, *primo*, *secondo*, and *dolce*, or you'll be missing the full experience. *Via Marmorata 39 (at Via Galvani).*

Snacking Like a Roman

Most locals don't eat full sit-down meals at lunch and dinner; you can save a bunch of euros by following their lead.

Panini & Pizza Instead of Lunch
Any time of day, grab a savory *pizza farcita* (stuffed pizza bread sandwich) from **Forno Campo de' Fiori** (Campo de' Fiori 22; open daily late), **Antico Forno Roscioli** (Via dei Chiavari 34; closed Sun), **Frontoni** (Viale Trastevere 52; closed Sun), or **Burro e Alici** (Via della Mercede 34, near the Spanish Steps; open daily); crisp fried cod fillets at **Dar Filettaro** (Largo dei Librari; opens at 5pm); or squares of pizza at **Panificio Renella** (Via del Moro 15–16 in Trastevere; open daily). For a more bare-bones experience, any *alimentari* (grocers) will make you a simple panino for

Apertivo, the Italian happy hour, is a good time to sample local specialties.

around 2.50€. Take it to Villa Borghese, or to a grassy site like the Palatine or Baths of Caracalla, for an afternoon picnic.

Aperitivo Instead of Dinner
Sundown is *aperitivo* time (happy hour) at most Roman bars, which means a free buffet of tasty Italian specialties for anyone who buys a drink. So that 8€ *prosecco* entitles you to a whole dinner's worth of food—and no one frowns on going back for seconds and thirds.

☎ 06-5742415. Entrees 12€–23€. AE, MC, V. Thurs–Tues lunch and dinner. Reservations recommended. Bus: 23, 75, 95, 170, or 280. Tram: 3. Map p 104.

★ **Pierluigi** CAMPO DE' FIORI ITALIAN Popular with older, well-heeled locals and tourists, this trusty indoor-outdoor trat does a mean octopus soppressata and tagliata di manzo (tender beef strips on a bed of rucola). Piazza de' Ricci 144 (at Via Monserrato). ☎ 06-6861302. www.pierluigi.it. Entrees 12€–28€. AE, MC, V. Tues–Sun lunch and dinner. Bus: 23, 40, 64, 116, 271, 280, or 571. Map p 103.

★ **Pigneto 41** PIGNETO/EASTERN SUBURBS ITALIAN In the trendy working-class district teeming with hip new eateries and wine bars, "41," with its warm lighting,

French jazz, and killer focaccia, is the area's best deal. Via del Pigneto 41 (near Via Giovanni de Agostini). ☎ 06-70399483. www.pignetoquarantuno.it. Entrees 7€–18€. AE, MC, V. Tues–Sun dinner. Bus: 105. Tram: 5 and 14. Map p 104.

★ **Ponte Sisto** TRASTEVERE ITALIAN/SEAFOOD With long, communal tables and red-check tablecloths, this bustling and well-priced joint, with its generous portions of Neapolitan fare, is great for groups. Via di Ponte Sisto 80 (at Piazza Trilussa). ☎ 06-5883411. Entrees 8€–14€. AE, MC, V. Daily lunch and dinner, till late. Bus: 23, 271, or 280. Map p 104.

★★ **Primo al Pigneto** PIGNETO/EASTERN SUBURBS NEW ITALIAN The hot address for new (and

Useful Italian Menu Terms

Agnolotti A crescent-shaped pasta shell stuffed with a mix of chopped meat, spices, vegetables, and cheese.

Antipasto Succulent tidbits served at the beginning of the meal (before the pasta), whose ingredients might include slices of cured meats, seafood (especially shellfish), and cooked and seasoned vegetables.

Aragosta Lobster.

Arrosto Roasted meat.

Baccalà Dried and salted codfish.

Bagna cauda Hot and well-seasoned sauce, heavily flavored with anchovies, designed for dipping raw vegetables; "hot bath."

Bistecca alla fiorentina Florentine-style steaks, coated before grilling with olive oil, pepper, lemon juice, salt, and parsley.

Bocconcini Veal layered with ham and cheese, and then fried.

Bollito misto Assorted boiled meats served on a single platter.

Braciola Pork chop.

Bresaola Air-dried spiced beef.

Bucatini Coarsely textured hollow spaghetti.

Busecca alla Milanese Tripe (beef stomach) flavored with herbs and vegetables.

Cacciucco ali livornese Seafood stew.

Cappellacci alla ferrarese Pasta stuffed with pumpkin.

Cappelletti Small ravioli ("little hats") stuffed with meat or cheese.

Carciofi Artichokes.

Cima alla genovese Baked filet of veal rolled with eggs, mushrooms, and sausage.

Coppa Cured morsels of pork filet encased in sausage skins, served in slices.

Costoletta alla milanese Veal cutlet dredged in bread crumbs, fried, and sometimes flavored with cheese.

Cozze Mussels.

Fagioli White beans.

Fave Fava beans.

Fritto misto A deep-fried medley of whatever small fish, shellfish, and squid are available in the marketplace that day.

Gnocchi Dumplings, usually made from potatoes *(gnocchi allà patate)* or from semolina *(gnocchi alla remana)*.

Granita Flavored ice, usually with lemon or coffee.

Insalata di frutti di mare Cold (not raw) seafood salad (usually including shrimp and squid) garnished with pickles, lemon, olives, and spices.

Involtini Thinly sliced beef, veal, or pork, rolled, stuffed, and fried.

Nervetti A northern Italian antipasto made from chewy pieces of calves' foot or shin.

Osso buco Beef or veal knuckle slowly braised until the cartilage is tender and then served with a highly flavored sauce.

Panna Heavy cream.

Pansotti Pasta stuffed with greens, herbs, and cheeses, usually served with a walnut sauce.

Pappardelle alle lepre Pasta with rabbit sauce.

Peperoni Green, yellow, or red sweet peppers (not to be confused with pepperoni).

Pesce al cartoccio Fish baked in a parchment envelope with onions, parsley, and herbs.

Piccata al Marsala Thin escalope of veal braised in a pungent sauce flavored with Marsala wine.

Piselli al prosciutto Peas with strips of ham.

Pizzaiola A process in which something (usually a beefsteak) is covered in a tomato-and-oregano sauce.

Saltimbocca Veal scallop layered with prosciutto and sage; "jump in your mouth," a reference to its tart and savory flavor.

Salvia Sage.

Seppia Cuttlefish (a kind of squid); its black ink is used in certain pasta sauces and in risotto dishes.

Sogliola Sole.

Stufato Beef braised in white wine with vegetables.

Tonno Tuna.

Trenette Thin noodles served with pesto sauce and potatoes.

Trippe alla fiorentina Beef tripe (stomach).

Vitello tonnato Cold sliced veal covered with tuna-fish sauce.

Zampone Pigs' feet stuffed with spicy seasoned port, boiled and sliced.

healthier) Roman cuisine in Rome's gritty-but-ever-gentrifying "it" neighborhood. The talented young chef, Marco Gallotta, prepares inventive and light fare, with superior fresh ingredients. The stylish space features lots of metal and glass and is open from breakfast to late night. *Via del Pigneto 46 (near Via Giovanni de Agostini).* ☎ *06-7013827. www.primo alpigneto.it. Entrees 10€–18€. AE, MC, V. Tues–Sun breakfast, lunch, and dinner. Bus: 81. Map p 104.*

★★★ **Quinzi e Gabrieli** PANTHEON *SEAFOOD* Local VIPs and visiting movie stars come here for the absolute best (and most expensive) seafood pastas and entrees in town. Lunch tasting-menus are a bit easier on the wallet. *Via delle Coppelle 5 (at Via degli Spagnoli).* ☎ *06-6879389. www.quinziegabrieli. it. Entrees 20€–35€. AE, MC, V. Mon–Sat lunch and dinner. Bus: 30, 70, 87, 116, or 492. Map p 103.*

★ **Remo** TESTACCIO *PIZZA* Don't let the spartan service and paper tablecloths fool you. Start by ordering beers and portions of bruschetta and beans while you wait for the crusty Roman pizza to arrive, possibly the best in Rome. *Piazza di Santa Maria Liberatrice 44 (at Via Giovanni Branca).* ☎ *06-5746270. Pizzas 5€–8€. No credit cards. Mon–Sat dinner only. Metro: Piramide. Bus: 23, 170, 280, 716, or 719. Map p 104.*

★★★ **Settembrini** PRATI *ITALIAN* Menu offerings on the handwritten chalkboard change daily, and Settembrini Caffé has light meals next door. The recently opened Set' bookstore serves drinks and nibbles. *Via Settembrini 27 (at Via Ricciotti).* ☎ *06-3232617. www.ristorantesettembrini.it. Entrees 14€–20€. AE, MC, V. Mon–Fri lunch and dinner, Sat only lunch. Metro: Lepanto. Map p 104.*

★★ **Spirito di Vino** TRASTEVERE *ROMAN* In a medieval synagogue atop a 2nd-century street, the Catalani family does exceptional modern and ancient Roman cuisine (like *maiale alla mazio,* a favorite pork dish of Julius Caesar's) and other plates as warm and comforting as the ambiance. *Via dei Genovesi 31 (at Vicolo dell'Atleta).* ☎ *06-5896689. www.ristorante spiritodivino.net. Entrees 15€–24€. AE, MC, V. Mon–Sat dinner only, with the possibility of booking for Sun and lunch 3 days in advance. Bus: 23, 271, 280, 780, or H. Tram: 8. Map p 104.*

★ **Taverna dei Quaranta** ANCIENT ROME *ROMAN* Honest eats by the Colosseum, with a mostly local clientele. The staff is friendly and the kitchen can be sophisticated, frequently offering regional menus of hard-to-find pastas and other specialties. Pizza at dinner only. *Via Claudia 24 (at Via Annia).* ☎ *06-7000550. www.tavernadeiquaranta.com. Entrees 10€–16€. AE, MC, V. Tues–Sun lunch and dinner. Metro: Colosseo. Bus: 75, 81, or 175. Tram: 3. Map p 104.*

★ **Taverna Romana da Tonino** MONTI *ROMAN* Sink your teeth into succulent roast lamb and other hearty *secondi* at this inexpensive, homey trat near the Forum. Come early or be prepared to wait. *Via Madonna dei Monti 79 (at Via dell' Agnello).* ☎ *06-4745325. Entrees 10€–17€. No credit cards. Mon–Sat lunch and dinner. Metro: Cavour. Bus: 60, 75, 85, 87, or 175. Map p 104.*

★★ **Trattoria Monti** ESQUILINO *REGIONAL/MARCHE* This cozy trat run by the earnest (and very good-looking) Camerucci family serves outstanding, hearty pastas and meat dishes from the Marche region. *Via di San Vito 13A (at Via Merulana).* ☎ *06-4466573. Entrees 10€–18€. AE, MC, V. Tues–Sat dinner, Sun lunch only. Metro: Vittorio. Bus: 714. Map p 104.* ●

Nightlife Best Bets

Best **Bar for Getting Wasted on 3€ Glasses of Wine**
★★ Vineria Reggio, *Campo de' Fiori 15* (p 125)

Best for **Hanging with the International In-Crowd**
★★ Salotto 42, *Piazza di Pietra 42* (p 124)

Most **Romantic**
★★ Etablì, *Vicolo delle Vacche* (p 124)

Best **Pub**
★★ Druid's Den, *Via San Martino ai Monti 28* (p 128)

Best **Aperitivo**
★★ Société Lutèce, *Piazza Montevecchio 17* (p 124); and ★★ Freni e Frizioni, *Via del Politeama 4–6* (p 124)

Best **People-Watching**
★★ Antico Caffè della Pace, *Via della Pace* (p 123)

Best **Summer Party**
La Terrazza dell'Eur, *Piazzale Kennedy* (p 127)

Best **Intimate Alfresco Spot**
★★ Le Coppelle 52, *Piazza delle Coppelle 52* (p 124); and June–Sept ★★ Salotto Gianicolo, *Piazzale Garibaldi* (p 127)

Best **Club-Hopping Zone**
Testaccio and Ostiense

Best **Live Music**
★★★ Big Mama, *Vicolo di San Francesco a Ripa 18* (p 128)

Best **Gay Disco**
★★ Alibi, *Via di Monte Testaccio 44* (p 126)

Aperitivo at Freni e Frizioni.

Previous page: Baccanale Pub in Trastevere.

Centro Storico Nightlife

Abbey Theatre 6
Antico Caffè della Pace 4
Bartaruga 10
Buccone 1
Enoteca Provincia Romana 9
Etablì 5
Freni e Frizioni 11
Isola del Cinema 12
Le Coppelle 52 7
Palatium 14
Portal 2
Salotto 42 8
Société Lutèce 3
Vineria Reggio 13

Rome Nightlife

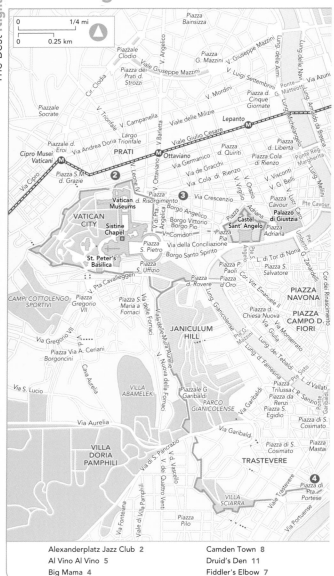

Alexanderplatz Jazz Club 2

Al Vino Al Vino 5

Big Mama 4

Camden Town 8

Druid's Den 11

Fiddler's Elbow 7

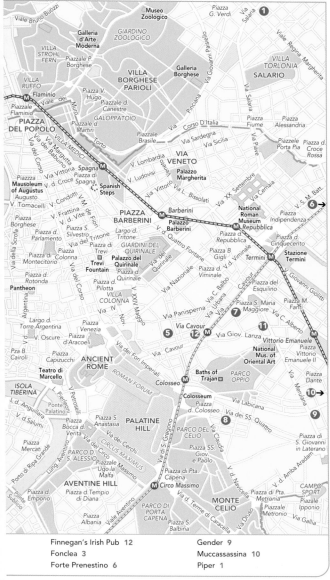

Finnegan's Irish Pub 12
Fonclea 3
Forte Prenestino 6

Gender 9
Muccassassina 10
Piper 1

Testaccio/Ostiense Nightlife

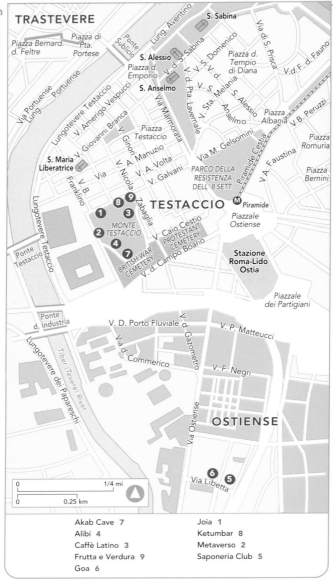

TRASTEVERE

Piazza Bernard. d. Feltre
Piazza di Pta. Portese
Lung. Aventino
S. Sabina
Ponte Sublicio
S. Alessio
Piazza d. Emporio
Via di S. Sabina
V. di Pta. Lavernale
V. di S. Sabina
V. S. Domenico
Piazza d. Tempio di Diana
V.d.F. d. Fauno
Via di S. Prisca
Via di S. Prisca
S. Anselmo
Via Marmorata
V. S. Melania
S. Alessio
S. Anselmo
V. Sta. Melania
Piazza Albania
V. B. Peruzzi
Via Portuense
Lung. Portuense
Lungotevere Testaccio
V. Amerigo Vespucci
Piazza Testaccio
Via M. Gelsomini
Piramide Cestia
Piazza Romuria
V. A. Faustina
S. Maria Liberatrice
Via Giovanni Branca
V. Ginori
V. A. Manuzio
PARCO DELLA RESISTENZA DELL' 8 SETT.
Piazza Bernini
Via B. Franklino
V. A. Volta
V. Nicola Zabaglia
V. Galvani
TESTACCIO
M Piramide
Piazzale Ostiense
8 **9**
1 **3**
MONTE TESTACCIO
2
4
7
V. Caio Cestio
PROTESTANT CEMETERY
BRITISH WAR CEMETERY
V. d. Campo Boario
Stazione Roma-Lido Ostia
Lungotevere Testaccio
Ponte Testaccio
Piazzale dei Partigiani
Ponte d. Industria
V. D. Porto Fluviale
V. d. Gazometro
V. P. Matteucci
Via d. Commerico
V. F. Negri
Tiber (Tevere) River
Lungotevere dei Papareschi
Via Ostiense
OSTIENSE
6 **5**
Via Libetta

0 _____ 1/4 mi
0 _____ 0.25 km

Akab Cave 7
Alibi 4
Caffè Latino 3
Frutta e Verdura 9
Goa 6

Joia 1
Ketumbar 8
Metaverso 2
Saponeria Club 5

Rome Nightlife A to Z

Bars & Lounges

★★ **Al Vino Al Vino** MONTI Cozy and convivial, this excellent wine bar feels like the neighborhood's living room. Great selection of antipasti, meats, and cheeses, too. Don't forego the house caponata. *Via dei Serpenti 19 (near Via Panisperna).* ☎ *06-485803. Metro: Cavour. Bus: 75. Map p 120.*

★★ **Antico Caffè della Pace** PIAZZA NAVONA   Known as "Bar della Pace," this boîte on a picturesque side street is the classic *centro storico* spot for people-watching with an entertaining mix of fashionable Romans and gawking tourists. *Via della Pace 5 (off Via di Parione).* ☎ *06-6861216. www.caffedellapace.it. Bus: 30, 70, 87, 492, or 628. Map p 119.*

★★ **Bartaruga** JEWISH GHETTO   A dark room with sagging armchairs and bright frescoes, sassy bar staff, and stiff drinks. The scene is arty and intellectual but unpretentious. *Piazza Mattei 9.* ☎ *06-6892299. www.bartaruga. com. Bus: 23, 271, or 280. Tram: 8. Map p 119.*

★★ **Buccone** PIAZZA DEL POPOLO   Once a Roman noble family's coach house, then a tavern in the '70s, now a refined wine merchant serving meals and quality wine by the glass alongside spirits and rare vintages. *Via di Ripetta 19.* ☎ *06-3612154. www.enoteca buccone.com. Metro: Flaminio or Spagna. Bus: 116, 117, or 913. Map p 119.*

When the (Roman) Lights Go Down

By night, Rome's palaces, ruins, fountains, and monuments are bathed in a theatrical white light. Few evening occupations are quite as pleasurable as a stroll past the solemn pillars of old temples or the cascading torrents of Renaissance fountains glowing under the blue-black sky.

The **Fountain of the Naiads** (Fontana delle Naiadi) on Piazza della Repubblica, the **Fountain of the Tortoises** (Fontana della Tartarughe) on Piazza Mattei, and the **Trevi Fountain** are particularly beautiful at night. The **Capitoline Hill** (or Campidoglio) is magnificently lit after dark, with its measured Renaissance facades glowing like jewel boxes. The view of the **Roman Forum** seen from the terraces behind the trapezoidal Piazza del Campidoglio (walk around the bell-towered Palazzo Senatorio to the left or right) is the grandest panorama in Rome, more so than even the Colosseum (which is also visible from here)

Piazza San Pietro (in front of St. Peter's) is impressive at night without the tour buses and crowds; to get there, the walk across Ponte Sant'Angelo and past Castel Sant'Angelo is perhaps even more beautiful. A combination of illuminated architecture, Renaissance fountains, and sidewalk shows and art expos enlivens Piazza Navona.

★★ **Enoteca Provincia Romana** PIAZZA VENEZIA/ MONTI   The newly inaugurated wine shop/wine bar in the hip Trajan's Forum area serves food and pours wines strictly produced in Rome and its suburbs. *Via del Foro Traiano 84 (off Via dei Fori Imperiali).* ☎ 06-67662424. Bus: 40, 64, or 70. Map p 119.

★★ **Etablì** PIAZZA NAVONA   Hip, romantic ambiance where young crowds chat, sprawled on plush sofas and armchairs, drinking their *aperitivo* in front of the blazing fireplace. *Vicolo delle Vacche 9 (off Via dei Coronari).* ☎ 06-97616694. www.etabli.it. Bus: 30, 70, 87, 492, 628. Map p 119.

★★ **Freni e Frizioni** TRASTEVERE   "Brakes and Clutches" is a former mechanics-garage-turned-nighttime-hot spot, with an ethnic-inflected *aperitivo* spread (think curried risotto). On the adjacent square, an effervescent crowd lounges against stone walls and parked *motorini*. *Via del Politeama 4–6 (near Piazza Trilussa).* ☎ 06-58334210. Bus: 23, 271, or 280. Map p 119.

★★ **Le Coppelle 52** PANTHEON   Occupying most of a wonderfully secluded piazza, this lounge catches all the evening traffic coming or going to the hip restaurants nearby. On balmy nights, the outdoor tables are highly prized real estate. *Piazza delle Coppelle 52 (off Via delle Coppelle).* ☎ 349-7404620. Bus: 30, 40, 62, 64, 70, 87, 492, or 571. Map p 119.

★★ **Palatium** SPANISH STEPS Government-sponsored wine bar that serves excellent wines and food from around the Lazio region. *Via Frattina 94 (off Via Belsiana).* ☎ 06-69202132. Metro: Spagna. Map p 119.

★★ **Salotto 42** PANTHEON   Jetsetters and wannabes congregate at this über-hip "book bar," run by a pair of Swedish and Roman models. Furnishings have a worn-in bohemian feel, and there's a Scandinavian smorgasbord for Sunday brunch. *Piazza di Pietra 42 (off Via del Corso).* ☎ 06-6785804. Bus: 30, 40, 62, 64, 70, 87, 116, 492, or 571. Map p 119.

★★ **Société Lutèce** PIAZZA NAVONA   One of the first bars to

La Vineria, Campo de'Fiori.

Outdoor performances abound in Roman summers.

introduce the Northern Italian *aperitivo* phenomenon to Rome, this stylish, laid-back spot is great for drinking and snacking before, after, or instead of dinner. *Piazza Montevecchio 17 (off Via dei Coronari).* ☎ 06-68301472. Bus: 30, 70, 87, 492, or 628. Map p 119.

★★ **Vineria Reggio** CAMPO DE' FIORI Night after night, this supercheap, social Campo drinking spot perpetuates *la dolce vita*. *Campo de' Fiori 15 (at Via Baullari).* ☎ 06-68803268. Bus: 30, 40, 62, 64, 70, 87, 116, or 492. Tram: 8. Map p 119.

Discos & Clubs

★★ **Akab Cave** TESTACCIO What was once a carpenter's workshop connected to stables below is now a London-inspired hip playbill for major up-and-coming Roman bands. Its large rooms, outdoor patio, and bars are also used for special events like tapestry classes, belly-dancing seminars, and Japanese cuisine workshops. *Via di Monte Testaccio 69.* ☎ 06-57250585. www.akabcave.com. *Metro: Piramide. Bus: 23, 30, 75, 95, 170, or 280. Tram: 3. After midnight, N3, N9, N10, or N11. Map p 122.*

★ **Forte Prenestino** CENTOCELLE No better way to feel the pulse of Rome's music scene than in its Centri Sociali—semi-legal squats. The Forte occupies a former 19th-century explosives depot, and features concerts, film screenings, and a slew of other social activities. *Via*

The Clubs of Monte Testaccio

Want to sample Rome's club scene but not sure where to start? **Monte Testaccio,** ancient Rome's pottery dump, is ringed with discos and lounges for all tastes, ages, and noise levels. Simply head for the three streets (Via Galvani, Via di Monte Testaccio, and Via Zabaglia) skirting the artificial mountain, and see what looks good to you. A few of my favorite standbys are **Metaverso** (Via di Monte Testaccio 38A; ☎ 06-5744712), **Joia** (Via Galvani 20; ☎ 06-5740802), and **Caffè Latino** (Via di Monte Testaccio 96; ☎ 06-57288556). Check the weekly listings mag *Roma C'è.* For Testaccio clubs, take the Metro to Piramide, or bus 23, 30, 75, 95, 170, or 280, or tram 3. After midnight, use bus N3, N9, N10, or N11.

A DJ spins at Akab Cave.

Federico Delpino. ☎ *06-21807855. www.forteprenestino.net. Bus: 5, 543, or 555. Tram: 19. After midnight, N12. Map p 120.*

★★ **Goa** OSTIENSE Consistently one of the best clubs in Rome, with an ethnic look, international DJs, and a *bella gente* crowd that's not too young, especially on weeknights. *Via Libetta 13 (off Via Ostiense).* ☎ *06-5748277. 20€ cover. Metro: Garbatella. Bus: 23, 271, or 280. Map p 122.*

★★ **Ketumbar** TESTACCIO Endorsing the nearby MACRO exhibit space, this disco-meets-haute-cuisine eatery caters to an arty clientele who dine and stay for the live music, DJ set, and drinks till the wee hours. *Via Galvani 24.* ☎ *06-57305338. www.ketumbar.it. Metro: Piramide. Bus: 23, 30, 75, 95, 170, or 280. Tram 3. After midnight, N3, N9, N10, or N11. Map p 122.*

★ **Piper** NORTHERN SUBURBS There's a winking, strutting, disco vibe at this historic venue. The multilevel dance floors make for good scoping of potential mates. Saturday nights are gay.

Via Tagliamento 9. ☎ *06-8555398. www.piperclub.it. 20€ cover. Bus: 63. Tram: 3 or 19. Map p 120.*

★ **Saponeria Club** OSTIENSE At this soap-factory-turned-dance-factory, the crowd tends to be squeaky clean and very good-looking—think Italian water polo players in Façonnable shirts and their female groupies. *Via degli Argonauti 20 (at Via Ostiense).* ☎ *06-5746999. www.saponeriaclub. it. 15€–20€ cover. Metro: Garbatella. Bus: 23, 271, or 280. Map p 122.*

Gay & Lesbian

★★ **Alibi** TESTACCIO This consistently good gay disco, with an infamously heavy pickup scene, features a happy mix of house and techno. In summer, the dancing spills out to the club's fabulous rooftop. *Via di Monte Testaccio 44 (at Via Galvani).* ☎ *06-5743448. www.lalibi.it. Metro: Piramide. Bus: 23, 30, 75, 95, 170, or 280. 12€–15€ cover (Fri–Sat only). Map p 122.*

★★ **Frutta e Verdura** TESTACCIO Gay after-hours club featuring two separate dark rooms, great

Oh, Those Roman Summer Nights

Every summer, the city does an epic job of erecting outdoor venues—part of a calendar of cultural events known as *Estate Romana*—where citizens party from June to September. In the *centro*, check out the breathtaking view, smooth cocktails, and hip DJ set in the ★★ **Salotto Gianicolo** lounge; live music and bars at **Portal,** the swimming pool/sun deck on the riverbank below Castel Sant'Angelo; or **Isola del Cinema,** the film festival on Tiber Island. In the fascist-era suburb of EUR to the south, **Le Terrazze** (Palazzo dei Congressi, Piazzale John F. Kennedy 1; ☎ 347-1167581) is a nightclub on the roof of an office building, and there's a **Gay Village** entertainment complex set up off EUR's man-made lake. *Estate Romana* also goes high-brow, with concerts and readings among the ruins. See www.estateromana.comune.roma.it and our favorites in the Arts & Entertainment chapter.

cruising scene, and huge dance floor, open from 4:30am. *Via di Monte Testaccio 94 (at Via Nicola Zabaglia).* ☎ *347-2446721. www.fruttaeverdura.roma.it. 12€ cover. Metro: Piramide. Bus: 23, 30, 75, 95, 170, or 280. Map p 122.*

★ **Gender** SAN GIOVANNI An intimate, erotic LGBT club with strip shows and private cabins—equal opportunity for exhibitionists and voyeurs alike. *Via Faleria 9 (at Via Appia Nuova).* ☎ *06-70497638.*

10€–15€ cover. Metro: San Giovanni or Re di Roma. Map p 120.

★★ **Muccassassina** EASTERN SUBURBS Friday night LGBT parties are hosted in the 2,500-sq.-m (27,000-sq.-ft.) multilevel Qube lounge. Music genres vary by guest/resident DJs; there are two live band/drag performance spaces, a garden, and white and dark rooms. *Via di Portonaccio 212.* ☎ *06-4385445. www.muccassassina.com. 15€ cover (Fri only). Metro: Stazione Tiburtina. Bus: 409. Map p 120.*

Rome glows by night.

Cafe culture is essential to Roman nightlife.

Live Music

★ Alexanderplatz Jazz Club
VATICAN Smooth and classy, this low-ceilinged jazz joint is one of the best in Italy. In summer, the club sponsors the super-fab jazz festival at Villa Celimontana. *Via Ostia 9 (at Via Leone IV).* ☎ *06-39742171. www.alexanderplatz.it. 10€ cover. Metro: Ottaviano. Map p 120.*

★★★ Big Mama TRASTEVERE With a reassuring reek of beer, this subterranean blues club is the closest thing in Rome to a honky-tonk. Top-notch blues, rock, and soul acts; the small, sticky wooden tables go fast. *Vicolo di Francesco a Ripa 18 (at Via San Francesco a Ripa).* ☎ *06-5812551. www.bigmama.it. Cover 8€–12€. Bus: 23, 271, 280, 780, or H. Tram: 3 or 8. Map p 120.*

★ Fonclea VATICAN This multi-room, English-style venue has a mellow happy hour and live sets of soul, funk, jazz, and rock. Pub food served. *Via Crescenzio 82A (at Piazza Risorgimento).* ☎ *06-6896302. www. fonclea.it. 10€ food/drink minimum. Metro: Ottaviano. Bus: 23, 81, 271, or 492. Tram: 19. Map p 120.*

Pubs

★ Abbey Theatre PIAZZA NAVONA A cozy and convenient stop for whetting a dry whistle after touring the centro storico, l'Abbey is also one of few pubs with a more robust food menu, including Irish dishes (beef in Guinness), Italian pastas, and bar snacks. *Via del Governo Vecchio 51-53 (at Via di Parione).* ☎ *06-6861341. abbey-rome.com. Bus: 30, 70, 87, 492, or 628. Map p 119.*

★ Camden Town ANCIENT ROME Owners Alberto and Carlo welcome a loyal young crowd nightly for pints and sporting events. Friendly English-speaking staff and a lively scene at the bar and tables prevail. *Via Ostilia 30A (at Via Capo d'Africa).* ☎ *06-7096322. Metro: Colosseo. Bus: 75, 81, or 175. Tram: 3. Map p 120.*

★★ Druid's Den MONTI Traditional Irish pub offering regulars and foreign visitors eight different types of cask beer, live Irish music (on Mon), live rugby and soccer coverage, dartboard tournaments, and arts and drama classes. Happy hour lasts till 8pm. *Via San Martino ai Monti 28 (off Via Merulana).* ☎ *06-48904781. www.druidspubrome.com. Metro: Cavour or Termini. Bus: 75, 84, 117, or 360. Map p 120.*

★ Fiddler's Elbow TERMINI/ MONTI The oldest Irish pub in Rome—always packed with a talkative crowd of locals, resident expats, travelers, and the odd priest. *Via dell'Olmata 43 (at Piazza Santa Maria Maggiore).* ☎ *06-4872110. Metro: Cavour or Termini. Bus: 75, 84, 117, 360, or 714. Map p 120.*

★ Finnegan's Irish Pub
MONTI Proudly self-proclaimed as the single 100% Irish-owned pub in the Eternal City, this watering hole welcomes expats and locals to join in the craic, shoot a game of pool, and enjoy a pint of dark ale. *Via Leonina 66 (off Via dei Serpenti).* ☎ *06-4747026. www.finneganpub. com. Metro: Cavour. Bus: 75, 84, 117, 360, or 714. Map p. 120.* ●

Arts & Entertainment Best Bets

Best **Entertainment, Period**
★★★ AS Roma or ★★ SS Lazio,
Stadio Olimpico (p 136)

Best **Classical Music**
★★ Accademia di Santa Cecilia,
Largo Luciano Berio 3 Auditorium
(p 133)

Best **Summer Festival**
★★ Villa Celimontana Jazz Festival, *Villa Celimontana (p 134)*

Best for **Living La Dolce Vita**
★★★ Baths of Caracalla, *Viale*
delle Terme di Caracalla (p 133)

Best **Excuse to Get Dressed Up**
★ Teatro dell'Opera, *Via Firenze 72*
(p 133)

Best **Place to Catch a Big-Budget American Action Flick in English or Italian**
★ The Space Cinema—Moderno,
Piazza della Repubblica 45 (p 135)

Best **Mellow Outdoor Concerts**
★★ Villa Giulia, *Piazza di Villa*
Giulia (p 135)

Best **Crosstown Rivalry**
★★★ Roma-Lazio derby games,
Foro Italico/Viale dello Stadio
Olimpico (p 136)

Best **Athletics Complex**
★ Foro Italico, *Viale del Foro Italico/Viale dei Gladiatori (p 136)*

Evening performance at the Villa Giulia.

Previous page: The Teatro dell'Opera.

Centro Storico Arts & Entertainment

Alcazar 5

AS Roma 2

Baths of Caracalla 8

Cinecittà 7

Cinema Nuova Olimpia 1

Teatro dell'Opera 4

The Space–Moderno 3

Villa Celimontana Jazz Festival 6

Northern Rome Arts & Entertainment

1. AS Roma
2. SS Lazio
3. Stadio Olimpico
4. Foro Italico
5. Auditorium–Parco della Musica
6. Accademia di Santa Cecilia
7. Villa Giulia

Rome A&E **A to Z**

Classical Music
★★ Accademia di Santa Cecilia
NORTHERN SUBURBS Rome's premier symphony orchestra, founded by Palestrina in the 16th century, performs in the brand-new concert halls at the Auditorium–Parco della Musica (see below). ☎ 06-80242355 (info) or 06-8082058 (tickets). www.santacecilia.it. Tickets 18€–52€. Bus: 53, 217, 231, 910, or M. Tram: 2. Map p 132.

★★ Auditorium–Parco della Musica
NORTHERN SUBURBS This exciting multipurpose center for the arts, designed by Renzo Piano, brings a refreshing breath of modernity to Rome. Some say the three lead-roofed concert halls look like giant beetles, but the architecture is undeniably dramatic and the acoustics outstanding. The schedule features lots of folk singer-songwriter acts as well as traditional orchestras. Great cafes and a bookstore on-site, too. Viale Pietro di Coubertin 30 (Corso Francia/Viale Tiziano). ☎ 06-80241281 (info), or 06-892982

(tickets). www.auditorium.com. Ticket prices vary. Bus: 53, 217, 231, 910, or M. Tram: 2. Map p 132.

★ Teatro dell'Opera
TERMINI Performances tend to be good, but seldom great, at the financially troubled city opera. Still, the theater's ornate 19th-century interior is a perfect setting for a sophisticated Roman night out. Recent productions have included La Bohème, Nabucco, and such ballets as Il Lago dei Cigni (Swan Lake) and Lo Schiaccianoci (The Nutcracker). Piazza Beniamino Gigli 7 (at Via del Viminale). ☎ 06-481601. www.operaroma.it. Tickets 115€–150€. Metro: Repubblica. Map p 131.

Summer Venues
★★★ Baths of Caracalla
AVENTINE Attend a production of Aïda here, amid the towering ruins of the 3rd-century-A.D. caldarium, and you'll know the meaning of la dolce vita. Viale delle Terme di Caracalla. July–Aug only. ☎ 06-5740796. www.operaroma.it. Ticket prices vary. Metro: Circo

Auditorium Parca della Musica.

Pianist performs in the Tempietto series at Casina delle Civette in Villa Torlonia.

Massimo. Bus: 30, 118, or 628. Map p 131.

★ **Tempietto** MULTIPLE LOCATIONS With outdoor classical concerts at the Theater of Marcellus and Villa Torlonia, or inside the Teatro Ghione, the Tempietto music series is an informal way to soak up some great atmosphere

and culture. ☎ 06-87131590. www. tempietto.it. Tickets 21€.

★★ **Villa Celimontana Festival Jazz** ANCIENT ROME In this gorgeous 16th-cenurty park, a summer-long festival offers nightly jazz, blues, and rock acts, as well as temporary, miniature versions of some of Rome's top restaurants. *Via della*

Rome Performs

The performing arts do exist in Rome, but they've never been the city's highest priority. Having said that, the symphony is excellent, and summer sees an explosion of cultural offerings, with romantic concerts among ruins, operas in church courtyards, and jazz in the parks. The best tickets in town, however, are to soccer games at the Stadio Olimpico. For the most detailed information about what's on, the weekly listings mag *Roma C'è* (1.20€ at newsstands) is an indispensable resource. Tickets for most events can be bought online at www.listicket.it.

Even if you don't speak Italian, you can generally follow the listings of special events and evening entertainment featured in **La Repubblica,** a leading Italian newspaper. **Wanted in Rome** has listings of jazz, rock, and such and gives an interesting look at expatriate Rome. And **Un Ospite a Roma,** available free from the concierge desks of top hotels, is full of details on what's happening.

Check the daily papers for information on **free church concerts** hosted around town, especially during the Easter and Christmas holiday seasons.

Navicella (at Via Claudia). ☎ 06-58335781. *For table bookings,* ☎ 06-5897807. www.villacelimontana jazz.com. *Tickets around 20€. Metro: Colosseo. Bus: 60, 75, 81, 87, 175, or 271. Tram: 3. Map p 131.*

★★ **Villa Giulia** VILLA BOR-GHESE It doesn't get much lovelier than an intimate classical concert here, in the *nymphaeum* (ornamental grotto built as a shrine to water nymphs) of a 16th-century villa. *Piazza di Villa Giulia (at Viale delle Belle Arti).* ☎ 06-9398003. *Ticket prices vary. Bus: 926. Tram: 3 or 19. Map p 132.*

Cinemas

Alcazar TRASTEVERE Single-screen cinema with films in *versione originale* on Monday. *Via Cardinale Merry del Val 14 (at Viale Trastevere).* ☎ 06-5880099. *Tickets 4.50–7€. Bus: H or 780. Tram: 3 or 8. Map p 131.*

★ **Cinecittà** SOUTHERN SUB-URBS Rome's legendary film lots had their heyday in the 1950s and '60s. Nowadays more reality shows than silver-screen classics are shot here, but film buffs will still want to check it out. Fascinating looks at the sets of HBO's *Rome* and *Gangs of New York* are available on guided tours (in English at 11:30am and 4pm), and a permanent exhibition spotlights Fellini. Cinecittà is developing a theme park to be called **Cinecittà World,** a 60-hectare (146-acre) park that will occupy a part of the current studios' premises. *Via Tuscolana 1055.* ☎ 06-722931. *Wed–Mon 9:30am–6:30pm. 10€. www.cinecittashowsoff. it. Metro: Cinecittà. Map p 131.*

★★ **Cinema Nuovo Olimpia** VIA DEL CORSO This modern two-screen cinema offers a wide selection of original language (VO) films, with air-conditioning and facilities for people with disabilities. *Via in Lucina 16G.* ☎ 06-6861068. *Tickets 6–8€. Bus: 62, 80, 81, 85, 95, 117, 119, 160, 175, 492, 628, or 850. Map p 131.*

★ **The Space–Moderno** TER-MINI One screen at this American-style multiplex is dedicated to films

On the sets at the Cinecittà film lots.

GOOOOOAL! Soccer, Rome-Style

To experience Roman culture at its most fervent, don't go to Mass—go to a soccer game. Full of pageantry, dramatic tension, and raw emotion, the home games of **Roma** and **Lazio,** the city's two *Serie A* (Italian premier league) teams, can be far more spectacular than any fancy theater event, and certainly more interactive (when was the last time you got beaned in the head by a sandwich, thrown by an irate fan, at *La Bohème*?). *Romanisti* far outnumber *Laziali*, but both fan bases pack the Stadio Olimpico, coloring the stands with the red and yellow of Roma or the light blue and white of Lazio, every weekend from September to June. If you go to a game, invest in a team scarf (sold at concession stands outside the stadium), and learn a few stadium choruses—both teams have a few easy ones set to the tune of "The Entertainer" and the march from *Aïda*. Buy game tickets at *tabacchi* stores bearing the LOTTOMATICA logo.

in *versione originale*—often the latest installment of an action franchise like *Fast & Furious*. *Piazza della Repubblica 45.* ☎ *06-47779111. www.thespacecinema.it. Tickets 6.50€–8.50€. Metro: Repubblica. Bus: 40, 64, 70, or 170. Map p 131.*

Sports
★★★ AS Roma NORTHERN SUBURBS La Roma wears yellow and red (*giallorosso*), draws fans from the city center and political left, and is Lazio's archrival. Team captain Francesco Totti is a local hero. See Stadio Olimpico, below. *Tickets can be purchased at the Stadio Olimpico on game day, at Lottomatica stores, or at the official Roma Store at Piazza Colonna 360.* ☎ *06-69200642. www.asroma.it. Tickets 30€–120€. Map p 131.*

★ Foro Italico NORTHERN SUBURBS This sprawling athletics complex, dotted with umbrella pines and Fascist-era mosaics and statues, is home to soccer games, the Italian Open tennis tournament, and various other sporting events.

Viale del Foro Italico/Viale dei Gladiatori. ☎ *06-36858218. Ticket prices vary by event. Bus: 32, 271, or 280. Tram: 225. Map p 132.*

★★ SS Lazio NORTHERN SUBURBS Rome's other *Serie A* soccer team wears light blue and white (*biancoceleste*); its followers hail from the monied suburbs. See Stadio Olimpico, below. *Tickets can be purchased at the Stadio Olimpico on game day, at Lottomatica stores, or at the Lazio Style on Via G. Calderini 66C.* ☎ *06-32541745. www.sslazio.it. Tickets 30€–120€. Map p 132.*

★★ Stadio Olimpico NORTHERN SUBURBS For better or for worse, there is no better place to soak up modern Roman culture than at the soccer stadium. The Olimpico, Rome's 73,000-capacity venue, is where the AS Roma and SS Lazio *Serie A* (premier league) teams play at least once a week from September to June. *Foro Italico/Viale dello Stadio Olimpico.* ☎ *06-36851 (switchboard). Tickets 20€–120€. Bus: 32, 271, or 280. Tram: 225. Map p 132.* ●

A Flash of Art

Lodging Best Bets

Best **"Only in Rome" Hideaway**
★★★ The Inn at the Roman Forum $$$$ *Via degli Ibernesi 30* (p 146)

Best **Stylish Retreat**
★★★ Villa Laetitia $$$ *Lungotevere delle Armi 22–23 (p 150)*

Best **Cheap & Centrally Located Accommodations**
★ Sole al Biscione $ *Via del Biscione 76 (p 150); and* ★ Ivanhoe $ *Via dei Ciancaleoni 50 (p 146)*

Best **for Hobnobbing with Hotshots**
★★★ Hotel de Russie $$$$ *Via del Babuino 9 (p 146); and* ★★★ Portrait Suites $$$$ *Via Bocca di Leone 23 (p 149)*

Best **Vacation-Rental Agency**
★★ Roman Reference $–$$$ (p 145)

Best **for Families**
★ Aldrovandi Palace $$$ *Via Ulisse Aldrovandi 15 (p 144); and* ★ Lancelot $$ *Via Capo d'Africa 47 (p 147)*

Best **Gem in an Overpriced Area**
★★ Modigliani $$–$$$ *Via della Purificazione 42 (p 148); and Mario de' Fiori 37 $$–$$$ Via Mario de' Fiori 37 (p 148)*

Best **in an Authentic Roman Neighborhood**
★★ Santa Maria $$ *Vicolo del Piede 2 (p 150); and* ★ Arco del Lauro B&B $ *Via dell'Arco de' Tolomei 27–29 (p 144)*

Best **Escape from Vespa Drone**
★★ Aventino Hotels $$–$$$ *Via S. Melania 19 (p 144)*

Best **for Artists & Poets**
★ Locarno $$–$$$ *Via della Penna 22 (p 147); and* ★★ Episcopo Lipinsky $$ *Via Margutta 33 (p 145)*

Best **for Visiting Cardinals**
★ Columbus $$–$$$ *Via della Conciliazione 33 (p 145)*

Best **Cheap Sleep (Minus the Bed Bugs)**
★ Mimosa $ *Via Santa Chiara 611 (p 148).*

Below: Terrace overlooking centro storico at the Hotel Modigliani.

Previous page: A suite at Portrait Studios.

Centro Storico Lodging

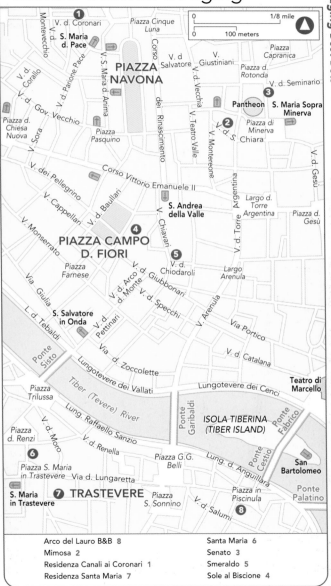

Arco del Lauro B&B 8
Mimosa 2
Residenza Canali ai Coronari 1
Residenza Santa Maria 7
Santa Maria 6
Senato 3
Smeraldo 5
Sole al Biscione 4

Rome Lodging

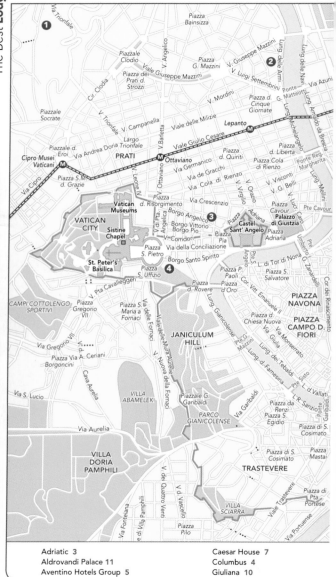

Adriatic 3

Aldrovandi Palace 11

Aventino Hotels Group 5

Caesar House 7

Columbus 4

Giuliana 10

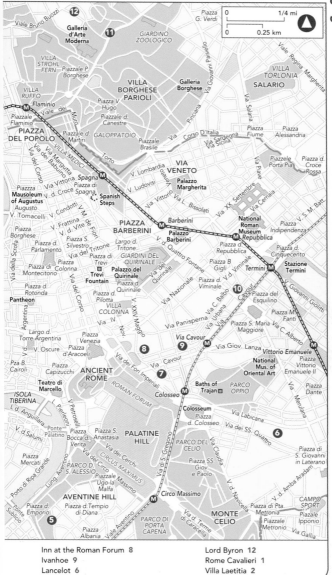

Inn at the Roman Forum 8
Ivanhoe 9
Lancelot 6

Lord Byron 12
Rome Cavalieri 1
Villa Laetitia 2

Tridente & Campo Marzio
Lodging

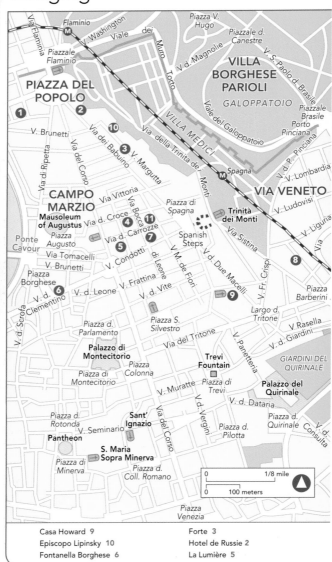

Casa Howard 9

Episcopo Lipinsky 10

Fontanella Borghese 6

Forte 3

Hotel de Russie 2

La Lumière 5

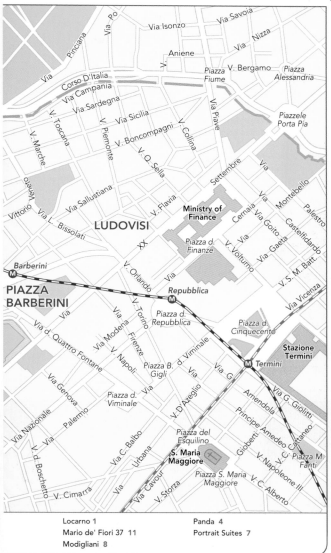

Locarno 1
Mario de' Fiori 37 11
Modigliani 8

Panda 4
Portrait Suites 7

Rome Hotels A to Z

Note: As of January 1, 2011, by order of the Rome City Council, all hotels now apply a sojourn tax of 2€ per person, per day—to be paid in cash, directly upon check-in. Children ages 9 and under are exempt.

★ **Adriatic** VATICAN   Within easy walking distance of the *centro storico*, Castel Sant'Angelo, and St. Peter's, the simple but spacious rooms here are perfect for budget-conscious travelers who want a convenient location but not a lot of amenities. A partly covered common terrace is great for sunning, reading, or sipping wine with fellow travelers. *Via Vitelleschi 25.* ☎ *06-68808080. www.adriatichotel. com. 42 units. Doubles 120€–260€. AE, MC, V. Metro: Ottaviano. Bus: 23, 40, 271, or 280. Map p 140.*

★ **Aldrovandi Palace** VILLA BORGHESE   Occupying some seriously prize real estate in the gorgeous greenery north of Villa Borghese, this classy hotel boasts a swimming pool and all modern amenities. *Via Ulisse Aldrovandi 15.* ☎ *06-3223993. www.aldrovandi. com. 108 units. Doubles 250€–400€. AE, MC, V. Bus: 52 or 53. Tram: 3 or 19. Map p 140.*

★ **Arco del Lauro B&B** TRASTEVERE   Vivacious Lorenza is your hostess at this clean and modern B&B on the quiet side of Trastevere, just across the river from Tiber Island and the Jewish Ghetto. Breakfast is served at a typical Roman bar on a nearby piazza. *Via dell'Arco de Tolomei 27–29.* ☎ *06-97840350 or 346-2443212. www.arcodellauro.it. 6 units. Doubles 85€–145€. No credit cards. Bus: 23, 271, or 280. Map p 139.*

★★ **Aventino Hotels Group** AVENTINE   Of these three converted villas on the leafy and prestigious Aventine Hill, the San Anselmo is the chicest and most luxurious, the Aventino has cheerful 1930s appeal, and the Villa San Pio is like visiting your long-lost, old-money Roman relatives. All are blessedly tranquil. *Via S. Melania 19.* ☎ *06-570057. www.aventinohotels. com. 100 units (in the Aventino Hotels Group). Doubles 115€–300€. AE, MC, V. Metro: Circo Massimo. Bus: 95 or 175. Tram: 3. Map p 140.*

★★ **Caesar House** ANCIENT ROME   Done up in a Roman palette of crimsons and golds, this family-run guesthouse has

Poolside at the Aldrovandi Palace.

Vacation Rentals (Short-Term Apartments)

Rome is among the growing number of cities where renting an apartment is often more attractive than staying in a hotel—especially for folks trying to stretch the U.S. dollar. In an apartment, you'll live like a Roman, and almost certainly save money, since nightly rates are usually lower than those of hotel rooms. And you'll be able to shop for food at the local markets and cook for yourself instead of going out for pricey meals. Located throughout the city, Rome's vacation rentals come in all sizes and price ranges, though amenities (satellite TV, washer/dryer, air-conditioner) vary from property to property. Most have a minimum-stay requirement of 3 nights. ★★ **Roman Reference** (☎ 06-48903612; www.romanreference.com) is a responsive and helpful agency with a large database of apartments, and my good friend Fulvia Angelini runs two lovingly appointed rental apartments in central locations (www.myromeapartment.com).

luxurious, homey rooms, some with picture-window views over ruins and rooftops. Warm hospitality makes this a personal, intimate place that's hard to leave. *Via Cavour 310.* ☎ *06-6792674. www. caesarhouse.com. 7 units. Doubles 170€–270€. AE, MC, V. Bus: 75, 85, 87, 175, 571. Map p 140.*

★★ **Casa Howard** SPANISH STEPS This stylish, intimate guest-house features luxe fabrics like Toile de Jouy and Shanghai silk, fresh flowers in every unique room, and a Turkish bath. Such luxury, at these prices, is unheard of in Rome. *Via Capo le Case 18 and Via Sistina 149.* ☎ *06-69924555. www.casa howard.com. 10 units. Doubles 170€– 250€. AE, MC, V. Metro: Spagna. Map p 142.*

★ **Columbus** VATICAN This upscale inn, a stone's throw from St. Peter's, was once home to a long line of popes and cardinals. Many of the somber-toned rooms preserve their original 16th-century wood ceilings and stucco work.

Via della Conciliazione 33. ☎ *06-6865435. www.hotelcolumbus.net. 92 units. Doubles 150€–280€. AE, DC, MC, V. Bus: 30, 40, or 64. Map p 140.*

★★ **Episcopo Lipinsky** SPAN-ISH STEPS Romantic, quiet, and overlooking the lush Villa Medici gardens, this two-room B&B in the artsy Via Margutta bohemia land is one of Rome's best-kept secrets. *Via Margutta 33.* ☎ *06-369994. www.bbepiscopolipinsky.it. 2 units. 190€–280€ according to season. AE, MC, V. Metro: Spagna and Flaminio. Map p 142.*

★ **Fontanella Borghese** PAN-THEON Occupying two floors of a palazzo that once belonged to the Borghese family, this is a noble address (equidistant from the Pantheon, Spanish Steps, and Piazza del Popolo) at sort-of-plebeian prices. It's not a fancy place, but the classically decorated, family-friendly rooms are bright and spacious. *Largo Fontanella*

Borghese 84. ☎ *06-68809504. www.fontanellaborghese.com. 29 units. Doubles 200€–250€. AE, MC, V. Bus: 70, 81, 87, 116, or 492. Map p 142.*

★ **Forte** SPANISH STEPS The location, on one of Rome's loveliest streets, can't be beat. The small-ish rooms are comfortable and (mostly) contemporary, and the prices are certainly low for this part of town. *Via Margutta 61.* ☎ *06-3207625. www.hotelforte.com. 18 units. Doubles 185€–300€. AE, MC, V. Metro: Spagna. Map p 142.*

Giuliana TERMINI The Santacroce family and their staff will bend over backwards to make you feel welcome at this moderate inn near the train station and Santa Maria Maggiore. Simple but comfy rooms are done up in crimson and buttercream, and the bathrooms are surprisingly large. *Via Depretis 70.* ☎ *06-4880795. www.hotelgiuliana. com. 11 units. Doubles 100€–190€. AE, MC, V. Metro: Cavour. Bus: 70 or 75. Map p 140.*

★★ **Hotel de Russie** PIAZZA DEL POPOLO It has the best location of Rome's five-star hotels, a clean neoclassical look, and tons of high-profile guests. The hotel's

Hotel de Russie.

U-shape encloses a fabulous terraced garden with bars, restaurants, and grottos sweeping up toward the Pincio. *Via del Babuino 9.* ☎ *06-328881. www.hotelderussie.it. 122 units. Doubles from 500€. AE, DC, MC, V. Metro: Flaminio. Map p 142.*

★★★ **Inn at the Roman Forum** MONTI This new boutique inn on a silent side street is one of most wonderful properties I've seen in recent years. Rooms are tastefully luxurious, with ethnic silks, soothing tones, and spacious bathrooms. The fifth-floor Master Garden Rooms (from 480€) have private patios surrounded by flowers and greenery, ocher walls, and busts of emperors. The hotel's roof lounge has views of the Campidoglio, and for archaeology buffs there's an ancient Roman *cryptoporticus* behind the lobby. *Via degli Ibernesi 30.* ☎ *06-69190970. www.theinnattheromanforum.com. 15 units. Doubles 240€–690€. AE, MC, V. Metro: Cavour. Bus: 75, 85, 87, 175, or 571. Map p 140.*

★ **Ivanhoe** ANCIENT ROME The rooms are all private, though there's a hostel-like feel to this basic but cheerful inn in the heart of the hip Monti neighborhood. A well-used common room off the lobby is great for meeting fellow guests. Those willing to rough it a bit can save by booking rooms without private bathrooms. *Via de' Ciancaleoni 49.* ☎ *06-486813. www.hotelivanhoe.it. 20 units. Doubles 90€–175€. AE, MC, V. Metro: Cavour. Bus: 75, 85, 87, 175, or 571. Map p 140.*

★ **La Lumière** SPANISH STEPS Country guesthouse feel in a cosmopolitan location. Spacious rooms feature soft blues and mauves and beautiful hardwood floors. *Via Belsiana 72.* ☎ *06-69380806. www.la lumieredipiazzadispagna.com. 10 units. Doubles 120€–350€. AE, MC, V. Metro: Spagna. Map p 142.*

Inn at the Roman Forum's rooms are boutique chic.

★ **Lancelot** ANCIENT ROME
This friendly three-star with surprisingly large and bright doubles (and free Wi-Fi) attracts a veritable United Nations of return guests. Full- and half-board options are great for families on a budget, and kids can play at the nearby Villa Celimontana. *Via Capo d'Africa 47.* ☎ *06-70450615. www.lancelothotel.com. 60 units. Doubles 150€–330€. AE, MC, V. Metro: Colosseo. Bus: 60, 75, 87, 175, or 571. Map p 140.*

★ **Locarno** PIAZZA DEL POPOLO   Artistic types love this shabby peacock of a hotel: The Art Deco furnishings are worn in places, but a feeling of old-world elegance remains. Ask for a deluxe

room in the eastern annex, as rooms in the main building are dowdy and a bit melancholy. *Via della Penna 22.* ☎ *06-3610841. www.hotellocarno.com. 66 units. Doubles 168€–390€. AE, MC, V. Metro: Flaminio. Map p 142.*

★★ **Lord Byron** PARIOLI   Bordering Villa Borghese, in Rome's most prestigious residential area, this elegant palazzo oozes Art Deco style. Guest rooms, done up in curved, lacquered wood and richly colored carpet, are romantic, sleek, and chic. Be sure to book a renovated room, as some floors have yet to be updated. The on-site restaurant, Sapori del Lord Byron, is outstanding. *Via Giuseppe de*

Hotel Ivanhoe.

View of the Colosseum from Hotel Lancelot.

Notaris 5. ☎ 06-3220404. www. lordbyronhotel.com. 32 units. Doubles 240€–540€. AE, MC, V. Tram: 3 or 19. Map p 140.

★★ Mario de' Fiori 37 SPANISH STEPS

Be the envy of all passersby when you enter this townhouse, equipped with 7 stylish luxury suites and a concierge. Prices are surprisingly moderate for the fancy location and rich interiors, and staff are as warm and helpful as can be. *Via Mario de' Fiori 37.* ☎ 06-69921907. www.romeluxury suites.com/mariodefiori. 7 units. Doubles 220€–370€. AE, MC, V. Metro: Spagna. Map p 142.

Mimosa PANTHEON

This budget stalwart in the heart of the *centro storico* enjoys great word of mouth, so book early. Decor is hodgepodge at best, but the rooms are bright, and there are larger units suitable for families with small children. Mention *Frommer's* for a 10% discount. *Via di Santa Chiara 61.* ☎ 06-68801753. www.hotelmimosa.net. 11 units. Doubles 95€–155€. MC, V. Bus: 40, 62, 64, 70, 87, 492, or 571. Map p 139.

★★ Modigliani VIA VENETO

Cheerful Roman hospitality and fantastic value near the top of the Spanish Steps. Accommodations are clean and classic, and there's a big common area off the lobby. West-facing rooms on the fifth and sixth floors have heart-stopping views over the *centro* and St. Peter's. Owners Marco and Giulia are a delight—be sure to read their "newsletter." *Via della Purificazione 42.* ☎ 06-42815226. www.hotelmodigliani.com. 23 units. Doubles 170€–230€. AE, MC, V. Metro: Barberini. Bus: 62, 95, 175, or 492. Map p 142.

A Note on the Grande Dames

Among Rome's well-known five-star hotels, there is no one "right" address, and they're all so astronomically expensive these days—especially owing to the weak U.S. dollar—that I've chosen to primarily review lesser-known, less-pricey, and more-interesting lodging options. For the record, the most prestigious big hotels in the city center are the Eden, the Excelsior, the Hassler, the Hotel De Russie (reviewed on p 146), and the St. Regis, while the Rome Cavalieri (reviewed on p 149), set in the hills above the Vatican, is a top choice for families looking for a bit more room and resort-style amenities.

Panda SPANISH STEPS   On a cafe-filled street in the heart of Rome's pricey shopping district, the Panda is a basic, pleasant choice, where a weeklong stay costs less than an Armani suit. *Via della Croce 35.* ☎ *06-6780179. www.hotel panda.it. 20 units. Doubles with en suite bathroom 85€–108€. MC, V. Metro: Spagna. Map p 142.*

★★★ Portrait Suites SPANISH STEPS   Fashionistas with money to spare, look no further than this boutique guesthouse run by the Ferragamo-owned Lungarno hotel group. Swanky and uncluttered are the keywords here, but warmth and amusing Italian flair aren't lacking in the ultra-stylish room decor. The roof terrace, with its overstuffed cushions, romantic candlelight, and exclusive company, is the epitome of modern Roman fabulousness. Superb staff. *Via Bocca di Leone 23.* ☎ *06-69380742. www.lungarno hotels.com. 15 units. Suites from 600€. AE, MC, V. Metro: Spagna. Map p 142.*

★★ Residenza Canali ai Coronari PIAZZA NAVONA   This delicious little guest house is in a meticulously restored historic building in Rome's antiques district. Furnishings are classic and sumptuous, and rooms are bright and surprisingly spacious. The Honeymoon Suite (from 160€) has a private terrace overlooking the rooftops near Piazza Navona. *Via dei Tre Archi 13.* ☎ *06-68309541. www.residenza canali.com. 10 units. Doubles 120€– 260€. AE, MC, V. Bus: 30, 70, 87, 492. Map p 139.*

★ Residenza Santa Maria TRASTEVERE   This spinoff of the Santa Maria (below) opened in 2007. It may lack the garden space of its older sister, but it makes up for it with more spacious, family-friendly rooms, high exposed-wood ceilings, ancient Roman artifacts uncovered during the restoration, and a warm staff. *Via dell'Arco di San Calisto 20.* ☎ *06-58335103. www.residenza santamaria.com. 6 units. Doubles 100€–260€. AE, MC, V. Bus: 23, 271, or 280. Tram: 8. Map p 139.*

★★★ kids Rome Cavalieri MONTE MARIO   A fresh and cosmopolitan air reigns at this 5-star hotel-resort on the hill above the Vatican. Now under Waldorf Astoria management after being a Hilton for decades, it has exceptionally livable rooms, the most comfortable beds in Rome, and spacious bathrooms clad with enough marble to satisfy an emperor. All rooms have

The dining room at Hotel Lord Byron.

balconies, most with dazzling city views, and the leafy grounds include several pools and restaurants, including critics' darling La Pergola. *Via Alberto Cadlolo 101.* ☎ *06-35091. www.romecavalieri. com. 370 units. Doubles 300€–700€. AE, DC, MC, V. Map p 140.*

★★ Santa Maria TRASTEVERE An amazing find in hotel-deprived Trastevere, the Santa Maria feels like a 16th-century motel, with simple chalet-style rooms and a pretty courtyard with orange trees. Comfy breakfast room/lounge/bar. *Vicolo del Piede 2.* ☎ *06-5894626. www.htlsanta maria.com. 19 units. Doubles 100€– 260€. AE, MC, V. Bus: 23, 271, or 280. Tram: 8. Map p 139.*

★ Senato PANTHEON Privileged location, mere feet from the Pantheon. Classically appointed rooms, some with direct temple views, make you feel like you're living in your own Roman palazzo. On the roof terrace, drink in the views from alfresco tables. *Piazza della Rotonda 73.* ☎ *06-6784343. www.albergodel senato.it. 57 units. Doubles 220€– 330€. AE, MC, V. Bus: 30, 40, 62, 64, 70, 87, 116, or 492. Map p 139.*

★ Smeraldo CAMPO DE' FIORI Well-priced but cramped, this *centro storico* "emerald" has a few shining facets, including Internet access and air-conditioning in

rooms, and a pretty roof garden. There's also a recently renovated 16-room rooftop annex across the street. *Vicolo dei Chiodaroli 9.* ☎ *06-6875929. www.smeraldoroma. com. 50 units. Doubles 110€–170€. AE, MC, V. Bus: 40, 62, 64, 70, 87, 492, or 571. Map p 139.*

★ Sole al Biscione CAMPO DE' FIORI Rooms are basic (and can be loud when school groups lodge here), but the multilevel courtyard garden, open to all guests, overflows with Roman charm. *Via del Biscione 76.* ☎ *06-68806873. www. solealbiscione.it. 60 units. Doubles 100€–170€. No credit cards. Bus: 40, 62, 64, 70, 87, 492, or 571. Map p 139.*

★★★ Villa Laetitia PRATI Set in the lush and tranquil back garden of a 100-year-old villa, each lovely suite at Anna Fendi's first Roman-lodging venture is decorated with 19th- and 20th-century antiques and original pieces—by the likes of Picasso and Lagerfeld—collected by Fendi herself. All rooms have kitchens, and all but one unit have an outdoor living space. The central building houses an events space, ample parking, and a state-of-the-art spa. *Lungotevere delle Armi 22–23.* ☎ *06-3226776. www.villalaetitia.com.14 units. Doubles 190€–350€. AE, MC, V. Tram: 19. Map p 140. ●*

At the Hotel Panda.

Tivoli: Hadrian's Villa

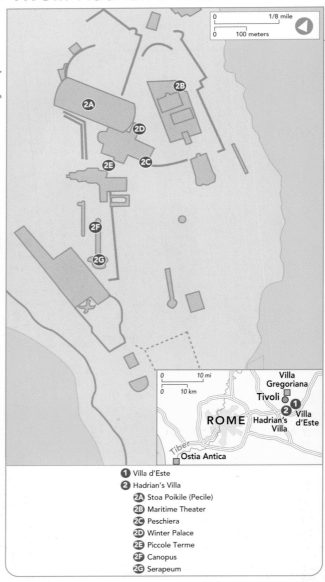

1 Villa d'Este
2 Hadrian's Villa
 2A Stoa Poikile (Pecile)
 2B Maritime Theater
 2C Peschiera
 2D Winter Palace
 2E Piccole Terme
 2F Canopus
 2G Serapeum

Previous page: Villa Adriana.

The most classic Roman day trip, Tivoli lies about 32km (20 miles) west of the city and is home to the fountain-filled 16th-century Villa d'Este and the fantastically unique ancient ruins of Villa Adriana. Transportation to Tivoli can be slow; allow a full day.

Neptune Fountain at Villa d' Este.

1 ★★★ Villa d'Este. It's all about the fountains at this pleasure palace, commissioned in 1550 by Renaissance noble and cardinal Ippolito d'Este. Throughout the lush, steeply sloping gardens, whimsical grottoes, rushing flumes, reflecting pools, musical fountains, and bizarre gurgling "trees" delight and charm. ⏱ *1 hr. Piazza Trento 1.* ☎ *0774-312070 or 199-766166 (toll-free from Italy). www.villadestetivoli.info. 8€, higher during special exhibitions. Tues–Sun 9am–7pm May–Sept; 8:30am–5pm Oct–Apr. From Rome: COTRAL bus from Metro Ponte Mammolo, about 45 min. From Villa Adriana, regional bus to Tivoli, about 15 min.*

2 ★★★ Hadrian's Villa (Villa Adriana). Hadrian's sprawling

estate (A.D.118–34) was as much a summer retreat from the stifling air in Rome as it was a place where the emperor could fulfill all his architectural fantasies.

Near the entrance, the **2A ★ Stoa Poikile** pool was once surrounded by a shady colonnade. The delightfully inventive **2B ★★★ Maritime Theater** was where the emperor meditated and swam laps. The **2C ★ Peschiera** was a giant aquarium, handy for seafood dinners this far inland. The attached **2D ★ Winter Palace** has some of its heating system intact, as well as great views toward Rome. At the **2E ★ Piccole Terme (Small Baths),** look for marvelous stuccoes on the ceiling vaults. The exquisite **2F ★★★ Canopus,** a long pool with broken Assyrian arcades and statuary, terminates in the **2G ★★ Serapeum,** a dining room whose front "wall" was a thin sheet of water, fed by the aqueduct above, that cooled the air. ⏱ *12 hr. Villa Adriana (Tivoli).* ☎ *0774-382733. www.villaadriana.com. 8€, higher during special exhibitions Daily 9am–6:30pm Apr–Sept; 9am–6pm Oct–Mar. From Rome: COTRAL bus to Villa Adriana from Metro station Ponte Mammolo, about 45 min. From Villa d'Este (Tivoli town), regional bus to Villa Adriana, about 15 min.*

Panoramic view at the historic Villa Adriana.

Ostia Antica

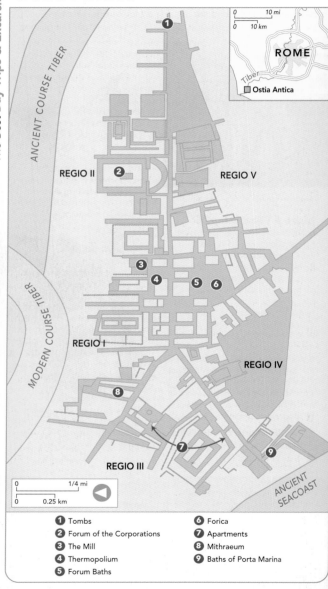

1. Tombs
2. Forum of the Corporations
3. The Mill
4. Thermopolium
5. Forum Baths
6. Forica
7. Apartments
8. Mithraeum
9. Baths of Porta Marina

The port of ancient Rome lay where the Tiber flowed into the Mediterranean (ostia is "mouth" in Latin). The seacoast receded, and the river course changed, leaving ★★★ **Ostia Antica** landlocked and obsolete. Surrounded by trees and rarely crowded, the ruins are varied, extensive, and fun to explore, even better than Pompeii for understanding how the ancients used to live. The visit can easily be done in half a day, or combined with a trip to the beach at Ostia Lido (p 161) for a full day's excursion. Bring a picnic, or eat at the site's pleasant cafe.

The mill at Ostia Antica.

❶ **Tombs.** The road leading into the ancient town proper is lined with tombs; as was the custom throughout Rome, burials had to be outside the city walls.

❷ ★★★ **Forum of the Corporations.** Farther into town, behind an ancient theater, is this wonderful former square where the shops of various importers have mosaics that indicate their cargo, from oil to elephants.

❸ ★★ **The Mill.** Here, grinding stones and bread ovens are still in place.

❹ ★★ **Thermopolium.** These hard-to-find ruins were once a stylish snack bar, serving hot and cold food and drinks.

❺ ★ **Forum Baths.** Notice especially the pipes that heated the marble-clad walls of these baths.

❻ ★★ **Forica.** This tour-group magnet was the public latrine, with neat rows of toilets still open to the sewer below (now neutral-smelling).

❼ ★ **Apartments.** All over the site, modest-to-extravagant apartment clusters are open for wandering—be sure to visit the posh ★ **Garden Apartments,** the ★ **Insula of the Charioteers,** and the ★ **House of the Dioscuri.**

❽ ★★ **Mithraeum.** This creepy chamber is found under the Baths of Mithras and was where 2nd-century-A.D. initiates of the god of Mithras performed rituals.

❾ ★★ **Baths of Porta Marina.** Check out the hilarious ancient mosaics of bodybuilders here. ⏱ *2–3 hr. Viale dei Romagnoli 717.* ☎ *06-56358099. www.itnw.roma.it/ostia/ scavi. 6.50€. Apr–Oct Tues–Sun 9am– 6pm; Nov–Mar 8:30am–4pm. Train to Ostia Antica from Stazione Porta San Paolo (Metro: Piramide), about 30 min.*

Brick ruins among the pines, Ostia Antica.

Pompeii & Naples

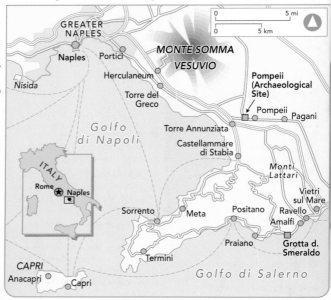

The ancient Roman town of Pompeii, buried by the devastating volcanic eruption of Mount Vesuvius in A.D. 79, is the most visited cultural site in Italy. At 3 hours away, Pompeii may not be the most convenient day trip from Rome, but it's worth the effort. For a real treat, stop in the city of Naples on the way back for a panoramic drive through Italy's most naturally stunning city.

Getting There

Take the train to Napoli Centrale station (about 2 hr.), then a Sorrento-bound Circumvesuviana (commuter train) to Pompei Scavi (about 30 min.). The Circumvesuviana also stops at Ercolano (the excavations of ancient Herculaneum).

★★★ **Scavi di Pompei.** Pompeii is a vast site—to see the best of it, you'll have to cover a lot of ground. Pick up a map at the entrance to get

your bearings. While not everything is well preserved, what has survived will strike you as uncannily sophisticated and often luxurious. The **Forum** was the center of civic life in Pompeii, but not its most interesting attraction today (except for the plaster casts of bodies stored along the north side). To the east are the **Forum Baths,** with their elegant condensation-management system and locker-room cubbyholes. **House of the Vettii** is popular for its racy frescoes and preserved kitchen implements. The fabulous **House of**

Plaster cast of a Pompei victim's body.

the Faun, **House of Menander,** and **House of the Tragic Poet** are where the wealthiest Pompeiians lived. At the eastern end of the site (a 20-min. walk from the entrance) is the **Amphitheater,** with the gladiators' barracks adjacent. On your way back, be sure to see the **Lupanare** (the town brothel, with X-rated frescoes above each door), the

charming and fantastically preserved **Small Theater,** and the **Stabian Baths,** which has great vaults and more plaster casts of crawling bodies caught in desperate attempts to survive. (Most deaths during the eruption were actually caused by asphyxiation from the volcano's toxic fumes.) **Villa of the Mysteries,** famous for its beautiful and enigmatic frescoes, is a good 10-minute walk north of the main part of the site.
🕐 *At least 3 hr. Entrance: Porta Marina.*
☎ *081-8575347. www.pompeii sites.org. 11€. Daily 8:30am–5pm Nov–Mar; 8:30am–7:30pm Apr–Oct.*

★★★ **Naples.** Sadly, most people associate petty scams and organized crime with Napoli, but it's still safer than most big cities—and heart-stoppingly beautiful. Don't miss characteristic neighborhoods **Spaccanapoli** and **Quartieri Spagnoli,** and knockout sights **Piazza Plebiscito** and **Castel Sant'Elmo.** Stroll, the waterfront from **Chiaia** to **Castel dell'Ovo,** and take the funicular to the heights of **Vomero.** Eat pizza at **Sorbillo** (Via dei Tribunali 32, ☎ 081-446643) in Spaccanapoli or seafood at seafood at **Giuseppone a Mare** (Via Ferdinando Russo 13, ☎ 081-5756002) in tony **Posillipo.**

Fat City

As the birthplace of pizza and Sophia Loren (in nearby Pozzuoli), bella Napoli is known for its bounty—even the main drag in Pompeii is called Via dell'Abbondanza (street of abundance). From Cape Misenum to Sorrento, the Bay of Naples is leaping with the best fish the Med has to offer. The fertile volcanic soil on the sunny slopes of Mount Vesuvius is home to citrus groves that yield softball-size lemons. Thanks to a unique combination of sea air and local grass, Naples's region, Campania, is the only place in the world where real *mozzarella di bufala* can be produced. Make time for sipping fresh-squeezed lemonade, crunching into amazing fried calamari, or sinking your teeth into a fat slice of Neapolitan pizza with a huge hunk of melted mozzarella on top.

Castelli Romani

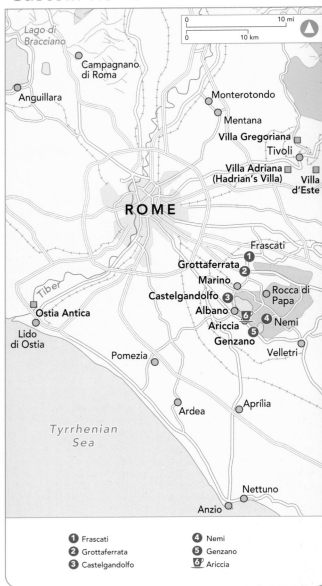

Lago di Bracciano

Anguillara

Campagnano di Roma

Monterotondo

Mentana

Villa Gregoriana

Tivoli

Villa Adriana (Hadrian's Villa)

Villa d'Este

ROME

Frascati ❶

Grottaferrata ❷

Marino

Castelgandolfo ❸

Rocca di Papa

Tiber

Albano ❻

Ariccia ❹ Nemi

Ostia Antica

Genzano ❺

Lido di Ostia

Velletri

Pomezia

Ardea

Aprília

Tyrrhenian Sea

Nettuno

Anzio

❶ Frascati
❷ Grottaferrata
❸ Castelgandolfo
❹ Nemi
❺ Genzano
❻ Ariccia

The best way to see these charming "Roman castles" (hill towns) just south of the city is to rent a car (p 165). On the way, stop and see the spectacular ruins of Roman aqueducts at the Parco degli Acquedotti (heading south on Via Appia Nuova, turn left on Viale Appio Claudio). Alternatively, the Castelli Romani are served by COTRAL buses from the Anagnina Metro station. There's also a direct train from Termini to Frascati.

❶ ★★ Frascati. The biggest but not the prettiest of the Castelli, Frascati is lively and has tons of restaurants and hole-in-the-wall *osterie* where townies (mostly old men) gather on rickety benches to sip the local *mescita* (rough-and-ready white wine, poured straight from great big wooden casks). Just below the town, adjacent to the train station, are the gardens and main house of the 17th-century **Villa Aldobrandini** (☎ 06-9422630), whose imposing, broken-pediment facade can be seen all the way from Rome's Janiculum Hill (p 59, ⓬) on a clear day. The main building and gardens were designed by Giacomo della Porta and Carlo Maderno.

❷ ★★ Grottaferrata. Henry James wrote that this town "has nothing to charm the fond gazer but its situation"—high on a hill, with dramatic views over the Appian Way and

Villa Aldobrandini, Frascati.

Rome—"and its old fortified abbey," the wonderful 11th-century **Abbazia di San Nilo** (☎ 06-9459309), an example of medieval architecture rare for the Roman region.

❸ ★★ Castelgandolfo. Overlooking volcanic Lake Albano, clean and elegant Castelgandolfo has been the popes' summer retreat since the 1500s—the 17th-century palace here is technically part of the Vatican. The town piazza has a fountain by Bernini, who also designed the Church of San Tommaso di Villanova, with its acrobatic stuccoes by Antonio Raggi.

❹ ★★ Nemi. Set on the lip of an ancient volcanic crater, Nemi is by far the most picturesque of the Castelli, and famous for its wild strawberries. Gorgeous Lake Nemi—formed by the water that collects in the crater—was called "Diana's Mirror" by the ancients because the surrounding woods seemed to suit the goddess of the hunt.

❺ ★ Genzano. On the other side of the lake from Nemi, Genzano is at its best the week after Corpus Christi, when the streets are covered with flower petals for the *Infiorata* festival.

The town of **❻ Ariccia** is famous for porchetta (pork roast with garlic and rosemary). Stop for lunch at the wonderfully simple Fraschetta dar Burino (Via dell'Uccelliera 46–50; ☎ 333-1828584; www.darburino.it), where you can get a tasting menu of the local specialties, including wine, for 12€. *$$.*

Beaches & Etruscan Sites
Near Rome

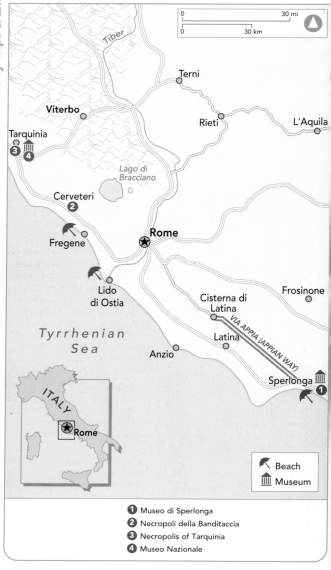

1 Museo di Sperlonga
2 Necropoli della Banditaccia
3 Necropolis of Tarquinia
4 Museo Nazionale

The Roman litorale (seacoast) has never won any Mediterranean beauty contests, but there are several convenient and pleasant places to escape when summer in the city gets to be too much. When you tire of beachcombing, head north along the coast-hugging Via Aurelia to the ancient sites of Cerveteri and Tarquinia. Here you'll find fascinating physical evidence of the Etruscans, the sophisticated culture that ruled Italy before the Romans. Much of the jewelry and other finds from these cavernous painted tombs can be seen at Rome's Villa Giulia museum (p 30, ❷).

★ **Fregene.** The preferred seaside destination for upper-middle-class Romans, Fregene lies right below the path of jets on the final approach to Fiumicino airport. The topography isn't particularly gorgeous, but the see-and-be-seen crowd of super-bronzed bathers makes for quite a spectacle on its own. Go to beachfront **Il Mastino** (Via Silvi Marina 18; ☎ 06-66563880) for a lovely-as-can-be lunch of spaghetti with clams. *COTRAL bus from Lepanto Metro station, about 1 hr.*

Ostia. Even if you have only half a day to spare, you can still make it to Ostia, Rome's closest seashore. The water here is far from sparkling, but it's lively, with plenty of beach clubs (and dark sand that Romans say accelerates tanning). At the ★★ *spiaggia libera*, or "free beach," bus no. 7 from Cristoforo Colombo train station takes you to "i cancelli," where rugged dunes and wider stretches of sand make for a much more attractive setting, but there are few facilities. *Train from Porta San Paolo (Piramide Metro station) to Ostia Centro, Stella Polare, or Cristoforo Colombo, about 35 min.*

★★ **Sperlonga.** Well worth the trek from Rome, charming Sperlonga has two main beach areas. The crescent-shaped bay south of the point is the more picturesque, with wide swathes of sand. On the headlands above, Sperlonga town looks like a Greek village, with whitewashed walls, narrow alleys, and spectacular

A Day at the Beach

The beaches here, like in so many of the country's best places, are bustling with a deeply rooted social culture. **Beach clubs** (*stabilimenti*)—pleasant, and nearly identical—consume much of the coast near Rome, and typically charge between 12€ to 18€ for access to their shores; the daily fee includes a **lounge bed** (*lettino*) and **shade umbrella** (*ombrellone*), and use of changing rooms and shower facilities. Regardless of shape or age, about half of Italian women go topless at the beach, and half of the men wear Speedos. As for the water, while it's not exactly crystalline near Rome, it's plenty clean for swimming—and no matter where you go, you'll find takeout huts serving delicious cold-mozzarella-and-tomato sandwiches or plates of steaming pasta with fresh Mediterranean seafood.

Sunbathers at Cerveteri Beach.

vistas over the water. At the southern end of the bay is **Museo di Sperlonga** (☎ 0771-548028), with its marble sculptures of Polyphemus, and the attached, 2nd-century **Villa di Tiberio,** with its whimsical sea-grotto dining room. *Train to Fondi (D or R train toward Napoli), then bus to Sperlonga, about 1½ hr.*

★★ **Cerveteri.** Called Kysry by the Etruscans and Caere by the Romans, this town near the seacoast was one of Italy's great Etruscan cities and may date back as far as the 9th century B.C. It is home to the immensely atmospheric main burial ground, the **Necropoli della Banditaccia,** whose labyrinth-like paths between thick

Etruscan ruins, Cerveteri.

trees and huge tumulus tombs feel like something out of an *Indiana Jones* adventure sequence. The typically Italian lax site supervision means you can clamber all over everything, which is great fun. Of the graves thus far uncovered, none is finer than the **Reliefs' Tomb (Tomba Bella),** the burial ground of the Matuna family. ⏱ *1 hr. Via della Necropoli.* ☎ *06-9940001. 6€. Tues–Sun 8:30am–sunset. COTRAL bus from Cornelia Metro station to Cerveteri, about 1 hr.*

★★ **Tarquinia.** The **necropolis** of Tarquinia may not be as lush or ancient-feeling as the one at Cerveteri, but the tombs here have vivid, beautifully preserved wall paintings. In the town, the **Museo Nazionale** (located in the noble Palazzo Vitelleschi) houses prized terra-cotta winged horses from the 4th century B.C., among the greatest Etruscan masterpieces ever found, as well as exhibits and sarcophagi excavated from the necropolis. Tarquinia itself is a very pretty medieval town, with several good restaurants. ⏱ *2½ hr. (necropolis and museum).* ☎ *0766-850080. 8€ for both sites. Necropolis Tues–Sun 8:30am–1 hr. before sunset; museum 8:30am–7:30pm. COTRAL bus from Cornelia Metro station to Civitavecchia, then change buses to Tarquinia, about 2 hr.* ●

The Savvy Traveler

Before You Go

Government Tourist Offices

In the U.S.: 630 Fifth Ave., Ste. 1565, New York, NY 10111 (☎ 212/245-4822); 500 N. Michigan Ave., Ste. 2240, Chicago, IL 60611 (☎ 312/644-0996); and 12400 Wilshire Blvd., Ste. 550, Los Angeles, CA 90025 (☎ 310/820-1898). **In Canada:** 175 Bloor St. E., South Tower, Ste. 907, Toronto, ONT, M4W 3R8 (☎ 020/7408-1254). **In the U.K. & Ireland:** 1 Princes St., London, W1B 2AY (☎ 020/7408-1254; www.italiantouristboard.co.uk). **In Australia:** Level 4, 46 Market St., Sydney, NSW 2000 (☎ 02/9262-1666).

The Best Times to Go

April to June and late September to October are the best months to travel in Italy. Starting in mid-June, the summer rush really picks up, and from July to mid-September the country teems with visitors. August is the worst month for touring: It can get uncomfortably hot, muggy, and crowded, and the entire country goes on vacation at least from August 15 to the end of the month. Many hotels, restaurants, and shops are closed (except at the spas, beaches, and islands, which are where 70% of the Italians head). From late October to Easter, most attractions go on shorter winter hours or are closed for renovation. Many smaller hotels and restaurants take a month or two off between November and February.

Festivals & Special Events

SPRING. The 42km (26 miles) of the **Maratona di Roma** are run the third Sunday in March. During the **Settimana dei Beni Culturali,** 1 week in April (www.beniculturali.it), admission is free to many museums and monuments. In late March and early April, azaleas cover the Spanish Steps in the **Mostra delle Azalee. Settimana Santa (Holy Week)** and **Pasqua (Easter)** in March or April are the biggest Catholic holidays of the year, with the pope partaking in dramatic ceremonies daily. Every April 21, Rome celebrates its birthday **(Natale di Roma)** with fireworks over the Campidoglio. Workers' unions organize a huge free rock concert at San Giovanni on **Primo Maggio** (May 1). The **Italian Open** brings the VIPs of the world tennis circuit to the Foro Italico (the Forum) for 10 days in May.

SUMMER. **Estate Romana** (June–Aug) brings concerts to the sites of ruins, and open-air cinemas to piazzas. The miraculous snowfall of August 5, A.D. 352, is reenacted every year in Santa Maria Maggiore with a flurry of white flower petals during the **Festa della Madonna della Neve.** Get out of town, or wish you had, on **Ferragosto** (beginning Aug 15)—a 2-week holiday when *everyone* in Rome takes a vacation.

FALL. The pope says Mass at the Verano Cemetery on **Ognissanti (All Saints' Day),** November 1. For the **Giornata dei Defunti (Day of the Dead)** on November 2, Romans visit the graves of family members.

WINTER. To celebrate the **Immacolata Concezione** (Dec 8), firemen shimmy up a column in Piazza di Spagna to place a wreath on the arm of the Virgin Mary. Nativity scenes *(presepi)* spring up all over town in the weeks leading to **Natale (Christmas).** Italians ring in **Capodanno (New Year's)** by partying in the streets, setting off fireworks, wearing red knickers, and casting unwanted furniture out windows. On

Previous page: Scooters buzz along the streets of the city.

ROME'S AVERAGE DAILY TEMPERATURE & MONTHLY RAINFALL

	JAN	FEB	MAR	APR	MAY	JUNE
Temp. (°F)	49	52	57	62	72	82
Temp. (°C)	9	11	14	17	22	28
Rainfall (in.)	2.3	1.5	2.9	3.0	2.8	2.9

	JULY	AUG	SEPT	OCT	NOV	DEC
Temp. (°F)	87	86	73	65	56	47
Temp. (°C)	31	30	23	20	13	8
Rainfall (in.)	1.5	1.9	2.8	2.6	3.0	2.1

January 5, a witch called **La Befana** "lands" at Piazza Navona, signifying the arrival of **Epiphany** (Jan 6) and the end of the holiday season.

Weather

Rome's generally mild climate means that you can enjoy visiting the city year-round, and can eat dinner outside April through October. Summer (especially late July and Aug) can be hot and humid. May and October are generally the best months for sightseeing, with sunny days and temperatures between 60° and 80°F (15°–26°C). March is often rainy, and November brings the first bite of autumn. January and February are the coldest months, though winter temperatures rarely drop below 40°F (4°C), and sunny, 70°F days, permitting alfresco dining, aren't unheard of over the Roman winter.

Useful Websites

- **www.adr.com:** Information about Rome's airports.
- **www.060608.it:** The official site of the Rome tourist board, with tons of info, downloadable brochures, and a list of accommodations.
- **www.trenitalia.com:** Schedules, fares, and online booking for the national train system.
- **www.vatican.va:** The Vatican's excellent official site; see also the comprehensive site for the Vatican Museums at http://mv.vatican.va.

Cellphones

World phones are the only U.S. phones that can be used in Italy. Italy is on the GSM (Global System for Mobiles) wireless network. GSM phones function with a removable plastic SIM card, encoded with your phone number and account information. In Italy, you can buy an inexpensive phone and SIM for 10€ and buy prepaid minutes in increments of 5€ to 20€.

You can also rent one in the U.S. before leaving home from **InTouch USA** (☎ 800/872-7626; www.intouchglobal.com), **RoadPost** (☎ 888/290-1606 or 905/272-5665; www.roadpost.com), or **Cellhire** (www.cellhire.com, www.cellhire.co.uk, www.cellhire.com.au).

U.K. mobiles all work in Italy; call your service provider before departing your home country to ensure that the international call bar has been switched off and to check call charges, which can be extremely high.

Even if you don't make any calls, bring your smartphone and charger with you. Wi-Fi hotspots are increasingly common (and often free) in Rome and can put useful tourist info at your fingertips.

Car Rentals

All roads might lead to Rome, but you don't want to drive once you get here. You're usually allowed to park in front of the hotel long enough to unload your luggage.

I've found **AutoEuropa (www. sbc.it)** to have the best online rental deals in Italy. If you want to book a car in Rome, all the agencies have desks inside Termini station and Fiumicino airport as well as city center locations in the vicinity of Via Veneto and Villa Borghese. **AutoEuropa** is at Via Calabria 11 (☎ 06-42019014); **Hertz** is on Viale del Galoppatoio 33, in the underground parking lot of the Villa

Borghese (☎ 06-3216886); and **Avis** is at Via Sardegna 38A (☎ 06-42824728). **Maggiore,** another Italian company, has an office at Via Po 8A (☎ 06-8548698).

From the U.K., I recommend **www.holidayautos.co.uk**. All prepaid vouchers include insurance—which can be astronomical in Italy. Book online for a guaranteed 10% discount.

Getting **There**

By Plane

Chances are you'll arrive at Rome's **Leonardo da Vinci International Airport** (☎ 06-65951 or 06-65953640), popularly known as Fiumicino, 30km (19 miles) from the city center.

After you leave Passport Control, you'll see two **information desks** (one for Rome, one for Italy; www.adr.it). At the Rome desk, you can pick up a general map and pamphlets Monday through Saturday from 8:15am to 7pm. The staff can help you find a hotel room if you haven't reserved ahead. A *Cambio* (money exchange) operates daily from 7:30am to 11pm, offering surprisingly good rates.

There's a **train station** in the airport. To get into the city, follow the signs marked TRENI for the 30-minute express train to Rome's main station, **Stazione Termini** (arriving on Track 22). The shuttle runs from 6:37am to 11:37pm for 14€ one-way. On the way, you'll pass a yellow machine dispensing tickets (cash or credit), or you can buy them from the news agent (cash only) near the tracks. When you arrive at Termini, get out of the train quickly and grab a baggage cart. Do watch out for pickpockets at Termini.

A **taxi** from Fiumicino airport to the city costs 40€ for the 30-minute to 1-hour trip if your central Rome location is inside the Aurelian Walls (most hotels are). There are always plenty of metered, white, official Comune di Roma cabs outside the terminal.

If you arrive on a charter or low-cost flight at **Ciampino Airport** (☎ 06-65959515), you can take the **Terravision** coach (☎ 06-97610632; 6€ one way) to Termini. Alternatively, the **Sit Bus Shuttle** (☎ 06-5916826) between Ciampino to Termini runs every 45 minutes and costs 4€. A **taxi** to Rome costs 30€.

By Car

From the north, the main access route is **Autostrada del Sole (A1),** which cuts through Milan and Florence; or you can take the coastal route, **SS1 Aurelia,** from Genoa. If you're driving north from Naples, you take the southern leg of **Autostrada del Sole (A1).** All the autostradas join with the **Grande Raccordo Anulare,** a ring road encircling Rome.

By Train, Bus, or Metro

Trains and buses arrive in central Rome at **Stazione Termini,** Piazza dei Cinquecento (☎ 06-478411); this is the train, bus, and Metro transportation hub for all of Rome and is surrounded by many hotels (especially cheaper ones).

If you're taking the **Metropolitana,** follow the illuminated red-and-white M signs. To catch a **bus,** go straight through the station's outer hall to the sprawling bus lot of

Piazza dei Cinquecento. You'll find **taxis** there as well. Note that taxis now charge a 2€ supplement for any fares originating at Termini. This is official city policy, though not well-marked, so don't feel that you're getting ripped off. Just make sure the meter reads 1, not 2, next to the price amount (2 being the higher, out of town applied fare).

Getting Around

By Car
Don't drive in the center of Rome. Period.

By Taxi
Licensed taxis are white and prominently feature the classic overhead taxi light. Be sure your cab has the red SPQR insignia on the driver's door. Cabs can be difficult to hail on the street, particularly during the day. Always insist on the metered fare, never an arranged price. The meter starts at 2.33€ from 7am to 10pm Monday to Saturday, and at 4.91€ from 10pm to 7am every day. On Sunday and holidays from 7am to 10pm, the meter starts at 3.36€. As a guideline, a daytime fare between Termini and the Vatican (one of the longer distances in the city center) should be 15€ to 20€, depending on traffic. Add the tip by rounding up to the next whole euro—if the fare is 7.40€, leave the driver 8€.

By Metro
The **Metropolitana,** or **Metro,** for short, is the fastest means of transportation, operating daily from 5:30am to 11:30pm. A big red M indicates the entrance.

Tickets are 1€ and are available from *tabacchi* (tobacco shops, most of which display a sign with a white

T on a brown background), many newsstands, and vending machines at all stations. Some stations have managers, but they won't make change. You can also buy **passes** for 1 to 7 days (see "By Bus & Tram," below).

By Bus & Tram
Roman buses and trams are operated by an organization known as **ATAC** (Azienda Tramvie e Autobus del Comune di Roma), Via Volturno 65 (☎ 800-431784; www.atac mobile.it for information).

For 1€ you can ride to most parts of Rome, although it can be slow going in all that traffic, and the buses are often very crowded. Your ticket is valid for 75 minutes, and you can get on many buses and trams (as well as one run on the Metro) during that time by using the same ticket. Ask your hotel where to buy bus tickets, or buy them in *tabacchi* or at bus terminals before boarding.

At Stazione Termini, you can buy a **1-day ticket** (*biglietto giornaliero*), which costs 4€, or a **weekly ticket** (*biglietto settimanale "carta"*), which costs 16€. A **tourist pass** costs 11€ and is valid for 3 days. The tourist pass, the 1-day ticket, and the weekly tickets are valid on buses, trams, and the

Metro. On the first bus you board, you place your ticket in the machine, which prints the day and hour you boarded.

Buses and trams stop at areas marked FERMATA. At most of these, a yellow sign displays the numbers of the buses that stop there and lists all the stops along each bus's route in order, so you can easily search out your destination. In general, they're in service daily from 6am to midnight. It's best to take a taxi in the wee hours—call 06-3570 for radiotaxi service.

At the **bus information booth** at Piazza dei Cinquecento, in front of the Stazione Termini, you can purchase a directory complete with maps summarizing the bus routes.

On Foot

Seeing the city on foot (and getting a little lost while you're at it) is the best way to get oriented. Many main sights are very close together, and the *centro* is mostly flat.

Fast **Facts**

APARTMENT RENTALS For short-term vacation rentals in Rome, check out **Roman Reference** (www.romanreference.com), **Rental in Rome** (www.rentalinrome.com), or **Rome-Accom** (www.rome-accom.com). For longer stays, see the classifieds in the English-language magazine *Wanted in Rome* at its website (www.wantedinrome.com/clas) or at newsstands. The most comprehensive classified newspaper for long-term room or apartment rentals is the Italian-only *Porta Portese,* at its website (www.portaportese.it) or at newsstands.

ATMS/CASHPOINTS There are **ATMs** *(bancomat)* all over central Rome; you'll be charged at least a 3€ fee (in addition to whatever your home bank charges for international withdrawals). Cash tends to run out by Saturday night and isn't replenished until Monday afternoon, so think ahead.

BANKING HOURS Teller windows are open Monday to Friday from 8:45am to 1:30pm and from 2:45 to 4pm. Queues can be painfully slow.

B&BS The **Bed & Breakfast Italia** agency, Corso Vittorio Emanuele 282 (☎ 06-6878618; www.bbitalia.it), has a dizzying array of accommodations. Rates range from 25€ to 80€ per person per night. **The bed-and-breakfast.it** online booking portal offers 1,200 (and counting) different tourist accommodations for Lazio alone.

BIKE RENTALS Rome's streets are busy and Vespa-infested, but the parks make for good riding, and Sundays are largely traffic-free. Just outside the entrance to the Spagna Metro station, **Spagna Rent,** Vicolo del Bottino (☎ 339-4277773), rents bikes by the hour or the day, convenient for riding in the Villa Borghese nearby. **On Road,** Via Cavour 80 (☎ 06-4815669; www.scooterhire.it), between Termini and the Colosseum, rents bikes as well as mopeds.

BUSINESS & SHOP HOURS Most Roman shops open at 10am and close at 7pm from Monday to Saturday, closing for 1 or 2 hours at lunch. Smaller shops are often closed Monday morning and Saturday afternoon. Most restaurants are closed for *riposo* (rest) 1 day per week, usually Sunday or Monday.

CLIMATE See "Weather," p 165.

CONCERTS See "Tickets," below.

CONSULATES & EMBASSIES **United States Consulate and Embassy,** Via Veneto 121 (☎ 06-46741; italy. usembassy.gov). **Canadian Consulate,** Via Zara 30 (☎ 06-854442912; www.canada.it). **British Embassy,** Via XX Settembre 80 (☎ 06-42200001; www.britain.it). **Australian Embassy,** Via Antonio Bosio 5 (☎ 06-852721; www.italy. embassy.gov.au).

CREDIT CARDS Credit cards generally offer good exchange rates. You can also withdraw cash advances from your credit cards at banks or ATMs (cashpoints), provided you know your PIN. Most banks assess a 2% fee above the 1% fee for currency conversion on credit charges.

CUSTOMS By law, anyone arriving from outside the E.U. is allowed to bring up to 200 cigarettes, two bottles of wine, and one bottle of liquor into Italy, duty-free. There are no limits for anyone, foreign nationals included, arriving from another E.U. country.

DENTISTS See "Emergencies," below.

DOCTORS See "Emergencies," below.

ELECTRICITY Like most of continental Europe, Italy uses the 220-volt system (two round prongs). American (110-volt) electronics with dual voltage (laptops and shavers) can be used with a simple adapter. Other appliances like hair dryers require a clunky voltage converter. U.K. 240-volt appliances need a continental adaptor, impossible to find once in Italy.

EMBASSIES See "Consulates & Embassies," above.

EMERGENCIES The *Polizia* are at ☎ 112; the *Carabinieri* (they speak more English than the regular police), ☎ 113. Call ☎ 115 for the **fire department.** For an **ambulance,** call ☎ 118. Should you find

yourself in need of medical attention, ask to go to the nearest *pronto soccorso* (emergency room). **Ospedale Fatebenefratelli** on Tiber Island (Piazza Fatebenefratelli 2, ☎ 06-68371; www.fatebene fratelli-isolatiberina.it), is one of the best hospitals. For dental emergencies, head for **Ospedale Dentistico George Eastman,** in the Policlinico medical complex at Viale Regina Elena 287B (☎ 06-844831).

EVENT LISTINGS The weekly *Roma C'è* (1.50€ at newsstands, or online at www.romace.it, in Italian) has the most thorough listings. The "Roma" sections of the daily newspapers *Corriere della Sera*, *La Repubblica*, and *Il Messaggero* list major events.

FAMILY TRAVEL Italian hotels and restaurants are generally very accommodating to children. Rome's many city parks (p 92) offer respite from the stress of sightseeing in a chaotic urban environment.

GAY & LESBIAN TRAVELERS **Circolo Mario Mieli di Cultura Omosessuale** (☎ 06-5413985; www.mario mieli.org) is the best gay and lesbian resource in Rome.

HOLIDAYS Celebrated in Rome are New Year's Day (Jan 1); Epiphany (Jan 6); Easter and Easter Monday (Mar or Apr); Liberation Day (Apr 25); Labor Day (May 1); St. Peter and Paul's Day (June 29, Rome only); Ferragosto (Aug 15); All Saints' Day (Nov 1); Immaculate Conception (Dec 8); Christmas (Dec 25); and St. Stephen's Day (Dec 26).

INSURANCE For trip-cancellation and lost-luggage insurance, try **Travel Guard International** (☎ 800/826-4919; www.travel guard.com) or **Travel Insured International** (☎ 800/243-3174; www.travelinsured.com). North Americans interested in getting medical insurance, including emergency evacuation coverage, can contact **Travel Assistance International** (☎ 800/821-2828; www.travelassistance.com). **For U.K. citizens,** insurance is always advisable, even if you have form E111.

INTERNET Most Roman hotels have Internet access—broadband connections in guest rooms, a hotel-wide wireless network, or an Internet terminal in the lobby. Otherwise, most have a small Internet/phone center where you can pay about 5€ an hour to log on. For those with laptops, many parts of the Villa Borghese have free Wi-Fi; the Internet cafe/tearoom **Gran Caffè La Caffettiera,** Piazza di Pietra 65 (☎ 06-6798147; www.grancaffelacaffettiera.com), near the Pantheon, has great atmosphere.

LOST PROPERTY Always file a police report if you wish to submit an insurance claim. Items left on buses and Metros, or at other city-run agencies, may turn up at the **Oggetti Smarriti (Lost Objects)** Circonvallazione Ostiense 191 (☎ 06-67693214). For property left on trains, try the Oggetti Smarriti desk at Termini station (near platform 24).

MAIL & POSTAGE STAMPS Stamps (francobolli) for the Poste Italiane can be purchased at post offices or at most tobacco shops and hotel reception desks.

MONEY Italy's currency is the euro (at press time, equal to $1.41/0.7%). For the most up-to-date currency conversion information, go to www.xe.com.

PARKING You don't want to drive a car once you're in Rome. Either turn in your rental car once you arrive or, if you plan to take a number of day trips while you're there, consider parking at the **ParkSì** underground lot at Villa Borghese, Via del Galoppatoio 33 (☎ 06-3225934). 20€ per day, 1.70€ per hour.

PASSES Rome does not have a fully comprehensive sightseeing pass, but the **RomaPass** (www.romapass.it; 34€ for 3 days) gets you free admission for two sites (most museums and monuments are covered AND passholders get to skip any queues), plus discounts on subsequent admissions, as well as free city public transportation. For Rome's major archaeological sites, one 12€ ticket gets you into the Colosseum, the Roman Forum, and the Palatine, but it must be used within 48 hours. The archaeological superintendency also offers a 7-day **Archeologia Card** (28€) that includes admission to the Colosseum, Roman Forum, Palatine, Baths of Caracalla, all three locations of the Museo Nazionale Romano, and Crypta Balbi, as well as Villa dei Quintili and the Tomb of Cecilia Metella on the Appian Way. The 7.50€ **Appia Antica card** is good for 7 days and includes the Baths of Caracalla, the Tomb of Cecilia Metella, and the Villa of the Quintili.

PASSPORTS Always keep a photocopy of your passport with you when you're traveling. If your passport is lost or stolen, it significantly facilitates the reissuing process at your consulate. While in Rome, keep your passport and other valuables in your room's safe or in the hotel safe (cassaforte). See "Consulates & Embassies," above, for more information.

PHARMACIES Farmacie are recognizable by their neon green or red cross signs. A few pharmacies, like those at Piazza Cinquecento 49–53 and at Via Nazionale 228, are open late. All closed pharmacies have signs in their windows indicating open pharmacies in the area.

SAFETY Violent crime is virtually nonexistent, but petty theft and scams can be a problem. Pick-pockets, some of them Gypsies, expertly work the tourist areas, crowded buses (especially N64), and Termini station. Gypsies normally travel in groups of two or three, with babies slung across their chests. Other pickpockets dress like typical businesspeople, so always be suspicious of anyone who tries to "befriend" you in a tourist area. In general, Rome is quite safe—walking alone at night is usually fine anywhere in the *centro storico*.

SCOOTER RENTALS The best way to "do as the Romans do" is to rent a scooter. You'll find agencies in all the tourist areas (or ask at your hotel)—expect to pay between 40€ and 50€ per day for a scooter. An agency I like is **RomaRent,** Vicolo dei Bovari 7A (☎ 06-6896555).

SENIOR TRAVELERS Non-E.U. seniors are entitled to precious few discounts while in Rome, although AARP (☎ 800/424-3410; www.aarp.org) members can save on airfare and car rentals arranged prior to departure. **Elderhostel/Road Scholar** (☎ 800/454-5768) organizes well-priced "study trips" to Italy, though accommodations may be spartan.

SMOKING A nationwide ban prevents smoking in bars and restaurants, but you can still puff away at sidewalk tables.

SPECTATOR SPORTS One of the best experiences you can have in modern Rome is going to a **Roma** or **Lazio** football (soccer) game at the Stadio Olimpico (p 136). Tickets go on sale 6 days before games and cost 25€ to 120€. The season runs from late August or early September to May or June.

TAXES Non-E.U. visitors (with the exception of citizens from the U.K. and Ireland) who spend 155€ or more at stores with TAX-FREE stickers are entitled to a VAT refund (up to 13% of the total purchase amount). The cashier will fill out a form, which you must present at the Customs office at the **last European point** of departure.

TAXIS It's usually (but not always) impossible to hail a taxi on the street. During busy hours, they're required by law to pick up fares only at taxi stands at the center of Rome, Piazza Venezia (east side), Piazza di Spagna (Spanish Steps), the Colosseum, Corso Rinascimento (Piazza Navona), Largo Argentina, the Pantheon, Piazza del Popolo, Piazza Risorgimento (near St. Peter's), and Piazza Belli (Trastevere). Taxis can also be requested by phone (☎ 06-3570, 06-88177, 06-6645, 06-4185, or 06-4994)—the meter starts from the moment your cab is dispatched. Early morning taxis to the airport can also be reserved in advance, at no extra charge. Fares within the city range from 6€ to 20€. Fare to or from the airport costs 40€ (flat rate to and from Fiumicino) or 30€ (flat rate to and from Ciampino). *Note:* The fixed airport fares are only valid if your city destination or point of origin is inside the old Aurelian Walls (Mura Aureliane)—otherwise, the metered rate applies.

TELEPHONES Italy phased out its coin phones long ago, and a government resolution was passed to remove all existing public phone booths in Italy within 2012.

TICKETS For concert and theater tickets, visit the venue box office or the **Orbis** agency, Piazza Esquilino 37 (☎ 06-4744776). For soccer tickets, go to the Roma Store, Lazio Point (p 136), or a **Lottomatica** (inside many, but not all, *tabacchi*). Your hotel concierge may be able to help you (offer a tip).

TIPPING Many Roman waiters have grown accustomed to receiving gratuities of 15% from tourists, but

Italians don't tip nearly that much, and waiters don't depend on them to feed their families. In general, rounding up a lunch or dinner bill is sufficient. (If, say, the check is 33€, leave 35€.) Check to see if the *servizio* is included; if it is, no additional gratuity is necessary. At the coffee bar, always add a few coins when you place your order (10¢ is perfectly acceptable, but 20¢ will get you faster service).

In hotels, a service charge of 15% to 19% is already added to the bill, but it's customary to give a small gratuity (50¢/day) to the housekeeping staff. You should tip a porter a few euros for each bag carried to your room. A helpful concierge should also get a tip. Taxi drivers should be tipped about 10% of the fare, more if heavy baggage lifting is involved.

TOILETS Cafes, bars, and restaurants are required by law to let even non-customers use their restrooms, so don't be shy; just ask politely for the *bagno*. You may be handed a key to access.

TOURIST OFFICES The state-operated tourist bureau, or **APT,** Via Parigi 5 (☎ 06-488991; www. turismoroma. it), provides maps, pamphlets, and info. Much more helpful and friendly is **Enjoy Rome,** Via Marghera 8A (☎ 06-4451843; www.enjoyrome. com), which also arranges tours.

TOURS Rome has plenty of tour companies, but I recommend **Enjoy Rome,** Via Marghera 8A (☎ 06-4451843; www.enjoyrome. com). For a more in-depth, academic experience, the specialized, small-group tours organized by **Context Rome** (☎ 800/691-6036 toll-free from the U.S., ☎ 06-97625204 in Italy; www.context rome.com) are outstanding.

TRAVELERS WITH DISABILITIES Many *centro storico* hotels and some lesser sites remain inaccessible to wheelchairs; call to inquire. The **COIN** agency, Via Enrico Giglioli 54A (☎ 06-23267695; www.coin sociale.it), provides up-to-date information about accessibility.

VAT See "Taxes," above.

A Brief History

6TH–5TH CENTURIES B.C. Following the expulsion of the seventh king of Rome, the Republic begins. Roman law is codified in 450 B.C.

3RD CENTURY B.C. Rome defeats Carthage in the Punic Wars.

2ND CENTURY B.C. Rome conquers Greece and adopts the Greek gods.

50S B.C. Caesar invades Britain and conquers Gaul (France).

44 B.C. Julius Caesar is assassinated on the Ides of March.

31 B.C. Octavian (Augustus) defeats Antony and Cleopatra at Actium, annexing Egypt.

A.D. **41** Caligula is assassinated; Claudius is emperor until he is poisoned in A.D. 54.

A.D. **64** The Great Fire destroys two-thirds of the city. Universally loathed emperor Nero is blamed for doing nothing to stop it.

A.D. **64 OR 65** St. Peter is crucified, upside down, at the Circus of Nero, on the future site of Vatican City.

A.D. **72–80** To satisfy the public's growing appetite for blood sport, the Colosseum is built.

A.D. **98–117** The reign of Trajan. The empire reaches its zenith;

Rome's power extends through Europe and the Mediterranean.

3RD CENTURY A.D. During the "troubled century," Rome loses territory to barbarian invaders.

313 Constantine legalizes Christianity.

330 Byzantium (modern Istanbul) is renamed Constantinople and becomes the new capital of the Roman Empire.

5TH CENTURY Rome is left defenseless and takes a beating from repeated barbarian invasions. Historians cite A.D. 476 as the end of the Western Empire.

7TH–9TH CENTURIES The popes govern a small and scattered population in Rome. The structures of antiquity fall into ruin.

9TH–11TH CENTURIES A conflict-ridden "alliance" between the popes and the Holy Roman Empire brings bloody warfare.

11TH–13TH CENTURIES The popes—now essentially princes, descended from Italian nobility—extend the reign of the Church throughout Italy.

1303–1377 Temporary removal of the papacy from Rome to Avignon.

1508 Michelangelo begins his frescoes in the Sistine Chapel.

1527 Charles V sacks Rome; the city is held hostage for 7 months.

1555 Roman Jews are ordered to live in the Ghetto.

1590S–1650S The baroque period flourishes: Caravaggio, Borromini, and Bernini reign the art world.

1798 Pope ousted by the invading French army.

1848 Rebels declare "the Roman Republic," which is quashed by French troops.

1870 Rome becomes the capital of a newly united Italy.

1922 Mussolini makes the "March on Rome" by train.

1929 Vatican City becomes a sovereign state with the signing of the Lateran Treaty.

1944 Rome is liberated from the Nazis.

1946 The *Repubblica Italiana* is created, ending the reign of the Savoia monarchs.

2001 The richest man in Italy, media tycoon Silvio Berlusconi, is elected prime minister for the second time. (He was prime minister very briefly in the 1990s.)

2001 AS Roma wins the *scudetto*, Italy's prized football (soccer) championship, for the third time.

2005 Pope John Paul II dies at the age of 84 after serving for 27 years. He is replaced by Pope Benedict XVI.

2006 Italia defeats France to win the World Cup. Rome is the epicenter of nationwide revelry.

2008 Berlusconi is voted back in as prime minister, for a third time. (He is later succeeded in office by Mario Monti, in 2011, and Enrico Letta, in 2013).

2012 Italy suffers massive losses of its market share of world trade with the global financial crisis.

2013 Benedict XVI shocks the Catholic world when he resigns from the papacy. Cardinal Bergoglio of Argentina becomes Pope Francis I.

Roman **Architecture**

Ancient Rome (6th c. B.C.–5th c. A.D.)

Everyone knows that arches and columns were the backbones of Roman buildings, but what about the rest of the buildings' structures? Some guidelines for making sense of the ruins:

- The lower the base of a building, the older its date; street level in Rome has risen about 9m (30 ft.) since ancient times. (Roman temples, such as the Pantheon, are a confusing exception to this rule, as temples were built on high podiums that are now flush with modern street level.)

- Round or irregular holes in ancient ruins indicate where metal has been removed (such as lead clamps that held a building together, or iron hooks that held decorations like sculpture or marble revetment).

- Rectangular holes are called "put-log holes," where beams were placed for scaffolding or to support a higher floor.

- Republican architecture was more modest than Imperial. Ruins with simple rectangular plans and plain tufa construction normally predate ruins with heavy marble or intricate vaulting.

- The use of concrete was perfected in the 1st century B.C.; any building utilizing concrete dates after that century.

- As lovely as they look to us today, brick walls never went naked in ancient Rome; they were always covered with marble paneling or stucco.

Early Christian & Romanesque (5th–9th c. A.D.)

The focus is on the interior. Churches are like geodes, with plain brick facades and dazzling jewel-tone mosaics inside.

Medieval (9th–14th c.)

The Middle Ages have largely disappeared from the architectural record in Rome. Santa Maria Sopra Minerva is the city's only Gothic church, its pointed arches and soaring vaults emphasizing heaven.

Renaissance (15th–16th c.)

Characterized by stateliness, symmetry, and a rebirth of the classical orders, the best Roman architecture of this period is at Piazza del Campidoglio and Palazzo Farnese. Painting and sculpture are balanced, harmonious, and idealistic.

Baroque (17th–18th c.)

Histrionic and playful, baroque defines the modern look of Rome. Architects like Bernini and Borromini employed such dynamic flourishes as jagged cornices and curvilinear tension (Sant'Agnese in Agone) to enliven monuments and public squares; sculptors (like Bernini) and painters (like Caravaggio) infused their subjects with naturalism and palpable, high-keyed emotion.

Rococo (18th c.)

Florid to the point of being frenzied—the baroque on methamphetamines.

Neoclassical (19th c.)

Safe and sedate, a return to the purest Greek and Roman forms.

Fascist/Rationalist (1920s–40s)

Buildings are bombastic, blocky caricatures of Roman Imperial monuments. Unweathered and insufficiently relieved by negative volume, they come off much harsher than their ancestors.

Useful Phrases

English	Italian	Pronunciation
Hello/Good morning	Buongiorno	bwohn-*djor*-noh
Hello/Good evening	Buona sera	*bwohn*-ah *say*-rah
Good night	Buona notte	*bwohn*-ah *noht*-tay
Goodbye	Arrivederci (formal)	hr-ree-vah-*dehr*-chee
Hi/Bye	Ciao (or "salve"; informal)	chow
Yes	Sì	see
No	No	noh
Please	Per favore	*pehr* fah-*vohr*-eh
Thank you	Grazie	*graht*-tzee-yey
You're welcome/ Go ahead	Prego	*prey*-go
Do you speak English?	Parla inglese?	*pahr*-lah *een*-gleh-zeh?
I don't speak Italian	Non parlo italiano	nohn *parl*-loh ee-tah-*lyah*-noh
Excuse me (apologizing, interrupting)	Mi scusi	mee *skoo*-ze
Excuse me (getting through a crowd	Permesso	pehr-*mehs*-soh
OK (agreeing)	Va bene	vah *beh*-neh
Where is . . . ?	Dov'è . . . ?	doh-*vey*
the station	la stazione	lah stat-tzea-oh-neh
the bathroom	il bagno	eel *bahn*-nyoh
a restaurant	un ristorante	oon reest-ohr-*ahnt*-eh
a hotel	un albergo	oon ahl-*behr*-goh
I am looking for . . .	Cerco . . .	*chehr*-koh
the check-in counter	il check-in	eel check-in
departures	l'area partenze	*lah*-reh-ah pahr-*tehn*-tseh
a security guard	una guardia di sicurezza	*ooh*-nah *gwahr*-dyah dee see-koo-*ret*-sah
the smoking area	l'area fumatori	*lah*-reh-ah foo-mah-*toh*-ree
the information booth	l'ufficio informazioni	loof-*fee*-choh een-*fohr*-mah-*tsyoh*-nee
a public telephone	un telefono pubblico	oon teh-*leh*-foh-noh *poob*-blee-koh
an ATM/cashpoint	un bancomat	oon *bahn*-koh-maht
baggage claim	il ritiro bagagli	eel ree-*tee*-roh bah-*gahl*-lyee

English	Italian	Pronunciation
a luggage cart	un carrello portabagagli	oon kahr-*rehl*-loh pohr-tah-bah-*gahl*-lyee
a currency exchange	un cambiavalute	oon *kahm*-byah-vah-*loo*-teh
a cafe	un caffè	oon kahf-*feh*
a restaurant	un ristorante	oon ree-stoh-*rahn*-teh
a bar	un bar	oon bar
a bookstore	una libreria	oo-nah lee-breh-*ree*-ah
a duty-free shop	un duty-free	oon duty-free
To the left	A sinistra	ah see-*nees*-tra
To the right	A destra	ah *dehy*-stra
Straight ahead	Avanti (*or* sempre diritto)	ahv-*vahn*-tee (sehm-pray dee-*reet*-toh)
How much does it cost?	Quanto costa?	*kwan*-toh *coh*-sta
What time is it?	Che ore sono?	kay *or*-ay *soh*-noh
The check, please	Il conto, per favore	eel kon-toh *pehr* fah-*vohr*-eh
When?	Quando?	*kwan*-doh
Yesterday	Ieri	ee-*yehr*-ree
Today	Oggi	*oh*-jee
Tomorrow	Domani	doh-*mah*-nee
Breakfast	Prima colazione	*pree*-mah coh-laht-tzee-*ohn*-ay
Lunch	Pranzo	*prahn*-zoh
Dinner	Cena	*chay*-nah
Monday	Lunedì	loo-nay-*dee*
Tuesday	Martedì	mart-ay-*dee*
Wednesday	Mercoledì	mehr-cohl-ay-*dee*
Thursday	Giovedì	joh-vay-*dee*
Friday	Venerdì	ven-nehr-*dee*
Saturday	Sabato	*sah*-bah-toh
Sunday	Domenica	doh-*mehn*-nee-kah

Numbers

English	Italian	Pronunciation
1	uno	*oo*-noh
2	due	*doo*-ay
3	tre	tray
4	quattro	*kwah*-troh
5	cinque	*cheen*-kway
6	sei	say
7	sette	*set*-tay
8	otto	*oh*-toh
9	nove	*noh*-vay

English	Italian	Pronunciation
10	dieci	dee-ay-chee
11	undici	oon-dee-chee
20	venti	vehn-tee
21	ventuno	vehn-toon-oh
22	venti due	vehn-tee doo-ay
30	trenta	trehn-tah
40	quaranta	kwah-rahn-tah
50	cinquanta	cheen-kwan-tah
60	sessanta	sehs-sahn-tah
70	settanta	seht-tahn-tah
80	ottanta	oht-tahn-tah
90	novanta	noh-vahnt-tah
100	cento	chen-toh

Useful Websites

Airlines

AER LINGUS
www.aerlingus.com

AIR CANADA
www.aircanada.com

AIR FRANCE
www.airfrance.com

AIR MALTA
www.airmalta.com

ALITALIA
www.alitalia.com

AMERICAN AIRLINES
www.aa.com

AUSTRIAN AIRLINES
www.austrian.com

BRITISH AIRWAYS
www.britishairways.com

DELTA AIR LINES
www.delta.com

EASYJET
www.easyjet.com

IBERIA
www.iberia.com

ICELANDAIR
www.icelandair.is

KLM
www.klm.com

LUFTHANSA
www.lufthansa.com

OLYMPIC AIRWAYS
www.olympicair.com
RYANAIRwww.ryanair.com

SCANDINAVIAN AIRLINES
www.flysas.com

SWISS INTERNATIONAL AIRLINES
www.swiss.com

TAP AIR PORTUGAL
www.flytap.com

TURKISH AIRLINES
www.turkishairlines.com

UNITED AIRLINES
www.united.com

US AIRWAYS
www.usairways.com

VIRGIN ATLANTIC AIRWAYS
www.virgin-atlantic.com

Car-Rental Agencies

ADVANTAGE
www.advantage.com

ALAMO
www.alamo.com

AUTO EUROPE
www.autoeurope.com

AVIS
www.avis.com

BUDGET
www.budget.com

DOLLAR
www.dollar.com

HERTZ
www.hertz.com

KEMWEL HOLIDAY AUTO (KHA)
www.kemwel.com

NATIONAL
www.nationalcar.com

THRIFTY
www.thrifty.com

Index

00100 Pizza, 74

A
Abbey Theatre, 128
abbreviations, meaning, vi
Accademia di Santa Cecilia, 130, 133
accessories, shopping, 76, 81–83
Adriatic, 144
Ai Monasteri, 77, 87
air travel, 166
Akab Cave, 125
Al Girarrosto Toscano, 107
Al Sogno, 77, 88
Al Vino Al Vino, 123
Alcazar, 135
Aldrovandi Palace, 138, 144
Alexanderplatz Jazz Club, 128
Alibi, 118, 126
Amarcord, 46–47
Ancient Rome, 22–27
    Arch of Constantine, 22, 26
    Bottega del Caffè, 22, 24
    Capitoline Hill, 22–23
    Circo Massimo, 22, 27
    Circus Maximus, 22, 27
    Colosseum, 22, 26–27
    Museum of the Imperial Forums, 22, 24
    Palatine Hill, 22
    Roman Forum, 22, 24–25
    Teatro di Marcello, 22–23
    Terme di Caracalla, 22, 27
    Trajan's Markets, 22, 24
    Via dei Fori Imperiali, 22–24
    Via di Monte Caprino, 22–23
ancient wall, 65
Anglo-American Book Co., 80, 83–84
Antica Enoteca di Sero, 71
Antica Pesa, 107
Antico Arco, 107
Antico Caffè della Pace, 118, 123
Antico Forno Roscioli, 57, 113
apartment rentals, 138, 145, 168
Apollo Belvedere, 49–50
apparel, shopping, 81–83

apperitivo, dining, 113
Appia Antica (Appian Way), 94–97
Appian Way (Via Appia Antica), 18–19
Ara Pacis, 62
Arch of Constantine, 22, 26
Arch of Septimius Severus, 25
Arch of Titus, 25
architecture, 174
Arco del Lauro, 138, 144
Area Sacra di Largo Argentina, 57
Ariccia, 159
Armani Jeans, 10, 81
arts, see entertainment
AS Roma, 130, 136
ATMs, 168
Auditorium-Parco della Musica, 133
Aurelian Walls, 91, 93
Aventine Hill (Aventino), 18–20
Aventino Hotels, 138, 144

B
B&Bs, 168
banks, 168
Bar Caffè dell'Appia Antica, 94, 97
Bar della Pace, 52–53
Bar Marzio, 36, 39
Bar Sant'Eustachio, 3, 107–108
Bar Stravinskij, 14, 17
Baroque Rome, 32–35
    Galleria Borghese, 32, 35
    Piazza Navona, 32, 34–35
    Piazza San Pietro, 32
    Ponte Sant'Angelo, 32, 34
    San Carlo alle Quattro Fontane, 32, 35
    Santa Maria della Vittoria, 32, 35
    Sant'Andrea al Quirinale, 32, 35
    Sant'Ivo alla Sapienza, 32, 35
    St. Peter's Basilica, 32–34
    Trevi Fountain, 32, 35
bars, 123–125
Bartaruga, 123
Basilica of Maxentius, 25
Basilica Santa Maria in Trastevere, 58–59
Baths of Caracalla, see Terme di Caracalla
Baths of Porta Marina, 155
beaches, 160–162
Belevedere Torso, 50

Beppe e I Suoi Formaggi, 78, 85
Big Mama, 118, 128
bike rentals, 168
Bioparco, 90–92
Bocca della Verità (Mouth of Truth), 18, 20, 69
Bocconcino Kosher, 67
books, shopping, 83–84
Botanical Gardens, 59
Bottega del Caffè, 22, 24
boutiques, 84
Brandy Melville, 76, 78, 81
Brioni, 78, 81
Buccone, 123
Burro e Alici, 113
bus travel, 166–167
business hours, 168

C
Caesar House, 144–145
Caffè della Arti, 90–91, 93
Caffè Italia, 9, 1
Caffè Latino, 125
Caffè Settimiano, 59
Caffè Teichner, 63
Camden Town, 128
Campidoglio (Capitoline Hill), 9–10, 44–45
Campo de' Fiori, 2, 4, 8, 13, 14–16, 36, 39, 56–57, 77, 86
Campo Marzio Design, 80, 88
Campo Marzio, 142–143
Capitoline Hill, 4, 22–23, 123
Capitoline Museums, 3, 5, 29, 31, 76, 78
car rentals, 165–166
car travel, 166–167
Casa Bleve, 108
Casa Howard, 145
Case Romane di Santi Giovanni e Paolo, 46–47
Casina Valadier, 44–45
Castel Sant'Angelo, 12–13, 52–53
Castelgandolfo, 159
Castelli Romani, 158–159
Castroni, 78, 85–86
Catacombs of San Callisto, 18–19, 46–47, 94–95
Catacombs of San Sebastiano, 46–47, 94–95
catacombs, 4, 94–96
Cavalieri dell'Appia Antica, 94, 97
Centro Storico
    dining, 103
    entertainment, 131
    lodging, 139
    nightlife, 119
    shopping, 77
Cerveteri, 162
Checchino del 1887, 108

children's books, best
    shopping, 76
churches, 40–43
    concerts, 134
    dress code, 43
    San Giovanni in
        Laterano, 41–43
    San Paolo Fuori Le
        Mura, 41, 43
    Santa Croce in Gerusa-
        lemme, 41–42
    Santa Maria in Traste-
        vere, 40, 43
    Santa Maria Maggiore,
        41–42
    Santa Maria Sopra
        Minerva, 41, 43
    Santa Sabina, 41, 43
    Santo Stefano Rotondo,
        41, 43
    St. Peter's Basilica,
        40, 43
Cinecittà, 135
Cinema Nuovo Olimpia, 135
cinemas, 135–136
Circo Massimo, 22, 27,
    98–100
Circus Maximus, 3–5, 22, 27
Città del Sole, 76–77, 88
classical music, 133
Cloaca Maxima, 69
clubs, 125–126
coffee, 102
COIN, 76, 78, 84
Colosseum, 4, 9–11, 22,
    26–27
Columbus, 138, 145
Column of Marcus Aurelius,
    52, 55
consulates, 169
contemporary fashion street,
    best shopping, 76
Craftsmen's Streets, 56
credit cards, 169
Crypt of the Capuchin
    Monks, 46–47
C.U.C.I.N.A., 80, 84–85
Cucina Romana, 102
Cul de Sac, 108
Curia Julia, 25
customs, 169

D
Da Bucatino, 108
D'Angelo, 36, 39
Danielle, 78, 87–88
Dar Filettaro, 113
Dar Poeta, 108
Davide Cenci, 77, 81
department stores, 84
design, shopping, 84–85
dining, 101–116
    Al Girarrosto Toscano,
        107
    Antica Pesa, 107
    Antico Arco, 107

Antico Forno Roscioli,
    113
apperitivo, 113
Bar Sant'Eustachio,
    107–108
best list, 102
Burro e Alici, 113
Casa Bleve, 108
Centro Storico, 103
Checchino del 1887,
    108
coffee, 102
Cucina Romana, 102
Cul de Sac, 108
Da Bucatino, 108
Dar Filettaro, 113
Dar Poeta, 108
Due Ladroni, 109
Eataly, 109
Enoteca Antica di Via
    della Croce, 109
Enoteca Cavour 313,
    109
Enoteca Corsi, 109–110
Felice, 110
Fiaschetteria Bel-
    tramme, 110
Flavio al Velavevdetto,
    110
food snobs, 102
Forno Campo de' Fiori,
    113
Frontoni, 113
'Gusto, 110
Hostaria, 111
Il Bacaro, 111
Il Margutta, 111
Insalata Ricca, 111
insider spots, 102
La Bottega del
    Caffè, 111
La Carbonara, 111
La Gensola, 111
La Montecarlo, 111–112
La Pergola, 112
La Veranda, 112
L'Asino d'Oro, 112
lunch, 102
menu terms, 114–115
Osteria del Gallo, 112
Osteria der Belli,
    112–113
outdoor, 102
Panificio Renella, 113
paparazzi, 102
Pastificio, 113
Perilli, 113–114
Pierluigi, 114
Pigneto 41, 114
pizzeria, 102
Ponte Sisto, 114
Primo al Pigneto,
    114, 116
Quinzi e Gabrieli, 116
Remo, 116
Rome, 104–105
ruins, 102

seafood, 102
Settembrini, 116
snacking, 113
Spirito di Vino, 116
splurge, 102
Taverna dei Quaranta,
    116
Taverna Romana da
    Tonino, 116
tips, 107
Trattoria Monti, 116
Tridente, 106
Via Veneto, 106
disability access, 172
discos, 125–126
Ditta G. Poggi, 77, 88
Dome of St. Peter's, 48–49
dress code, churches, 43
Druid's Den, 118, 128
Due Ladroni, 109

E
Eataly, 78, 86, 109
Eden, 148
electricity, 169
embassies, 169
emergencies, 169
Energie, 76, 80–82
Enjoy Rome tour, 95
Enoteca Antica di Via della
    Croce, 14, 17, 109
Enoteca Cavour 313, 109
Enoteca Corsi, 109–110
Enoteca Provincia
    Romana, 124
entertainment, 129–136
        best list, 130
    Centro Storico, 131
    cinemas, 135–136
    classical music, 133
    Northern Rome, 132
    performing arts, 134
    sports, 136
    summer festival, 130
    summer venues,
        133–135
Episcopo, 138, 145
Etabli, 118, 124
Ethic, 77–78, 82
Etruscan Museum at Villa
    Giulia, 28, 30
Etruscan Museum, 50
Etruscan sites, 160–162
Excelsior, 148

F
family travel, 169
Felice, 110
Feltrinelli Libre e Musica,
    77, 84
festivals, 164–165
Fiaschetteria Beltramme,
    110
Fiddler's Elbow, 128
Finnegan's Irish Pub, 128
Flavio al Velavevdetto, 110

Fonclea, 128
Fontanella Borghese, 145–146
food, shopping, 85–86
football games, 6
Forica, 155
Forno Campo de' Fiori, 113
Forno del Ghetto, 67
Foro Italico, 130, 136
Forte Prenestino, 125–126
Forte, 146
Fountain of Neptune, 34
Fountain of Santa Sabina church, 19
Fountain of the Four Rivers, 34
Fountain of the Naiads, 123
Fountain of the Tortoises, 123
Franchi, 76, 78, 86
Frascati, 159
Fregene, 161
Freni e Frizioni, 118, 124
Frontoni, 58, 113
Frutta e Verdura, 126–127
Fuori Orario, 78, 82

G

Galleria Borghese, 6, 14, 16, 28, 30, 32, 35, 78
Galleria Doria Pamphilj, 29, 31, 52, 55
Galleria Spada, 57
Gallery of the Maps, 50
Gardens at Villa Medici, 91, 93
gay nightlife, 126–127
gay travelers, 169
Gay Village, 127
Gender, 127
Gente, 76, 80, 82
Genzano, 159
Ghezzi, 76–77, 87
Gianicolo, 44–45, 59
gifts, best shopping, 76
Giolitti, 9, 13
Giuliana, 146
Goa, 126
gourmet foods, best shopping, 76
Gran Caffè la Caffeteria, 52, 55
Grottaferrata, 159
Gucci, 5
'Gusto, 110

H

Hadrian, 5
Hadrian's Villa, 152–153
Hall of Constantine, 50
Hassler, 148
history, 172–173
holidays, 169
home furnishings, shopping, 84–85

Homer, 5
Hostaria Antica Rome, 94, 96
Hostaria, 111
Hotel de Russie, 138, 146, 148

I

Ibiz, 76–77, 88
icons, meaning, vi
Il Bacaro, 111
Il Margutta, 111
Il Mattatoio, 74
Il Seme e la Foglia, 18–20, 73
Imperial Fora, 9, 11
The Inn at the Roman Forum, 138, 146
Insalata Ricca, 111
insurance, 169–170
Internet access, 170
Isola del Cinema, 127
Italian menu terms, 114–115
Italian phrases, 175–177
Ivanhoe, 146

J

Jewish Catacombs, 94–95
Jewish Ghetto, 18, 20, 66–69
Joia, 125

K

Ketumbar, 126

L

L.E.I., 77, 82
La Bottega del Caffè, 65, 111
La Carbonara, 111
La Gensola, 111
La Lumière, 146
La Montecarlo, 111–112
La Pergola, 112
La Repubblica, 134
La Rinascente, 80, 84
La Terrazza dell'Eur, 118
La Veranda, 112
Laghetto di Villa Borghese, 44–45
Laghetto, 90–91, 93
Lancelot, 147
Laocoon, 50
Largo 16 Ottobre, 68
Largo della Fontanella Borghese, 62
L'Asino d'Oro, 112
Le Coppelle 52, 118, 124
Le Terrazze, 127
Leone Limentani, 79, 85
lesbian nightlife, 126–127
lesbian travelers, 169
Libreria Godel, 80, 84
Limoni, 77, 87
Locarno, 138, 147
Loco, 77, 87

lodging, 137–150
Adriatic, 144
Aldrovandi Palace, 138, 144
apartment rentals, 138, 145
Arco del Lauro, 138, 144
Aventino Hotels, 138, 144
best list, 138
Caesar House, 144–145
Campo Marzio, 142–143
Casa Howard, 145
Centro Storico, 139
Columbus, 138, 145
Eden, 148
Episcopo, 138, 145
Excelsior, 148
Fontanella Borghese, 145–146
Forte, 146
Giuliana, 146
Hassler, 148
Hotel de Russie, 138, 146, 148
The Inn at the Roman Forum, 138, 146
Ivanhoe, 146
La Lumière, 146
Lancelot, 147
Locarno, 138, 147
Lord Byron, 147–148
Mario de' Fiori 37, 148
Mimosa, 138, 148
Modigliani, 138, 148
Panda, 149
Portrait Suites, 138, 149
Residenza Canali ai Coronari, 149
Residenza Santa Maria, 149
Roman Reference, 138
Rome Cavalieri, 148–150
Rome map, 140–141
Santa Maria, 138, 150
Senato, 150
Simeraldo, 150
sojourn tax, 144
Sole al Biscione, 138, 150
St. Regis, 148
Tridente, 142–143
Villa Laetitia, 138, 150
Lo Yeti, 70–71
Lord Byron, 147–148
Loren, Sophia, 157
lost property, 170
lounges, 123–125
lunch, 102

M

mail, 170
Mamertine Prison, 46–47

Mario de' Fiori 37, 148
markets, 76, 86–87
Martina Novelli, 76
Mausoleum of Augustus, 62
Mausoluem of Cecilia
   Metella, 94, 96–97
menu terms, 114–115
Mercato delle Stampe, 80, 86
Mercato di Testaccio, 3, 6, 74
Metaverso, 125
metro travel, 166–167
Mia Market, 65
Mimosa, 138, 148
Mithraeum, 155
Modigliani, 76, 80, 85,
   138, 148
money, 170
Monte Testaccio clubs, 125
Monte Testaccio, 74
Monti neighborhood, 20,
   64–65
Mouth of Truth, see Bocca
   della Verità
mozzarella di bufala, 157
Muccassassina, 127
multi-label boutique, best
   shopping, 76
Murphy & Nye, 80, 82
Museo della Civiltà Romana,
   29, 31
Museo delle Mura, 94–95
Museo Nazionale Romano-
   Palazzo Massimo, 30
Museum of the Imperial
   Forums, 22, 24, 79
museum stores, 76, 85
museums,28–31
   Capitoline Museums,
      29, 31
   Etruscan Museum at
      Villa Giulia, 28, 30
   Galleria Borghese, 28,
      30
   Galleria Doria Pamphilj,
      29, 31
   Museo della Civiltà
      Romana, 29, 31
   Museo Nazionale
      Romano-Palazzo
      Massimo, 30
   Terrazza Caffarelli, 29,
      31
   Vatican Museums, 28,
      30
music, live, 128

N

Naples, 156–157
Necci dal 1924, 71
Necropolis of St. Peter's,
   46–49
neighborhoods, 52–74
   Campo de'Fiori, 56–57
   Jewish Ghetto, 66–69
   Monti, 64–65
   Pantheon, 52–55

Piazza Navona, 52–55
Pigneto, 70–71
Testaccio, 72–74
Tiber Island, 66–69
Trastevere, 58–59
Tridente, 60–63
Nemi, 159
nightlife, 117–128
   bars, 123–125
   best list, 118
   Centro Storico, 119
   clubs, 125–126
   discos, 125–126
   gay, 126–127
   lesbian, 126–127
   lounges, 123–125
   Monte Testaccio
      clubs, 125
   music, live, 128
   Ostiense, 122
   pubs, 128
   Rome map, 120–121
   summertime, 127
   Testaccio, 122
Northern Rome, entertain-
   ment, 132
Nuyorica, 77, 82–83

O

Ombre Rosse, 14, 16
one-day tours, 8–13
   Campo de'Fiori, 8, 13
   Piazzo Navona, 8, 13
   Caffè Italia, 9, 1
   Imperial Fora, 9, 11
   Vittoriano, 9, 11
   Giolitti, 9, 13
   Vatican Museums,
      10, 12
   Campidoglio (Capito-
      line Hill), 9–10
   Roman Forum, 9–10
   Colosseum, 9–11
   Trevi Fountain, 9–10, 13
   Pantheon, 9, 11–12
   Castel Sant'Angelo,
      12–13
   St. Peter's Basilica, 8,
      12–13
Orologio ad Acqua, 91, 93
Osteria del Gallo, 112
Osteria der Belli, 112–113
Ostia Antica, 154–155
Ostia, 161
Ostiense, 118, 122
outdoor attractions, 89–100
   Appia Antica (Appian
      Way), 94–97
   Aurelian Walls, 91, 93
   Bar Caffè dell'Appia
      Antica, 94, 97
   Bioparco, 90–92
   Caffè della Arti,
      90–91, 93
   Catacombs of San
      Callisto, 94–95

Catacombs of San
   Sebastiano, 94–95
catacombs, 94–96
Cavalieri dell'Appia
   Antica, 94, 97
Circo Massimo, 98–100
Enjoy Rome tour, 95
Gardens at Villa Medici,
   91, 93
Hostaria Antica Rome,
   94, 96
Jewish Catacombs,
   94–95
Laghetto, 90–91, 93
Mausoluem of Cecilia
   Metella, 94, 96–97
Museo delle Mura,
   94–95
Orologio ad Acqua,
   91, 93
parks, 98–100
Piazza di Siena, 90–92
Piazzale delle Canestre,
   90–91, 93
Piazzale Napoleone,
   90–91, 93
Pincio Hill, 91, 93
Porta Pinciana, 90–92
Porta San Sebastiano,
   94–95
Temple of Aesculapius,
   90–91, 93
Terme di Caracalla
   Greenbelt, 98–100
Via Appia Antica, 94, 97
Viale del Museo Bor-
   ghese, 90–92
Viale delle Magnolie,
   90–91, 93
Villa and Circus of
   Maxentius, 94, 96
Villa Borghese, 90–93
Villa Celimontana,
   98–100
Villa Pamphilj, 98, 100
outdoor dining, 102
O.X.O., 80, 88

P

Palatine Hill, 5, 22
Palatine, 4
Palatium, 124
Panda, 149
Panificio la Renella, 59
Panificio Renella, 113
Pantheon, 9, 11–12, 52–55
papal vestments, best
   shopping, 76
paparazzi, dining spots, 102
parking, 170
parks, 98–100
passes, 170
passports, 170
Pastificio, 113
People, 77, 83
performing arts, 134

perfumery, 87
Perilli, 113–114
personal care, shopping, 87
pharmacies, 170
phrases, Italian, 175–177
piazzas, 36–39
  Bar Marzio, 36, 39
  Campo de'Fiori, 36, 39
  D'Angelo, 36, 39
  Piazza Borghese, 62
  Piazza del Parlamento, 62
  Piazza del Popolo, 14, 17, 37–39, 60–61
  Piazza della Minerva, 52, 54–55
  Piazza della Rotonda, 37–38
  Piazza di Montecitorio, 52, 55
  Piazza di Pietra, 52, 55
  Piazza di Siena, 90–92
  Piazza di Spagna, 36, 39, 62–63
  Piazza Farnese, 14, 16, 36, 39, 56–57
  Piazza Madonna dei Monti, 64–65
  Piazza Margana, 67
  Piazza Mattei, 37, 39, 67
  Piazza Navona, 8, 13, 32, 34–36, 38, 52–55
  Piazza San Lorenzo in Lucina, 37–38, 63
  Piazza San Pietro, 32, 48, 123
  Piazza Santa Maria in Trastevere, 14, 16, 36, 39, 58–59
  Piazza Testaccio, 76, 79, 87
  Piazza Trilussa, 59
Piazzale delle Canestre, 90–91, 93
Piazzale Napoleone, 90–91, 93
Piazzo del Campidoglio, 10, 24
Piazzo dell'Ara, 10
pickpockets, 10
Pierluigi, 114
Pigneto 41, 114
Pigneto, 70–71
Pinacoteca, 49
Pincio Hill, 91, 93
Pincio terraces, 2, 4, 14, 17, 44–45
Pinko, 80, 83
Piper, 126
pizzeria, 102
plane travel, 166
Pompeii, 156–157
Pont Sant'Angelo, 52–53
Ponte Rotto, 69
Ponte Sant'Angelo, 32, 34, 44–45

Ponte Sisto, 44–45, 114
Porta Maggiore, 71
Porta Pinciana, 90–92
Porta Portese market, 79, 87
Porta San Paolo, 73
Porta San Sebastiano, 94–95
Portal, 127
Portico d'Ottavia, 68
Portrait Suites, 138, 149
postage, 170
Posto Italiano, 2, 76–77, 88
Prada, 5
pricing guide, vii
Primo al Pigneto, 71, 114, 116
Protestant Cemetery, 73
Prototype, 77
Prototype, 83
pubs, 128
Pyramid of Gaius Cestius, 73

Q

Quinzi e Gabrieli, 116

R

Raphael Hotel, Roof Bar, 44–45
Raphael Rooms, 50
Regina Viarum, 4
religious, shopping, 87
Remo, 116
Residenza Canali ai Coronari, 149
Residenza Santa Maria, 149
rigatoni alla carbonara, 5
Roma-Lazio games, 130, 136
Roman Forum, 3–4, 9–10, 22, 24–25, 123
Roman Reference, 138
romance, 44–45
Rome
  dining map, 104–105
  lodging, 140–141
  nightlife map, 120–121
  shopping map, 78–79
Rome Cavalieri, 148–150
Roof Bar at Raphael Hotel, 44–45
Roscioli, 14, 16, 77, 86
Rostra, 25

S

safety, 170–171
sale season, 83
Salotto 42, 118, 124
Salotto Gianicolo, 118, 127
saltimbocca alla romana, 5
San Carlo alle Quattro Fontane, 32, 35
San Clemente, 46–47
San Francesco a Ripa, 58
San Giovanni in Laterano, 41–43
San Luigi dei Francesi, 52, 54

San Paolo Fuori Le Mura, 41, 43
Santa Cecilia, 14–16, 58
Santa Croce in Gerusalemme, 41–42
Santa Maria dei Monti, 65
Santa Maria del Popolo, 61
Santa Maria della Vittoria, 32, 35
Santa Maria in Trastevere, 40, 43
Santa Maria Maggiore, 41–42
Santa Maria Sopra Minerva, 41, 43
Santa Maria, 138, 150
Santa Sabina, 41, 43
Sant'Agnese in Agone, 34
Sant'Agnese in Agone, 52, 54
Sant'Agostino, 52, 54
Sant'Andrea al Quirinale, 32, 35
Sant'Andrea della Valle, 57
Sant'Ignazio, 52, 55
Sant'Ivo alla Sapienza, 32, 35, 52, 54
Santo Stefano Rotondo, 41, 43
Saponeria Club, 126
scooters, 5–6, 171
seafood, 102
Senato, 150
seniors, 171
Settembrini, 116
shoes, shopping, 5, 76, 87–88
shopping, 75–88
  accessories, 81–83
  apparel, 81–83
  best list, 76
  books, 83–84
  boutiques, 84
  Centro Storico, 77
  department stores, 84
  design, 84–85
  food, 85–86
  home furnishings, 84–85
  markets, 86–87
  museum stores, 85
  perfumery, 87
  personal care, 87
  religious, 87
  Rome, map, 78–79
  shoes, 87–88
  Spanish Steps, 80
  stationers, 88
  toys, 88
  VAT refund, 81
  Wine, 85–86
Simeraldo, 150
Sistine Chapel, 50
smoking, 171
snacking, 113
Société Lutèce, 118, 124–125